THE SNAKE HANDLER

BY

JAI BEZ
杰贝兹

For information, to make comments, and to purchase copies of this book address:
THE SNAKE HANDLER
736-D St. Andrews Road #151
Columbia, South Carolina 29210

Visit our website at www.thesnakehandler.com

American and Canadian Edition 2009 – Yi Chou 4707

ISBN 978-0-615-33856-9

"Blessed are they that hunger and thirst for justice:
for they shall have their fill."

Sermon on the Mount

**Dedicated to the brave souls who champion the
cause of Justice and battle the forces of evil
throughout the World.**

CONTENTS

CHAPTER I

SNAKEBITTEN

The Virginian received two anonymous phone calls at his home in the middle of the night. The angry caller threatened to "burn you out" if he continued with his lawsuit.

Paull Anderson took the threats very seriously, recalling Garvin Wells' explicit warning that "Nick Johnson has mob connections and he has no qualms about using violence to get his way."

He removed his old German Lugar pistol from his sea chest and, after cleaning, oiling and firing two clips of 9 mm rounds to insure its serviceability and to refresh himself with its handling, he placed it close at hand in his bedside table. He also took measures to more closely monitor and control both the open and the wooded acreage around his home and to insure that his home's alarm system was in excellent working order. But the anonymous threats could not deter his resolve to press on with his lawsuits and his quest for justice.

Paull Anderson never suspected he would soon be battling a den of snakes when his phone rang in September of 1990.

The gentle-natured farmer and his wife had just moved to the rural outskirts of Bristol, Virginia, from their farm eighty miles to the east—nestled in the lush, rolling foothills of the Blue Ridge Mountains in Carroll County. The Andersons had spent the previous decade rehabilitating a thoroughly run-down, 130 acre, Civil War farmstead in Carroll County where they had designed and then built by themselves, an efficient, New England, Quaker-style farmhouse. It sat on a knoll with a commanding view of their valley of sweeping pastureland and deep, rich bottomland.

They had reclaimed and restored the entire farm with hard work, lime and fertilizer, and miles of New Zealand high-tensile fencing and cross-fencing. They purchased the steel I beams and supporting struts from an old and abandoned ninety-foot-long railroad bridge and reassembled the steel to span the stone and concrete pylons they built on each side of an old ford used to cross the wide Little Reed Island Creek that gently coursed through the center of their farm. They built a quality herd of commercial cattle from fine Simmental and Black Angus blood stock to exploit the grasslands. They constructed three acres of raised, irrigated seedbeds where they grew Fraser fir and blue spruce seedlings and transplants to sell to commercial Christmas tree growers in Virginia and North Carolina.

All the while, June Anderson had held down a fulltime job teaching English at a nearby high school. During the later years of that decade, Paull Anderson began to manage some local, commercial tree farms for their absentee owners, whose ranks included physicians, dentists, lawyers and a judge. Eventually, his expanding management responsibilities included a large tree farm in eastern Tennessee that necessitated their move to the headwaters of the Shenandoah Valley in Bristol, Virginia.

In 1990, the gravelly voice on the phone introduced himself as Nick Johnson from Madison, Tennessee, with an interest in purchasing a tree farm in southwestern Virginia. Anderson was aware that one of his clients had put out feelers but was not actively pursuing such a sale. He assured Johnson that he would touch base with the owner and forward the information. He asked Johnson to provide some *bona fides* to pass on to his client. Johnson replied that he was a wealthy and highly successful businessman and venture capitalist dedicated to his philanthropic work assisting the plight of American Indians. He said he would send information about himself and was looking forward to reviewing the information about the tree farm.

A week later, the Virginian mailed out information about the tree farm. A few days later he received a packet of information from Johnson. It included a copy of Johnson's biography from Who's Who of the South and Southwest and an informational brochure describing the Foundation for the Advancement, Education and Employment of American Indians.

Johnson's biography stated that he was an insurance executive and real estate developer and had been president or chairman of several prominent businesses and corporations. He had served in the military, been a Kentucky state senator representing the twenty-first district of Harlan-Leslie counties and had been active with programs for the physically and mentally handicapped.

The Foundation information included copies of its 1976 Oklahoma Charter, Articles of Incorporation and By-Laws, its IRS certification as a non-profit, and descriptions of its good works, projects and activities. These included its "scholarship and medical assistance programs which have been able to help thousands of Indians improve their lives and Project New Hope, building a private boarding school complex to prepare Indian students from across the nation for college." The brochure emphasized "the Foundation's dedication to the betterment of America's Forgotten Minority, the American Indians, to overcome the tragic fact that society has imposed a barbaric vengeance on the American Indian."

Two weeks later, Johnson called back to express his satisfaction with the tree farm information and figures. He announced his plans to have his associate fly in to tour the facility as a due diligence to the purchase. Johnson then inquired about Anderson's reaction to the Indian Foundation materials. Upon receiving a favorable response, he began to enthusiastically expound upon its good works and latest notable projects: "to build our home and school for orphaned and deprived American Indian children, and our special AIDS project to bring medical help to the many unfortunate American Indians afflicted with AIDS who are treated as lepers and stigmatized with no one else but us to help them."

Paull Anderson had long been active supporting a few of his favorite charitable causes with cash and other valuable gifts that he conveyed discreetly and anonymously. He also had a tender spot for the plight of American Indians that had been sensitized by his personal relationship and deep respect for his Cherokee friends, Goingback Chiltosky, John Wilnoty, and Virginia Standingdeer. A few days later, the Virginian sent Johnson a personal check for $2,500 as a donation to the Foundation for use in the AIDS project.

Two weeks later, Johnson's associate, John Baumhoefner, flew into Tri-Cities airport from Cedar Rapids, Iowa, to tour the tree farm. On the hour-long trip from the airport to the Wythe County, Virginia, tree farm, Baumhoefner expounded upon the methods and practices of moving and marketing trees and shrubbery. As Anderson slowly drove him through the rows and stands of well-groomed conifers, the incessant chatter continued but switched to the botany and field practices of raising quality conifers and shade stock. His comments were laced with compliments.

"Good uniform color and quality. Looks like you have the nitrogen, phosphorus and potash balances in tight control. No sign of aphid, bagworm or spider mite probs. Shearing looks good and the semi-sheared configurations are just right. Good ground cover control. Nice lateral and terminal growth whirls and extension." Baumhoefner paused often to closely examine a single tree, press his fingernail into some new growth and ruffle branches to check for needle retention.

On the return trip to the airport the chatter continued, covering the "great dynamics, synergy, and fantastic future of the tree business." With a firm handshake and pat on the back, Baumhoefner assured Anderson that his report would be "totally positive" as he headed for the boarding gate.

A week later, Johnson called Anderson to announce that he was ready to finalize the purchase arrangements and he wanted Anderson to stay on as manager with Baumhoefner handling the moving and marketing of the stock through his Wood Creek Nursery in Cedar Rapids. Johnson also noted that he would structure the transaction as a combination sale/donation by the owner to the Foundation to be bonded through Johnson's Chase Holding Company. That arrangement would insure that the owner received the full asking price of $340,000 in cash in addition to a hefty IRS tax deduction credit which would be based upon the maximum market value of the stock, calculated at its peak, and which his IRS tax lawyer had figured to be a million dollars. Johnson's final good news was that in keeping with Foundation policy and by-laws, Anderson could expect to receive ten percent of that tax deduction credit in cash as a "finder's fee" for "originating" the donation.

"I thought you would appreciate the policy. Someone has to get it to comply with our by-laws. Might as well be you. Any other donations you help originate for the Foundation will likewise benefit you, as a matter of standard procedure. Look at it as a small gesture of appreciation for assisting the great work of the Foundation. Do whatever you please with the finder's fee. Give it to your favorite charity or do whatever you chose with it."

The Virginian was pleasantly surprised to learn of the Foundation's finder's fee policy and to realize that by doing good he would also be doing well and generating monies he could pass on to worthy causes of his choice.

In October of 1990, Anderson received a letter, on Indian Foundation letterhead, from Johnson and Baumhoefner confirming that "the Foundation can grant the owner of the Virginia tree farm a $1,000,000.00 tax deduction which could be taken over a five year period, either forward or backward, and the Foundation will get an approval of this transaction from the I.R.S. in Washington DC, prior to the property being transferred."

A month later, Anderson's lawyer informed him that that the bonding documents provided by Johnson and Baumhoefner appeared irregular and insufficient to properly protect the seller. When Anderson subsequently conveyed that information to Johnson, his miffed response was that he did not understand the problem, did not care to get involved in any drawn-out legalities over a simple transaction, and was forthwith withdrawing the offer to purchase the tree farm

In October of 1991, Johnson again contacted the Virginian to request assistance in facilitating the donation of a Limestone, Tennessee, tree farm to the Indian Foundation. The Riverview Farm was owned by one of Anderson's clients, Dr. Walter Harber, a dentist from Johnson City, Tennessee. Anderson subsequently discussed the matter with Harber and informed him of his previous experience with Johnson. The Virginian suggested Harber proceed cautiously, through his attorney, and deal only with the top authority in the Foundation.

Two weeks later, Johnson again phoned Anderson to announce that the chairman of the board of directors of the Foundation would be personally handling the Riverview Nursery farm donation negotiations and his credentials were on the way. A fax followed with the biography of Chairman Edward M. Mezvinsky:

Edward Mezvinsky, an attorney specializing in international trade and government relations, is a member of the Pennsylvania Bar Association. He is founder and chairman of the board of American Federal Insurance Company.

Mezvinsky was a member of the US Congress from Iowa from 1973 to 1977, and prior to his election to Congress, he served as a state representative.

In 1977, President Carter appointed Mezvinsky to serve as US Representative to the United Nations Commission on Human Rights, a post he held through 1979. He played an important role in formulating US human rights policy.

Mezvinsky is married to Emmy award-winning TV news reporter and journalist, Marjorie Margolies, a native Pennsylvanian and graduate of the University of Pennsylvania. They reside in Penn Valley, Pennsylvania, with their eight children and a Vietnamese family of five.

Mezvinsky holds a Master of Arts degree in political science and a J.D. degree in Law from the University of California. He received his B.A. from the University of Iowa.

He is the author of "A Term to Remember," published in 1977, and has written articles and opinions for the Georgetown Law Journal, The Philadelphia Inquirer, The New York Times, The Washington Post and The Boston Globe.

Shortly thereafter, Anderson received a phone call from Chairman Mezvinsky who casually introduced himself in the smooth, pleasant, relaxed voice that Anderson would expect from an old and trusted friend.

"Hi, Paull—Ed Mezvinsky here. Good to chat with you. Heard some great things about you and your compassionate concern for our nation's deprived Native Americans. I just want to add my congratulations and warmest personal greetings welcoming you aboard in our efforts to help our fellow Americans through our Foundation and its wonderful work..."

Mezvinsky was lavish with praise for the Foundation's activities and projects and its unselfish, dedicated staff and supporters. He noted that it would be his pleasure to personally handle the Riverview Nursery farm donation negotiations and he looked forward to meeting both Anderson and the donor in the near future. His conversation ended with his assurance that he would be sending out his biography and written confirmation of the finder's fee arrangement.

Days later, another Mezvinsky biography, similar to the one sent by Johnson, arrived followed by a finder's fee Agreement, dated January 23, 1992, executed by Mezvinsky on his letterhead as chairman of the board, memorializing Johnson's earlier assurances concerning Anderson's entitlement to a ten percent finder's fee for any donations received by the Foundation which originated from any of his clients or business associates.

Mezvinsky lost no time in establishing contact with Dr. Harber and facilitating the donation of the Riverview Nursery farm. He made several trips to Johnson City to confer with Harber and his attorney and to tour the Riverview Nursery Farm.

In early March of 1992, Mezvinsky persuaded Paull Anderson to participate, along with John Baumhoefner, in brokering the sales of the nursery stock on the Riverview Nursery farm. Mezvinsky subsequently executed a brokerage agreement to that affect, dated March 23, 1992. He urged Anderson to begin lining up wholesalers to purchase the nursery stock in advance of the actual donation. Anderson immediately commenced efforts to initiate sales to wholesalers he knew in both Maryland and South Carolina. Mezvinsky, as he had requested, was kept fully informed of all of Anderson's efforts to market the nursery stock. Mezvinsky had insisted upon and maintained tight, hands-on control.

In September of 1992, Mezvinsky flew in to Tennessee to execute the necessary transfer documents, in his official capacity as chairman of the Foundation, and to complete the donation of Harber's Riverview Tree Farm to the Foundation. The Foundation issued Harber a $2.8 million dollar IRS Form 8283 Tax Deduction certification. That evening, Harber phoned Anderson to relate the news and note that he had been surprised to learn, at the last minute, that it was necessary for him to make a $50,000 personal loan to Mezvinsky. Otherwise, as Mezvinsky had assured him, "the deal won't close, and you will be out in the cold on what you need from the IRS."

Anderson could only reply that he knew nothing at all about any such loan or even that the transfer date for the donation had been arranged.

The next day, Anderson phoned Mezvinsky to inquire further. Mezvinsky appeared to be in high spirits, describing how much the donation would mean to the

Foundation, "to further our great programs and projects that help so many of these deprived American Indians, and I can personally thank you for your help on behalf of every one of them." When Mezvinsky finally paused in his lavish praise, Anderson asked him about the $50,000 loan. There was a distinct silence, then more of the smooth colloquy. "That really is confidential, Paull. I certainly don't mind Walt sharing it with you. However, I must honor my commitment to Walt to keep it confidential. All I can say is I appreciated his interest in supporting the last, big push to get my wife elected and when she is in the House he will have a powerful friend there who won't forget who came through for her when it counted. If you care to get aboard, I am sure she would appreciate your matching Walt's gesture."

The Virginian ignored Mezvinsky's solicitation on behalf of his wife's election campaign for Pennsylvania's 13th Congressional District seat in the US House of Representatives, and he decided to say no more about the Harber loan to Mezvinsky.

A week later, Anderson received a letter from Foundation president, Johnson stating that "as a result of the Riverview Nursery farm donation $280,000.00 has been credited to your Finder's Fee Account with our Foundation."

A few days later, Anderson received a phone call from Sam F. Grigsby, Sr., the president of the Bank of East Tennessee. The Virginian had met Grigsby a year earlier when one of Grigsby's properties, the Bert Smith Cattle Farm in Church Hill, Tennessee, went up for sale. After several months of meetings and negotiations with Grigsby, Anderson had decided against the purchase.

Grigsby's phone conversation was pleasant. He invited Anderson to attend a scheduled meeting with Johnson at Grigsby's bank office in Morristown, Tennessee. Grigsby expressed "an interest in making a serious donation to the Foundation to obtain a much-needed tax deduction benefit." He had been informed that Anderson had "made a cash donation to the Foundation" and encouraged Anderson "to attend the meeting to facilitate the discussion and provide some help in working out the details between Johnson and I."

Anderson confirmed having given a cash contribution to the Foundation and assured Grigsby that he would consider the invitation. Two hours later, Anderson received a phone call from Johnson extending his invitation to the meeting and emphasizing that Anderson "really should participate in a discussion that could result in a serious donation from Grigsby for the AIDS Project and to the New Hope Home and School for Indian Children. These needy children really need our help and, of course, your participation resulting in a Grigsby donation would justify another finder's fee for you to pass on to your favorite charity."

On November 10th, Anderson met with Grigsby and Johnson in Grigsby's plush office at the Bank of East Tennessee in Morristown. Grigsby and Johnson were already having a serious discussion when Anderson was ushered into the room by Grigsby's secretary. Both men barely nodded to Anderson and continued to discuss the particulars of the Indian Foundation's IRS tax deduction benefits. Anderson stood by, listening.

Grigsby and Johnson presented an interesting contrast.

The banker was tall, lean, and comfortably attired in a conservative, expensive, pin-striped suit with starched shirt and subtle paisley tie. His naturally silvering hair was well groomed. His wing tip shoes gleamed. He stood calmly with arms crossed before him looking down at Johnson, who was shuffling through and emphasizing sections of the IRS and Foundation documents he was holding.

Johnson was slight and wore a wrinkled and loose-fitting shirt and soiled slacks that would have been more appropriate doing yard work. He had a shifty manner that kept him constantly moving side-to-side so that he never fully faced either Grigsby or Anderson. He also kept from looking directly at them and spoke to the documents he held or some focus point beside them. Johnson had small, dark eyes, set closely together in a deeply lined face with craggy features. His slick helmet of dyed, raven black hair was smeared down with a slick, glistening pomade that was stylish in the fifties. He exuded a hard-edged personality that had the air of a steel trap with a hair trigger. He was emphatically driving home the points he was trying to make and frequently tapped at a highlighted area of a document. His voice was raspy and frequently paused when unable to find an appropriate word or phrase to express itself. Notwithstanding, Johnson pushed on through his spiel like a determined used car salesman.

Grigsby listened attentively, infrequently interrupting to ask a terse, pointed question that Johnson immediately answered from what seemed like his stock of well-rehearsed responses.

Although both men appeared to be in their seventies, they shared nothing else in common. One was obviously the educated, well-polished, highly professional bank president who comported himself with the comfortable self-assurance of one used to exercising authority and handling serious responsibility, while the other stood out as a slick, streetwise, wheeler-dealer with a game plan and the brass to sell it.

Eventually, Johnson's sales pitch ended and he handed over the documents to Grigsby, who indicated that he was ready to do business with Johnson and take advantage of the Foundation's tax benefits in return for donations.

Grigsby turned and smiled at Anderson. "Well, Paull, looks like we both will be doing some Indians some good and doing our bottom line some good at the same time. I plan to pick up that Unisys property up your way and turn it to do us all some good. Nick assures me that the Foundation will accept the donation of the Unisys property along with its EPA cleanup problem and responsibilities that come with it. Later, the Foundation can resell it by providing the purchaser with an affidavit and assurance of liability that the Foundation will retain the responsibility and has the financial ability to cover any cleanup costs. That will allow the Foundation to convey the property on to the purchaser clear of any EPA responsibility."

The Virginian nodded and replied, "I understand that the Unisys property has a significant EPA pollution problem that has kept it from selling for some time and I can understand that you plan to move it through the Foundation to strip away that problem and leave it clear to sell on the market. But it seems to me that EPA liability and the cleanup costs down the road could leave the Foundation with some big problems and major expenses."

Johnson scowled at the comment. "The Foundation will handle that down the road, as you say. Our people and lawyers will handle the situation. Sam and I will see that your interests are protected." Grigsby nodded in agreement.

"Sounds like you both have a deal, so if you will excuse me I have to head back to Bristol for another matter."

On the return drive, Anderson reviewed the meeting and concluded that it had been largely a waste of time for him. But, apparently, his presence had provided a neutral, third party presence that made Grigsby and Johnson more comfortable and in some abstract way could have contributed to their seemingly successful meeting. And if it all worked out, Anderson would be assured of a finder's fee that he could pass on to do some good. The meeting, and his first personal contact with, and observation of, H. Nickolas Johnson had left Anderson with the firm, uncomfortable impression that he needed to keep a close eye on Johnson. This man bore too close a resemblance to a snake-oil salesman. He made a note to himself to closely monitor this man in any future dealings. He also resolved to keep a close eye on the banker.

The meeting subsequently proved to be mutually productive for Grigsby, the Foundation and Johnson— personally. In May of 1993, Grigsby took out two loans for $2.2 million, which he used to purchase the vacant

Unisys Corporation industrial property in Bristol, Tennessee. In January of 1994, Grigsby donated it to the Foundation, which issued him an IRS form 8283 tax deduction certificate for that amount.

It was discovered later that an hour after receiving the donation, the Foundation sold the property to the Exide Corporation for $3.5 million, of which $2.2 million went to pay off the Grigsby loans and the remaining $1.3 million profit reverted back to Grigsby in the form of a "loan" from the Foundation. The result left Grigsby with a handsome net profit of $1.3 million and a huge tax deduction for his troubles. Later, Grigsby wired a $150,000 "donation" to the Foundation, which Johnson quickly diverted to his own private account and use. While Grigsby and Johnson reaped considerable benefits from their "deal" the American Indian tribes gained nothing and the Indian Foundation was left with the Unisys property EPA cleanup responsibility.

During the last week of November, in 1992, Harber sent Anderson a copy of a letter from Johnson, on Foundation letterhead, promoting the purchase of a 24,700 acre tract of mineral-rich and timber-laden property in Eastern Kentucky:

> *November 12, 1992*
> *RE: 24,700 Acres in Kentucky*
> *Dear Walter:*
> *The above captioned properties are located in Breathitt, Perry and Knott counties. They are covered by the enclosed Title Policy in the amount of $25,000,000. No. 88-022 issued by First American Title Company of the Midwest.*

We have on hand in excess of $200,000. worth of geology, engineering, coal, oil, gas and timber evaluations up to date. Some of their analyses are as follows:

A. G.M. Andreen and Associates, 235 Rockbell Drive, San Antonio, Texas cover letter of September 3, 1987 states:

'Our primary conclusions are that proper development of the resources your property could yield over $800,000,000. (Eight hundred million dollars) in future net operating income.'

This is for the mining of the proven coal reserves.

B. The same report states the following opinion as to the value of the proven oil and gas reserves (Note there are 62 oil and/or gas wells on the property at the present time.):

'With current well completion techniques and improved prices, the oil and/or gas reserves of this property have an estimated economic potential of 70 million dollars after all expenditures except that required for income tax.'

C. Timber Resources – data prepared by the Forestry Department of the University of Kentucky when they cruised this property and their findings, samplings and evaluation are as follows:

The types of timber found were beech, black walnut, black oak, white oak, chestnut oak, chestnut poplar, white pine, maple.
Total gross acreage...............24,700+ acres

Estimated timber acreage.........20,000+ acres
Estimated average recoverable board feet per
acre.................................5,000 board feet
Estimated value of standing timber, total at
$40/thousand board feet..........$4,000,000.00
Estimated board feet.............. 100,000,000
Estimated gross value of timber, delivered to
mill, at $100/thousand board feet.............
..................................$10,000,000.00
-- by Hunt Perwick, Consultant Geologist
On June 1, 1989, Will Horton, Land and
Timber Consultant and Partner in North Florida
Timberlands and Investments, wrote the
following:
"I am familiar with these properties having
aided in the blocking up and the cruises over the
years. I unhesitantly endorse the reports of
Petrolane Corporation and the report of B.M.
Andreen and Associates as to the valuation and
economic potential."
Our maps, drill logs, analyses, cruises etc.
are available upon request.
Respectfully submitted,
H. Nicholas Johnson

In compliance with Harber's attached note, to "check this out," Anderson phoned Johnson for further information. Johnson enthusiastically noted that "This a real gold mine of an investment. An old widow in North Carolina inherited it from her late husband and doesn't know what's going on or the value of what she has. She is just interested in unloading the property for a few million in cash and needs the money."

Anderson decided to contact a trusted business associate, Michael Middleton, in Greenville, South Carolina, to inquire if anyone in the Middleton Group could be dispatched to eastern Kentucky to investigate the situation.

Mike Middleton was a brilliant MBA with an uncanny ability to develop creative, and often unorthodox, underwriting packages to provide venture, refinancing, and newco capital. He had a solid reputation for being a straight arrow who wanted nothing to do with any deal that was not fair to everyone involved. He was more interested in the challenges and dynamics of putting a deal together that is too difficult, or impossible, for his peers, than in the amount of his compensation. He frequently ended up with an inordinately modest fee for an excessive investment of his time, effort and expenses. All of his spare time was usually spent fishing on nearby Lake Jocassee.

Anderson faxed Middleton a copy of Johnson's letter, then rang him up. They spent the first half-hour discussing the fishing on Jocassee and the Saluda River, the latest flies and plugs on the market, and the secrets to smoking a trout. Eventually, they got around to the fax and Middleton said he would prefer to send his "miner, Frank Lynch, to Kentucky to do the ground work and check out the numbers but Lynch wouldn't be available to go for a couple of months."

On December 10, 1992, one of Anderson's wholesalers contracted with the Indian Foundation, Johnson and Mezvinsky to purchase a large number of the mature nursery stock on the Riverview Nursery farm for $2,250,000. Mezvinsky and Johnson phoned Anderson to express their satisfaction with their contract and to assure him that he should expect to receive a $225,000 check from the Foundation from the sale as his part of their brokerage agreement.

In February of 1993, Frank Lynch finally broke away from his work with the Middleton Group in South Carolina to travel to Kentucky to spend a week in Eastern Kentucky traveling around the country roads of Breathitt, Perry and Knott counties looking over the 24,700 acre tract, talking to the folks in the area along his way, and trying to locate specific sites of the coal, oil and gas reserves designated on the geological maps he had obtained after two days of research at the University of Kentucky. He was unable to complete his mission at that time and had to return for another ten days in March, after which he phoned Middleton with a favorable preliminary report.

Middleton passed the news on to Anderson, who relayed the information to Dr. Harber who decided he was too heavily invested and active with an ongoing real estate development project in Arkansas to get involved in the Kentucky matter. After Middleton expressed confidence in readily obtaining underwriting capital using the proven mineral reserves as collateral, Anderson decided to continue investigating the property's investment potential for his own interests. Lynch was instructed to set up a meeting with the owner and to start looking to market the mineral reserves. Middleton contacted Rick Whitworth in Tallahassee, Florida, to get The Whitworth Group involved marketing the timber.

Whitworth contacted fellow Floridian Bert Theriault, of Leeway Marketing, to exploit his international network of timber buyers.

A few days later, Theriault reported that the China timber market was hot to purchase big shipments of construction-grade timber at discount prices and he already had two very interested agents, from Beijing, ready to fly in to tour the stands of timber and sign contracts, subject to a timber cruise verification.

On April 30, 1993, Anderson's group met with the lawyers of the purported owner of the Kentucky property at their law offices in Charlotte, North Carolina. Middleton, his partner, Judson Decell, and Frank Lynch drove up together from Greenville to join Anderson and his assistant, Greg Childress. At the other end of the long, polished conference table, in their opulent office surroundings, sat the father/son lawyers, Julius Jennings "Jake" Wade, Jr. and James H. Wade. Between the Wades, and behind a mound of geological and topographical charts, maps and reports, sat their Kentucky geologist, Denver Andrews.

Introductions were made, business cards were exchanged, and Jake Wade went straight to the business at hand. He represented that his client, Margaret L. Godley of Charlotte, held and could convey good title to the 24,700 acres in Kentucky through her Kentucky corporation, Godley, Inc., which held that title as its sole asset and which she owned and controlled as the sole stockholder. She would also provide good title insurance and set aside funds to pay for a good, current survey which was readily available.

Denver Andrews then took over with a thorough presentation that ran for an hour and extolled the property's vast mineral reserves and timber stands. He repeatedly referred to the charts, maps and studies to point out specific locations and data supporting his representations.

As previously agreed, Mike Middleton was the spokesman for Anderson's group and he crisply noted that Anderson was interested in acquiring the property for its timber and crude reserves and he had timber sales ready to contract once he held a good option to purchase.

After a short break, there was discussion concerning the purchase price and the terms and price for an option, after which it was finally agreed that Anderson would pay $15,000 for a thirty day option to purchase the Godley, Inc. stock for $3,000,000.

On May 7, Anderson wired $15,000 to the bank account of Wade & Wade and notified his team to shift into high gear. Whitworth scheduled the timber buyers to fly into Greenville, within the week, to cover the preliminary work negotiating timber sales contracts. Lynch contacted C.C. Canada, of Camden, South Carolina, who arranged and managed large scale timber harvesting projects, to formulate harvest plans and expedite a comprehensive timber cruise of the 24,700 acre tract. Lynch also commenced firming up commitment letters and contract proposals with the most promising coal and gas markets in the Southeast. Decell and Childress began shaping up plans to purchase a small oil refinery in Somerset, Kentucky, which owned and operated a three state network of gas station and convenience stores.

Anderson also directed his Bristol attorney, Christen W. "Chip" Burkholder, to conduct a routine search of Godley's title.

A week later Middleton, Anderson, Whitworth, and Theriault met in Middleton's office with Guoming Song and Gong Mingxi, who had flown in from Beijing to negotiate contracts for the sale of the Kentucky timber. By the end of the following day a deal had been struck to sell the timber, for $11 million, to Guoming Song's Company, SDD, subject to confirmation of the standing timber quantity and quality by C.C. Canada's timber cruise. Mr. Guoming then announced that SDD had already entered into a contingent agreement to resell the timber to the China Timber Importing Company and would immediately deposit a $300,000 performance bond with China Timber.

Two days later, Anderson received a phone call from Mezvinsky expressing his enthusiastic satisfaction with the Kentucky purchase and the arrangements with the timber buyers from China. Mezvinsky assured Anderson that he was "prepared to arrange any Foundation tax credits that would be helpful" and he wished to bring "Roger Clinton and his associates, into the loop."

Mezvinsky informed Anderson that "Roger is well connected all around at the highest levels, as the brother of President Clinton and a close business associate of J.T. Lundy, the head of the famous Calumet Farms' thoroughbred dynasty in Kentucky." Mezvinsky gushed that his wife's recent "landslide victory over John Fox and election to the US House of Representatives and our close friendship with Bill and Hillary gives the Foundation real clout. I want you to plan to do lunch with us at the White House and to spend the night in the Lincoln bedroom My wife looks forward to meeting June and suggested we all plan to spend the next Renaissance Weekend together at Hilton Head."

Anderson congratulated Mezvinsky on his wife's election and suggested that he take up the Roger Clinton matter with Mike Middleton, who was taking care of the financing, and with Burton Theriault, who was handling the business with China.

On May 19, Burkholder phoned Anderson to inform him that his routine Westlaw search of the Godley title had uncovered 1992 and 1993 opinions, from the Federal District Court in Pikeville, Kentucky, and the Sixth Circuit Court of Appeals in Ohio, holding the title null and void and that Godley had been a party in the action and the Wades had represented her. The news shocked Anderson and he asked Burkholder to double-check the opinions language and legal impact on the title. Anderson passed the information on to Middleton who was also incredulous.

The next day, copies of the actual opinions in the case, captioned *Berry v. Cyprus Coal Co.*, were carefully reviewed by the three, prior to phoning Wade for an explanation. Burkholder noted that the first opinion holding the title "null and void" was handed down by Federal District Court judge, Henry Wilhoit in March of 1992 and he was affirmed by the Sixth Circuit's opinion which came down in March of 1993, a month before the Charlotte meeting. Burkholder maintained that there was no way the Wades or Godley should have maintained they held good title at the meeting and, at the very least, those opinions should have been disclosed. Burkholder phoned Wade for an explanation.

Jake Wade insisted that Burkholder was misinterpreting the legal effect of the opinions, "which were decided upon a narrow trespass issue that did not affect the validity of the DeGroot patents—which are the basis of Godley's title." Wade chastised Burkholder for daring to challenge his assurance that the title was good and noted that Burkholder was "a young lawyer who had not been involved in the case and who was totally misreading the case." Wade insisted "the title is good and that the sale must close or we will sell it to another party lined up with a contingency option on the property." When Burkholder asked Wade to provide written assurances of his position and representations, Wade refused to do so.

Several days later, Mike Middleton called Anderson with more troubling news. After receiving Mezvinsky's call and recommendation that Roger Clinton be "brought into the loop" of the Kentucky and China business ventures, Mike Middleton had done some due diligence checking into Clinton's *bona fides*. The information verified that he was the brother of the president and, consequently, had great influence with Bill and Hillary Clinton and, indirectly, through their contacts in high places. However, information about the dark side of the president's brother had convinced Middleton that Anderson should avoid doing any business with any of the Clintons or their business associates.

"These people are all bad news, Paull, regardless of their façades as president, first lady and first brother. Bill Clinton is real garbage as his record while governor of

Arkansas reflects. His wife is also a piece of work and her activities with her Rose Law Firm and the whitewater scandel, back in Arkansas, has the same stench. First brother, Roger, appears to be cut out of the same rotten wood. He has a bad drug history and did some serious prison time a few years back, in the eighties, for dealing cocaine as part of a drug ring with a big time, Little Rock, Arkansas, money man by the name of Dan Lasater. It appears that when Clinton was released from prison he did go on to work for another buddy, J.T. Lundy, who was running the Calumet Farms' stud farm in Kentucky.

My guy is still looking into any nexus between Clinton and Lundy with the Kentucky property and the Mezvinskys, the Wades, the Godleys, Hugh Rakes, and the rest of those thieves. It will be interesting to learn how Bill and Hillary Clinton fit into all this and nothing would surprise me. I don't intend to return any of Mezvinsky's or Roger Clinton's calls and I have left instructions with the secretary to pass on any messages from them but to always tell them I am unavailable. We have problems enough with that Kentucky mess and we don't want anything to do with Clinton and his sorry crowd."

Paull Anderson agreed and advised Mike Middleton to stay on top of the situation on his end and to keep him posted regarding developments.

In early June, Anderson and Middleton accepted the reality that the sale could not proceed, despite Jake Wade's continuing insistence that the title was good, that Burkholder was wrong, and that the sale must close. Anderson instructed Burkholder to demand the return of his option money and compensation to cover his mounting damages.

Wade scoffed at the demand and phoned Anderson to threaten to destroy him financially and tie him up with endless, expensive litigation if Anderson or Burkholder tried to make trouble for either Wade or his client, Margaret Godley.

Meanwhile, Anderson's team immediately acted to terminate their efforts and actions to market the mineral resources and to acquire the Somerset Refinery and its complex of service stations. Anderson contacted Guoming Song and Bert Theriault to advise them of the developments and suggested that he would search for substitute timber to meet the obligations to SDD and China Timber.

During the next two months, Anderson and Theriault searched for substitute timber sources within the same price range as the Kentucky timber, in the United States, Canada, and even the Lake Baku area of Russia.

In September, Guoming Song was advised that the effort to find substitute timber had failed; however, Anderson assured him that he would take all possible legal action to recover SDD's forfeited performance bond.

The Virginian later learned that the Wades and Godley did indeed have another party lined up behind Anderson to purchase an option to buy the Godley title. On the eighteenth of June, such an option was sold to a Texan, John Wolcott, for $25,000 and in July, that option was extended for an additional $25,000, notwithstanding the opinions of the federal courts, which had held that the title was "null, void and worthless."

Anderson, Burkholder, and Middleton were also surprised to learn that on the third of September, 1993, Godley had sold one-half of her Godley, Inc. stock to Johnson's and Mezvinsky's Indian Foundation for $3 million and she had conveyed the remaining shares to the Foundation as a charitable contribution and for which she received a $3 million IRS form 8283 tax deduction certificate from the Foundation. Johnson and Grigsby had earlier teamed up to arrange the acquisition of the Godley title by the Foundation through a loan from the Christ Is Our Savior (C.I.O.S.) organization, using the Godley, Inc. stock as collateral to secure the loan. Later, Johnson, Mezvinsky and Grigsby would repeatedly attempt to peddle the Godley stock for $28 million, despite their knowledge of the federal court opinions, ruling the Godley title "null, void and worthless."

In January of 1994, Anderson saw a local television news report announcing the sale of the old Unisys property, in Bristol, Tennessee, by the Indian Foundation to the Exide Corporation for $3.5 million and how Exide planned to convert the large industrial facility into a modern battery production plant. He phoned Johnson to inquire about the news and was told that the parties involved in the transaction had tried to keep it private and quiet. However, the information had somehow leaked out to the press. Johnson assured Anderson that all had gone well, nevertheless, and the results would greatly benefit the Foundation's work. In addition, several hundred thousand more dollars had been credited to Anderson's account as a finder's fee for assisting in originating the donation.

Anderson replied that since the Foundation was now obviously flush with significant funds he wished to withdraw the accumulated finder's fees credited to his account and convey the funds to three of his favorite charitable causes: St. Jude Children's Hospital, Shriners Children's Hospital, and Doctors Without Borders. Johnson said the checks would be cut and he would meet with Anderson for lunch in Bristol a week later to personally deliver the checks for Anderson to present to the three charities.

A week later, Johnson was a no-show at The Vineyard Restaurant and he kept dodging Anderson's subsequent calls and messages.

Anderson phoned Mezvinsky to relate his disappointment with Johnson's failure to appear at their scheduled meeting or to return his calls. Mezvinsky smoothly reassured Anderson that it must have been a simple misunderstanding that he would discuss with Johnson.

The next day, Mezvinsky called Anderson back to reschedule the meeting for the following week with his assurance that both he and Johnson would be there.

When neither Mezvinsky or Johnson appeared at that meeting place, Anderson phoned his lawyer to schedule a conference to discuss the failure of Johnson and Mezvinsky to honor their word and commitments, and the way their associates, Godley and the Wades, had defrauded Anderson with their Kentucky land scam.

The Virginian was deeply troubled by the fact that Mezvinsky, Johnson, Godley, and the Wades had all scoffed at his demand that they simply return the money they had defrauded him. They also had refused to comply with their frequent assurances that they would release the money he had earned through his service to the Foundation. Their brash arrogance and total lack of remorse amazed him.

Anderson and Burkholder discussed Anderson's legal options available to recover his damages. Civil litigation could be initiated in the Virginia state court against Mezvinsky, Johnson and their Indian Foundation. Similar civil litigation could be pursued against Godley and the Wades in either North Carolina or Kentucky state courts. However, since both lawsuits involved diversity of citizenship actions by Anderson, a Virginia citizen, against citizens of different states, and since the amount in controversy was in excess of $50,000 in each case, both cases qualified for federal jurisdiction.

Anderson knew he would be far better off pursuing both cases in the federal district court forums where the federal courts and federal laws could be relied upon to deal evenhanded justice. The prospects of pursuing the cases in the Virginia or Kentucky state courts were not particularly worrisome because both state courts had high standards and solid reputations for dispensing evenhanded justice.

On the other hand, the Virginian was well aware of the acute danger he would face by filing his suit against Godleys and the Wades in their Charlotte, North Carolina, state court before one of their notorious "juice judges." Anderson realized that his best chance to recover his losses lay in initiating a civil RICO racketeering, fraud and conspiracy lawsuit against Johnson, Mezvinsky, and their Foundation in the Federal District Court at Abingdon, Virginia, while pursuing a similar lawsuit against Godley and the Wades in the Federal District Court at Pikeville, Kentucky. He began to consider his options for simultaneously prosecuting the companion lawsuits.

Paull Anderson had confidence that Burkholder and his Bristol law firm, Woodward, Miles & Flannagan, could handle the Virginia case. However, they were not licensed to practice in Kentucky. He soon located several reputable firms in the Pikeville, Kentucky, area and one in Knoxville, Tennessee, that appeared capable of prosecuting the Kentucky action; he scheduled meetings with a senior partner in each firm to discuss the prospects of representation. Their response was uniformly discouraging and dwelt upon the fact that Anderson was going up against a father/son team of highly experienced lawyers with top A/V Martindale-Hubbell ratings. They conceded that the litigation was certain to be protracted over many years. It would be very expensive; the wealthy defendants had huge resources to retain a stable of top notch lawyers. In addition, such civil RICO/fraud cases were very difficult to win.

None of the attorneys would even consider pursuing the case on a contingency fee basis—where they would provide their legal services in return for a share of the proceeds recovered from the defendants if Anderson prevailed and received a money judgment. Finally, each demanded a large initial retainer to be followed by monthly sustainers and reimbursements for expenses.

Undaunted by his fruitless efforts to find counsel to represent him in the Kentucky case, Paull Anderson considered pursuing the litigation *pro se*, representing himself, and scheduled a meeting with Burkholder to discuss the situation.

Attorney Burkholder slowly paced about the conference room, deep in introspective thought, as Anderson discussed the *pro se* prospects. "I grant you that it will be another David versus Goliath battle for me going up against the Wades and their Kentucky lawyers but I have been there before. There is something about this situation—the total arrogance of those Wade lawyers and their wealthy client who think they can steal with impunity and that they are above the law. They paint you as some greenhorn lawyer and they denigrate me as some old farmer they can fleece and laugh at."

Burkholder was aware that many years earlier, Anderson had intensely studied and read the law under the private mentorship of a distinguished American judge and successfully pursued litigation *pro se*.

Regardless, Burkholder's advice was sobering. "I wouldn't advise you to pursue the Kentucky case *pro se* for several reasons that you already are aware of. Any civil case is difficult enough; a civil fraud, conspiracy, RICO racketeering case such as this will be most difficult for even the best of lawyers to handle. Only after carefully considering all of the factors—especially the negative ones—should you head down that slippery slope," Burkholder advised solemnly.

As Paull Anderson mulled over the wise advice from the young, trustworthy lawyer he turned to look out, beyond the tall windows in the conference room, and down to the park below and its war memorial to Bristol's veterans. Five realistic, life-sized, bronze figures, representing each of the military services stood around the reflecting pool, gazing upon the single jet of water that shot up from the center of the pool for ten feet and then cascaded back upon itself in eternal motion. The Virginian's gaze focused on the figure of the bronze sailor and his thoughts revisited memories of his days in the submarine service during the Vietnam conflict. He wound through some of the old reels, images and sounds gathering dust in the dead files of his fading memories. He was surprised at their clarity as his mind sifted through them, focusing on personal recollections of his distant past that had once been an important part of his life during the difficult, dangerous period of his early manhood.

He reviewed the thirty year-old film bites of his days aboard the diesel "smoke boat" submarines, USS Sirago and USS Bang, and one especially dangerous "Northern Run" in enemy waters. He was further surprised at the clarity of his old memories of the first three "gold war patrols" aboard the nuclear-powered, fleet ballistic missile submarine, USS George Washington.

The images took him back to the night, in October of 1962, on the "boomer" when they suddenly went to "battle stations missile:"

The unexpected call over the ships 1MC sound system had alerted and sent all of the submarine's crew scrambling to their battle stations. The two thirds the ship's company that was off-watch, asleep, eating or relaxing in the mess hall, or somewhere in a private recess studying, quickly moved about and throughout the submarine to their battle stations. The entire crew's mindset had shifted instantaneously to their most heightened sense of alertness and mental acuity—ready to perform at their maximum level of professional ability.

Paull Anderson had been off-watch, nestled in his bunk in a deep sleep, when the 1MC squawked the call to battle stations. He reacted instinctively, still half-asleep, along with several others in the berthing compartment, quickly rolling out of their "nests." He slipped into his shoes then turned sideways in the narrow passageway to allow Jack Evans to brush by him on his way to the nearby Gyro Room. Evans would "fire up" the huge, two ton stabilizing gyro whose tremendous precession forces would steady the gargantuan submarine at its launch depth, some eighty feet beneath the ocean surface—regardless of surface turbulence.

Jim Rebman emerged from the "goat locker" bitching about "another damn drill as soon as I get settled into my rack," and passed Denny Yure, headed to his battle station in the opposite direction. Quartermaster Bob Gilmore brushed past Anderson on his way to the control room to assume control of their navigation and launch course. Denny Denniston, and Tony Iacavelli joined Anderson in the dash toward their battle stations in missile control center and the missile compartment. As they moved through the mess hall, they each grabbed a hot cinnamon bun off a fresh stack that the crew's favorite "stewburner,"

Ken Szablewski, had just set out for the interrupted "soup call."

Beyond the mess hall, Doug Yauchler joined the group. Yauchler was on route to the scrubber room to "max up" the submarine's sophisticated oxygen generator, carbon dioxide scrubber, and atmospheric control system. He was grumbling about having his sleep disturbed, especially after having spent two straight days working to replace one of the cells that blew out on his oxygen generator.

"Sure wished you guys had given me a few more hours in the sack before deciding to run another drill. Hell, we just had one yesterday. Are we starting to get two a week, now?"

"This is no drill, Doug," replied Iacavelli as he stepped through the hatch and into the missile compartment, with Yauchler close behind. Anderson and Denniston had turned off before the hatch and entered the missile control center.

The missile launch fire control team smoothly ran through their well-practiced launch protocol to quickly bring up all sixteen missiles to condition 2 SQ—ready for immediate launch. With all sixteen "birds" spun up and ready to fire, an uncomfortable, eerie silence hung over missile control center as the launch team stood quietly awaiting and dreading the order to start the launch sequence that would unleash the horrific devastation of their nuclear arsenal. The solemn, worried faces of Paull Anderson, Denny

Denniston, Pete DePedro, Bob Mills, and Bob Stewart reflected the intense drama of that night.

They all stood around the launch panel, awaiting the command from Captain J. Larry From, up in the control room, to "initiate launch sequence." The order would turn the launch control panel "Christmas tree" lights from steady amber to flashing red and green. Waves of launching effects would ripple through the submarine as each Polaris missile sequentially blasted up from its missile tube in a bubble of compressed air to break through the surface as the huge, solid propellant rocket motors ignited with a roaring, searing, white-hot flame. Simultaneously and automatically, the complex gyros and accelerometers in each missile's guidance package would immediately stabilize and direct its pre-programmed flight path orientation and trajectory to insure that the deadly warhead would be carried high, far and fast to its doomed target thousands of miles away.

As the George Washington hovered at launch depth at condition 2SQ, many of the same dreaded thoughts were shared by every member of the crew. The launching of their missiles would signal that the deterrent intention and effect of the Polaris missile submarines had failed. Everyone knew that they would launch only in retaliation to a massive missile attack upon the United States and in so doing insure the total devastation of the enemy's major cites and weapons bases, and the unleashing of a vast nuclear cloud of radioactivity that would destroy all life under it. They also knew that such a highly radioactive cloud would have a long, deadly half-life of many years as the high, atmospheric winds slowly moved it around the world, indiscriminately raining death upon everything it passed over. That deadly cloud could one day end up passing over the very nation that unleashed its horrific, destructive force.

Two hours later, Captain From received a second transmission over the WRT-2 Bravo from COMSUBLANT – FBM Missile Control that allowed him to order the launch crew to "stand down to Condition 4SQ." A collective sigh of relief could be heard as the tense faces relaxed for the first time in hours in missile control as they stood down from their "ready to fire" status and allowed the missiles to return to the less ominous "general ready" status of 4SQ. The relief quickly flooded throughout the submarine and the somber melancholy gave way to small talk and banter intended to try to make light of having been on the edge of unleashing a doomsday scenario. Each submariner was thankful for having stepped back from the brink.

On the following day, Captain From announced over the 1MC speakers throughout the submarine the details of how President Kennedy had successfully forced the Russian General Secretary of the Communist Party, Nikita Khrushchev, to back down from the imminent threat of nuclear war by turning his missile-laden ships away from their planned delivery of their deadly cargo to Cuba. Only then did the entire crew fully grasp the gravity of their earlier situation.

Paull Anderson still held that experience vividly in his memory, along with other trying events that had tested his mettle, both during and after his military service. Those unique memories had remained long after he had finally been released from St. Alban's Naval Hospital–after recuperating from his serious military injuries.

He had packed away his military uniform, decorations, and medals in his sea chest to gather dust in the attic and only allowed his wife to display his special, personal commendation from President Jimmie Carter for "service to the Nation in time of war and outstanding community service in time of peace."

The Virginian's military service and experiences had left him more than capable of dealing with intense pressure and huge adversity.

After leaving the military, he found himself caught up in legal battles that also tested his character and perseverance. They had taught him that he could win battles against corrupt lawyers and judges on their own turf. He had become deeply involved in antiwar activities and in a difficult, protracted, legal battle championing a righteous cause against flagrant injustice, ruthless adversaries and corrupt lawyers. He had learned painful and expensive lessons but he persevered and eventually prevailed in the courts. Later, he began advocating as a court-appointed special advocate and officer of the court representing the *guardian ad litem* legal interests of abused and neglected children.

As the myriad memories had flashed before him, he had felt his face flush and his spirit girding for yet another confrontation up ahead. He smiled ever-so-slightly to himself and the spark in his eyes intensified when he turned to face attorney Burkholder.

"Maybe it's time for this old sodbuster and deep-water sailor to let Congressman Mezvinsky, those high and mighty big-time lawyers and their wealthy client see that I won't let them cheat and beat me with impunity. You prosecute the Virginia case, Chip, and I'll handle the Kentucky case as best I can."

Later, Paull Anderson informed his old friend, Idaho district judge, Sherman J. Bellwood, about the situation and soon received further sobering advice:

> *It is noble of you to have assured your business associates who suffered far greater monetary losses than you in the Kentucky land fraud that reimbursement of their losses will be the priority from any recovery proceeds resulting from your lawsuits and I agree with Attorney Burkholder's disenchantment with your plans to proceed pro se in the Kentucky case. However, having said that but knowing you I can appreciate the impetus driving your decision and it reminds me of the interesting and accurate way "the Teach" characterized you: "That Paull is a modern day Don Quixote or white knight from Idylls of the King; one of those champions*

of righteousness and justice that is simply destined to battle the forces of evil and injustice that the Good Lord confronts him with from time to time to test his mettle."

When I passed her remarks on to your good friends, Governor West and Judge Haynsworth, they both agreed with her and indicated that those who know you well would likewise concur. If Eleanor were still with us she would likely smile at this development and cheer you on. So buckle on your silver spurs, Sir Knight, mount your faithful charger, and go forth to battle the forces of evil in the Kentucky arena. Godspeed, and know that the loyal spirits of Eleanor and Shermie L. will be with you on your noble quest.

Keep your wits about you and remember well some of the sound legal advice and lessons you have picked up along the way during your past battles. Hope for the Court "to do justice above all else," in keeping with the splendid and exemplary tradition of the Warren and Haynsworth Courts, but be ever mindful that the measure of justice one receives depends not upon the laws and rules and courts, but upon the presiding judges and how they decide to apply the laws and rules to be just or otherwise. The competence and integrity of your presiding judge, or lack thereof, will make all the difference.

Enclosed is information concerning the Bellwood Lectures I am endowing at the University College of Law and I hope you will consider participating to share some of your inspirational legal insight and experiences."

The Virginian appreciated both the sound advice and the assurance that the best wishes of Judge Bellwood's beloved and deceased wife and son would be with him on his crusade.

In April of 1994, Burkholder filed the Virginia Complaint, *Anderson v. Foundation, et al.* and Anderson simultaneously filed, *pro se*, the companion Kentucky Complaint, *Anderson v. Wade, et al.*

Soon after Mezvinsky learned he was a party in the Virginia action, he phoned to schedule "a meeting to reconcile our differences."

On April 19, 1994, Anderson and Burkholder agreed to meet with Mezvinsky and Johnson at a Bristol, Virginia, motel. Mezvinsky was waiting outside as they drove up.

Edward Maurice Mezvinsky was tall and lean with an appearance that attested to his penchant for distance running and the healthy habits of a dedicated athlete. However, every inch of him was clearly the seasoned politician and lawyer. His neat, charcoal grey, glen plaid suit fit him perfectly, as one would expect from such an expensive, custom-made and hand-tailored garment. The matching Brooks Brothers, pale blue shirt framed one of their exclusive, finely woven, silk ties in a subdued Regimental Black Watch pattern. His English, black patent leather shoes looked brand new. He knew how to look the part and play the role.

Mezvinsky flashed the wide, disarming smile of a polished politician. However, the affected smile, trying to appear warm and genuine, was betrayed by the tightly clinched, thin lips and mouth that turned down at the corners in a sneer. Mezvinsky's steel grey eyes reflected two sinister, cold pupils that also contradicted the joyful and friendly nature that his face mask was trying to exude. His receding and thinning grey hair had been carefully left loose and gently disheveled to soften his facial appearance.

He threw out a wide open, friendly handshake at Anderson, "Good to get to meet with you and talk this little problem out, Paull." Mezvinsky pumped Anderson's firmly grasped hand and then extended the same greeting to attorney Burkholder. "Good to also meet you, Chip. So glad you could come. Let's step inside where Nick is waiting for us." Mezvinsky gestured toward the motel restaurant, holding the door open and with his wide smile still diligently frozen across his face.

As they moved toward the table where Johnson was seated, Anderson caught Burkholder's eye, smiled slightly, and barely said "slick suit," as he rolled his eyes back towards Mezvinsky. Burkholder grinned in spite of his attempt to keep it hidden and nodded back.

Johnson sat silently, glowering and openly hostile, as the three pulled out chairs and settled in.

"Guess you two already know, Nick, here," Mezvinsky continued the friendly banter. Neither Anderson nor Burkholder wasted more than the briefest glance towards Johnson as Mezvinsky kept center stage. "Well, we are all reasonable men and I am sure we can end this ridiculous litigation and get on with our affairs. Right?"

"It's pretty simple, Ed," Anderson replied. "Ante up what you owe me, fair and square. Give that money to the charities I have designated and we all live happily ever after."

"We're not turning over a goddamn nickel of that money and we're ready to whip your ass in the courtroom if this goddamn lawsuit continues," Johnson snapped.

Johnson's remark shattered Mezvinsky's attempt to present a diplomatic face to the proceedings. There was no more smoothing over the waters; from that point on, the discussion hardened as both sides quickly retreated from any chance of reaching a reasonable settlement. After further sharp, profane remarks from Johnson, Burkholder opined that it was obvious that he and his client were "wasting our time in our *bona fide* attempt to avoid litigation," as he gathered up his legal pad, acknowledging that the meeting had proven fruitless. It was hastily concluded.

Mezvinsky's smile was suddenly replaced with a hard and threatening scowl. His forefinger jabbed at the air as he arrogantly berated Anderson and Burkholder for daring to defame him by including him in the lawsuit. He insisted they would have no chance whatsoever in any courtroom contest against him.

"See you in court, counselor. Have a safe return trip," Anderson replied pleasantly, as he and Burkholder left Mezvinsky and Johnson fuming.

Later that evening, Mezvinsky phoned Anderson to threaten and intimidate him if the lawsuit was not immediately withdrawn.

"You had better think long and hard about who I am and the very powerful friends I have in high places that can make your life miserable and destroy your business. The IRS will come down on you like a ton of bricks and I will have my Philadelphia law firm tie you and Burkholder up in lawsuits that will break the both of you two fools…"

Paull Anderson simply smiled to himself as he cut off the conversation and hung up the phone.

CHAPTER II

SNAKEHUNTING: KENTUCKY

US FEDERAL DISTRICT COURT,
Pikeville, Kentucky
*Paull Anderson v. Margaret L. Godley, Julius J. Wade,
Jr., James H. Wade, Godley, Inc., Wade & Wade,
Attys. At Law*

Paull Anderson realized that the Kentucky case would present a great challenge, but he was encouraged by the fact that he would be advocating in a federal court where the judges were highly competent and sensitive to insure that *pro se* litigants receive justice.

The Virginian planned to work closely with attorney Burkholder, since the companion Virginia and Kentucky RICO racketeering/fraud/conspiracy cases were closely intertwined and shared many common factual and legal issues. He realized he was undertaking a difficult legal battle going up against the powerful, influential, father/son lawyers, Julius and James Wade, and their wealthy client, Margaret Godley. However, he looked forward to the opportunity to champion a righteous cause against the corrupt defendants. He also was pleased to have an opportunity to interface with and learn from the highly skilled and dedicated young lawyer as they worked together simultaneously pursuing Anderson's common foes in the Virginia and Kentucky federal district courts.

Anderson's Kentucky Complaint laid out the basis of his jurisdictional claim which established that Court's authority to hear the case, his factual allegations supporting his Complaint, and the three counts of his legal allegations against the defendants:

Jurisdiction

This Court has subject matter jurisdiction as to the Count One of this Complaint pursuant to the provisions of the Racketeer Influenced and Corrupt Organization Act. 18 USC. Section 1964(c)(1991 and Supp. 1993).

This Court has subject matter jurisdiction as to the remaining Counts of this Complaint pursuant to 28 USC. Section 1332 based on diversity of citizenship between the parties and an amount in controversy in excess of $50,000.

Plaintiff at all times relevant hereto is and has been a citizen of the Commonwealth of Virginia.

Defendants Julius Jennings Wade, Jr, James H. Wade, and Margaret L. Godley are all citizens of the State of North Carolina.

Defendant Wade and Wade, Attorneys at Law is a business in North Carolina whose principals are all citizens of the State of North Carolina.

Defendant Godley, Inc. is a Kentucky Corporation with its principal place of business in Kentucky.

Factual Allegations Common to All Counts

On or about April 30, 1993, the plaintiff, Paull Anderson, and certain of his business associates met with defendants Julius and James

Wade at their law offices in Charlotte, North Carolina to discuss the opportunity to acquire some 24,700 acres of mineral and timber bearing land located in Knott, Perry and Breathitt Counties Kentucky.

Defendant Margaret Godley is the purported owner of said property, having inherited her interest from her late husband.

Defendants Julius and James Wade and their law firm, Wade and Wade, are the attorneys for Mrs. Godley and the estate of M.R. Godley, deceased. Defendant Godley, Inc. is a corporation wholly owned by Margaret Godley to which she has transferred her title to the 24,700 acres of mineral property. The title to said property is the only asset of Godley, Inc.

Following the April 30, 1993 meeting, plaintiff purchased an option from Mrs. Godley to enter into a contract to purchase 100 percent of the stock in Godley, Inc. and thus acquire the 24,700 acres. True copies of that option and the proposed contracts documents for the purchase and sale of the Godley, Inc. stock are attached as Exhibits.

The chain of title by which Mrs. Godley and Godley, Inc. claim ownership of the 24,700 acres is commonly referred to as the "DeGroot patents," so named for a series of some 119 deeds originally coming out of the Commonwealth of Kentucky in 1870.

This Court, under the Honorable Federal District Judge Henry R. Wilhoit, Jr., has previously held that the DeGroot patents are void in their entirety as a matter of law in an unpublished opinion dated March 20, 1992 rendered in Civil Action No: 84-53, styled *Bessie Berry, et al v. Cyprus Coal Co., et al.* A true copy is attached as an Exhibit.

Judge Wilhoit's ruling was appealed to the United States Court of Appeals for the Sixth Circuit. That appellate court affirmed Judge Wilhoit in an unpublished *per curium* decision handed down March 19, 1993, Record No: 92-5543. A true copy of the Sixth Circuit's opinion is attached as an Exhibit.

Defendant Margaret Godley was a party to said litigation in both the district and circuit courts. Her attorneys in both courts were defendants Julius and James Wade and their law firm Wade and Wade.

Defendants never revealed the existence of these court decisions despite having direct knowledge thereof.

At all times pertinent hereto, defendants have maintained that they hold good title to the 24,700 acres.

Defendants have attempted to sell the 24,700 acres knowing that the title was void.

<u>Count I–RICO Racketeering</u>

The 24,700 acres contain coal mines, oil reserves, gas wells, pipelines and timber. As such, the property constitutes an enterprise engaged in, and the activities of which affect, interstate commerce.

The law firm Wade and Wade and the company Godley, Inc. are enterprises engaged in, and the activities of which affect, interstate commerce.

All defendants are associated in fact in an organization having an ascertainable structure and which functions as a continuing unit for the common purpose of selling the DeGroot patents despite the adjudication of these instruments as legal nullities. As such, the defendants' association in fact is an enterprise engaged in, and the activities of which affect, interstate commerce.

The defendants have knowingly and intentionally committed acts of racketeering activity in furtherance of a scheme to defraud plaintiff and obtain money by means of false and fraudulent pretenses, representations, and promises.

In furtherance of said scheme, the defendants have knowingly and intentionally transmitted the aforesaid option and proposed contracts, and between April and June, 1993, knowingly and intentionally transmitted numerous other telephone, telefax and mail communications to the plaintiff and his associates through the United States mail and by telefax wire communication in interstate commerce, all in violation of 18 USC. Sections 1341 & 1343.

In furtherance of said scheme, defendants solicited and received a wire transfer in interstate commerce of $15,000 from plaintiff in exchange for the aforenoted option, in violation of 18 USC. Sections 1341 & 1343.

Defendants have maintained an agent in this judicial district for the purpose of furthering said attempts to sell the DeGroot patents in the personage of Atty. Robert M. Pfeiffer of Lexington who performed title work for the defendants as indicated on a purported commitment for title insurance which accompanied the proposed contract for the purchase and sale of Godley, Inc.

In addition to the scheme to defraud the plaintiff, the defendants have engaged in acts of racketeering activity with respect to attempts to sell the subject property to other individuals and entities both before and after the events complained of in this action, including transferring an option to an entity identified as the Foundation for the Advancement, Education and Employment of American Indians, and despite knowledge of the decisions of this Court and of the Sixth Circuit both the defendants and the Foundation are attempting to sell the subject property to unsuspecting buyers through mail and wire communications in violation of 18 US C. Sections 1341 & 1343.

The defendants acts of racketeering activity all relate to schemes to obtain money from the sale of the subject property by false or fraudulent pretenses, representations and promises, their racketeering activities amount to a pattern and a regular way of conducting their affairs and threaten future criminal activity, and they have received income from the pattern of racketeering activities and used said income to operate Wade and Wade, Godley, Inc. and their association in fact, and conspired, all in violation of 18 USC. Section 1962(a) b)(c).

As a direct and proximate result of the racketeering activities of the defendants the plaintiff has been injured in his business and property and demands judgment against the defendants, jointly and severally, in the principal amount of $7,500,000 trebled to $22,500,000 pursuant to 18 USC. Section 1964(a).

Count II – Fraud

Defendants have made knowing, intentional, deliberate, willful and wanton misrepresentations of material facts regarding the state of their title to the subject property and concerning the effect of the decisions by this Court and the Sixth Circuit upon their title for the purpose of deceiving the plaintiff and which the plaintiff has relied upon to his detriment.

As a direct and proximate result of the defendants' actions the plaintiff has been injured in his business and property and demands judgment against the defendants, jointly and severally, in the principal amount of $7,500,000 and punitive damages in the amount of $15,000,000.

Count III – Conspiracy

Defendants have made materially false representations regarding the state of their title to the subject property and concerning the effect of the decisions by this Court and the Sixth Circuit upon their title intending that the plaintiff act upon said representations and plaintiff believing said representations entered into contractual relationships in reliance upon them.

As a direct and proximate result of the defendants' actions the plaintiff has been injured in his business and property and has suffered lost earnings, profits and business opportunities and incurred incidental and consequential damages and demands judgment against the defendants, jointly and severally, in the principal amount of $7,500,000 and punitive damages in the amount of $15,000,000.

Trial by jury of all issues so triable is hereby demanded.

Paull Anderson, *pro se*

Thirty days later the defendants submitted timely Answers denying all the allegations. The case then advanced into the discovery phase of the litigation. Discovery is vital because it allows both sides to utilize interrogatory and production vehicles to force their opponents to provide accurate and complete information, records, and documents necessary to develop important case information and evidence.

However, early on in the discovery phase it became obvious that although Paull Anderson was strictly complying with the Federal Rules of Civil Procedure the defendants had decided to flagrantly defy and violate those Rules. The defendants' obvious strategy was to delay and obstruct the due process of the case rather than turning over incriminating evidence in compliance with the Rules. Although that strategy seriously jeopardized their defense in Anderson's civil case, disclosing the incriminating evidence would have left the defendants in greater jeopardy of collateral criminal prosecution by the state and federal authorities. Consequently, they chose to take their chances by defying the Rules in the civil case to avoid facing criminal prosecution.

Anderson filed motions to compel the required discovery information and vigorously objected to the defendants' adamant refusal to comply with the discovery rules and disclose the requested information and documents. Anderson's motions were sustained by both Magistrate Judge Peggy Patterson and US Federal District Judge Joseph M. Hood, who ordered the defendants to comply with the discovery rules and provide the requested information and documentation. The orders explicitly chastised the defendants':

> **...deplorable stonewalling tactics and gamesmanship intended to flagrantly abuse and defy the Rules.**

Notwithstanding, the recalcitrant defendants stubbornly refused to modify their tactics and to comply with the Rules. Anderson filed additional motions to compel and Magistrate Judge Patterson and Judge Hood imposed large monetary sanctions as the first level of punishment against the intractable defendants. The defendants scoffed at the sanctions and intensified their egregious and defiant misconduct.

In addition to the defendants' repugnant courtroom antics in attempts to defeat Anderson's efforts to seek justice, another more sinister development raised its ugly presence when the Virginian received two anonymous phone calls at his home in the middle of the night, threatening to "burn you out" if he continued with his lawsuit.

Paull Anderson took the threats very seriously, recalling Garvin Wells's explicit warning that "Nick Johnson has mob connections and he has no qualms about using violence to get his way."

The Virginian removed his old German Luger from his sea chest and, after cleaning, oiling and firing two clips of 9 mm rounds through it, to insure its serviceability and to refresh himself with its handling, he placed it close at hand in his bedside table. He also took measures to more closely monitor and control both the open and the wooded acreage around his home and to insure that his home's alarm system was in excellent working order. But in no way did the anonymous threats deter his resolve to press on with his lawsuits and his quest for justice.

In December of 1995, Anderson received a favorable ruling from Judge Hood concerning the important issue of whether the defendants knew their title was bogus when they tried to sell it to Anderson:

...as a matter of law, the defendants herein had knowledge of the March 1992 opinion of the United States District Court, and the March 1993 opinion of the United States Court of Appeals for the Sixth Circuit, in the Berry v.

Cyprus Coal Co. case, which held that the DeGroot patents were null and void in their entirety.

Judge Hood's ruling affirmed the prior rulings by the federal courts and served to destroy the defendants' defense, which rested on their contention that the DeGroot patents, the basis of the Godley title, were not null and void. Nevertheless, the recalcitrant defendants continued to defiantly ignore and violate Judge Hood's rulings, to flagrantly abuse and flaunt federal discovery rules, and to support further attempts by their cronies to peddle the worthless title for $28 million.

The defendants' defiant actions greatly disturbed their lawyers at the distinguished Lexington, Kentucky law firm of Landrum & Shouse. Lead defense lawyer, John H. Burrus, Esq., repeatedly complained to the court that Godley and the the Wades "adamantly refuse to end their defiant misconduct and they have disregarded my repeated threats to withdraw from the case."

On February 1, 1996, Judge Hood signed an Order granting Mr. Burrus' motion to withdraw as the defendants' counsel. The defiant defendants began to search around for new counsel and eventually convinced Pikeville, Kentucky attorney David C. Stratton and his law firm to take the case. However, barely a month later, Stratton and his law firm also moved to withdraw from representing the defendants after learning of the conflicting problems in the case. Finally, in April of 1996, the defendants were able to bring in attorney Paul Franklin Heaberlin, of Prestonsburg, Kentucky, as replacement counsel. Attorney Heaberlin immediately began to try to convince the defendants to change their ways and to respect and comply with the orders and Rules of the Court. However, his diligent efforts also proved fruitless. The defendants' pusillanimous disrespect and defiance only intensified.

After the defendants defied three more distinct warnings from the Court, threatening default judgment, on September 29, 1997, Judge Hood issued his Order granting a default judgment against the defendants on the issue of liability:

> **Notwithstanding the numerous warnings from the Court and the imposition of monetary sanctions against them, the defendants have continued to engage in a pattern of obstruction and delay in response to not only Anderson's discovery requests but to the Court's orders compelling such discovery. Only the harsh sanction of default judgment on the issue of liability will serve to deter future litigants from engaging in this type of behavior, adequately punish these defendants, and preserve the integrity of the Court. Hence, the defendants will have default judgment entered against them on the issue of liability, and the issue of damages will go forward on the merits.**

In April of 1998, a trial was held in the federal district court to determine Anderson's damages. Anderson took the stand and testified. He put Mike Middleton and attorney Burkholder on the stand to testify and he introduced into evidence the lengthy depositions of Judson Decell, Greg Childress, and Guoming Song. He submitted the convincing testimony of Lee Theriault, the wife and business partner of Bert Theriault—who had recently died.

Finally, Anderson introduced a plethora of further damaging documentary evidence proving that the defendants had been vigorously peddling their bogus title to several other victims between 1992 and 1995. That evidence included Johnson's 1992 letter to Harber, documents evidencing the sale of the Wolcott option and extension in July of 1993 for $50,000, the sale/donation to the Indian Foundation for $3 million in cash and $3 million in tax deductions in September of 1993, and the defendants' 1995 attempt to peddle their bogus title for $28 million to the Wolford brothers, of Louisa, Kentucky.

Anderson's irrefutable evidence documented the severe damages, amounting to several hundred thousands of dollars, that he had suffered as a result of the defendants' illegal acts.

Although the Wades attended the hearing neither one dared take the stand and their lawyer called no witnesses to the stand to testify on their behalf.

On May 22, 2000, Judge Hood issued a blistering Memorandum Opinion and Order awarding Anderson $111,200.53 in compensatory damages and $500,000.00 in punitive damages that soundly chastised:

the evil nature of the defendants and their actions.

Judge Hood's characterization of the defendants as "evil" amazed everyone. It was highly unusual for a federal judge to independently volunteer such a drastic finding of fact and conclusion of law in a civil case and it reflected his most severe condemnation of the defendants' *mens rea* —evil minds.

The defendants appealed but in March of 2002, the United States Court of Appeals for the Sixth Circuit fully upheld Judge Hood's award of $611,200.53 in damages which concluded the Kentucky litigation with legally binding, *res judicata*, finality.

Early on in the Kentucky litigation, Paull Anderson had filed complaints with the North Carolina Bar Association to bring the Wades up on charges and have them disbarred. He also initiated actions with the FBI, the Criminal Investigation Department of the IRS, and the North Carolina authorities to investigate the Wades for their criminal conduct.

Paull Anderson's relentless and dedicated efforts to bring the Wades to justice eventually resulted in the convening of a grand jury in Virginia and the subsequent disbarment of both Julius Jennings Wade, Jr. and James H. Wade for their pattern of criminal activities which included stealing huge sums from their clients' trust accounts, subornation of perjury, and lying under oath.

Paull Anderson was pleased that his long and difficult battle against the Wades and Godley had resulted in a favorable judgment in the Kentucky case, exposed their illegal activities, cost the Wades their law licenses, and spared others from being victimized by their Kentucky land scam.

CHAPTER III

SNAKEHUNTING: VIRGINIA

US FEDERAL DISTRICT COURT,
Abingdon, Virginia
Paull Anderson v. Howard N. Johnson, Edward M.
Mezvinsky, Foundation for the Advancement,
Education & Employment of American Indians

On April 7, 1994, Attorney Burkholder filed a Complaint against Johnson, Mezvinsky, and their Indian Foundation before the US Federal District Court in Abingdon, Virginia.

The Complaint carefully laid out the basis of Anderson's jurisdictional claim, his factual allegations and the four counts of his legal allegations against the defendants:

Jurisdiction

This Court has subject matter jurisdiction as to the Count I of this Complaint pursuant to the provisions of the Racketeer Influenced and Corrupt Organization Act. 18 USC. Section 1964(c)(1991 and Supp. 1993).

This Court has subject matter jurisdiction as to the remaining Counts of this Complaint pursuant to 28 USC. Section 1332 based on diversity of citizenship between the parties and an amount in controversy in excess of $50,000.

Plaintiff at all times relevant hereto is and has been a citizen of the Commonwealth of Virginia.

Defendant Indian Foundation is an Oklahoma Corporation with its principal place of business in the District of Columbia. Defendant Johnson is the President of the Foundation and a citizen of the State of Tennessee. Defendant Mezvinsky is the Chairman of the Foundation and a citizen of the State of Pennsylvania.

Factual Allegations Common to All Counts

On or about January 23, 1992, plaintiff and the Foundation entered into a contract (the Finders Fee Agreement) whereby the plaintiff would procure donations to the Foundation and receive a finder's fee for his services. A true copy of said contract is attached as an Exhibit as well as a letter dated October 2, 1992 sent to the plaintiff by Johnson affirming said contract agreement.

On or about March 23, 1992, plaintiff and the Foundation entered into a separate contract (the Brokerage Agreement) whereby the Foundation would pay plaintiff a brokerage commission for sales of nursery stock. A true copy of said contract is attached as an Exhibit and referenced in the aforesaid Johnson letter.

Pursuant to the Finder's Fee Agreement plaintiff procured substantial donations to the foundation. On or about September 25, 1992, plaintiff secured the donation to the Foundation of the nursery stock on the Riverview Nursery, a tree farm at Limestone, Tennessee with the value of its nursery stock $2,837,088.

On or about January 14, 1994, plaintiff arranged for the donation to the Foundation of a Bristol Tennessee industrial property commonly known as the Unisys or Exide plant and which the defendants recognized had a value of $6,000,000.

Pursuant to the Brokerage Agreement, plaintiff arranged a sale of nursery stock by the Foundation to a purchaser for the sum of $2,500,000 as memorialized by a contract (the Nursery Stock Sales Contract) dated December 10, 1992; a true copy is attached as an Exhibit.

Under the terms of the Brokerage Agreement plaintiff is owed some $225,000 and under the Finder's Fee Agreement plaintiff is owed some $883,708 for his services.

The Finder's Fee Agreement, Brokerage Agreement and the Nursery Stock Sales Contract were all negotiated and executed by defendants Johnson and Mezvinsky.

Count I – RICO Racketeering

The Foundation, Riverview Nursery, and the Unisys/Exide plant are enterprises engaged in, and the activities of which affect, interstate commerce.

The defendants have knowingly and intentionally committed acts of racketeering activity in furtherance of a scheme to defraud plaintiff and obtain property by means of false and fraudulent pretenses, representations, and promises.

In furtherance of said scheme, the defendants have knowingly and intentionally transmitted the aforesaid exhibits to the plaintiff through the United States mail and by telefax wire communication in interstate commerce, all in violation of 18 USC. Sections 1341 & 1343 without any intention of honoring said contracts.

In furtherance of the scheme to defraud plaintiff, the defendants have knowingly and intentionally transmitted numerous telephone communications in interstate commerce to the plaintiff between January 1992 and January 1994 pertaining to said contracts without any intention of honoring same, all in violation of 18 USC. Section 1343.

In addition to the scheme to defraud the present plaintiff, the defendants have engaged in acts of racketeering activity with respect to a second scheme to defraud the buyer under the Nursery Stock Sales Contract. Said contract was negotiated and achieved by multiple acts of mail and wire fraud in interstate commerce, occurring between April and December 1992 in violation of 18 USC. Sections 1341 & 1343 without any intention of honoring said contract.

The defendants have also knowingly and willfully engaged in acts of racketeering activity with respect to a separate fraudulent scheme to sell some 24,700 acres of mineral property in Knott, Perry and Breathitt Counties, Kentucky while having knowledge that the purported title to said property has been declared factually void as a matter of law by a decision of the US District Court for the Eastern District of Kentucky, London Division, which ruling has been affirmed by the US Court of Appeals for the Sixth Circuit. True copies of the decision and ruling are attached as Exhibits.

Despite knowledge of these decisions, the defendants have acquired an option to purchase said void title and have attempted to sell same to unsuspecting buyers through mail and wire communications in interstate commerce in violation of 18 USC. Sections 1341 & 1343.

The defendants' acts of racketeering activity all relate to schemes to obtain property or money by false or fraudulent pretenses, representations and promises, which schemes have similar purposes, results, participants and methods of commission.

The defendants racketeering activities are a pattern and amount to a regular way of conducting their affairs and threaten future criminal activity.

Defendants Johnson, Mezvinsky, and Foundation have received income from a pattern of racketeering activity in which they participated as principals and have used said income to operate the Foundation and to acquire the Riverview Nursery and the Unisys/Exide plant all in violation of 18 USC. Section 1962(a).

Defendants Johnson and Mezvinsky have acquired and maintained interests in and control of the Riverview Nursery and the Unisys/Exide plant and control of the Foundation through a pattern of racketeering activity in violation of 18 USC. Section 1962(b).

Defendants Johnson and Mezvinsky are employed by or associated with the Foundation, and they have conducted and/or participated in the conduct of the Foundation's affairs through a pattern of racketeering activity in violation of 18 USC. Section 1962(c).

Defendants Johnson and Mezvinsky have conspired to violate 18 USC. Section 1962(a)(b)(c), and as a direct and proximate result of the racketeering activities of the defendants in violation of 18 USC. Section 1962, the plaintiff has been injured in his business and property.

WHEREFORE, plaintiff demands judgment against the defendants, jointly and severally, in the principal amount of $1,500,000 trebled to $4,500,000 and his costs in this action pursuant to 18 USC. Section 1964(c).

Count II – Fraud

Defendants' promises of performance under the foregoing contracts were willfully and deliberately made with the present intention not to perform the defendants' obligations thereunder and for the purpose of misleading the plaintiff

Plaintiff has relied on the defendants' misrepresentations to his detriment.

As a direct and proximate result of the defendants' actions, plaintiff has been injured in his business and property and has suffered lost earnings, profits and business opportunities and incurred incidental and consequential damages.

WHEREFORE, plaintiff demands judgment against the defendants jointly and severally, for compensatory damages in the amount of $1,500,000 and punitive damages in the amount of $3,000,000 and his costs in this action.

Count III – Conspiracy

Defendants Johnson and Mezvinsky have knowingly, willfully and intentionally conspired to breach the foregoing contracts with the plaintiff, and as a direct and proximate result of the defendants' actions, plaintiff has been injured in his business and property and has suffered lost earnings, profits and business opportunities and incurred incidental and consequential damages.

WHEREFORE, plaintiff demands judgment against the defendants, jointly and severally, for compensatory damages in the amount of $1,500,000 and punitive damages in the amount of $3,000,000 and his costs in this action.

Count IV – Breach

Demand has been made upon the defendants to honor the foregoing agreements and they have refused thereby breaching the terms of the contracts.

As a direct and proximate result of the defendants' actions, plaintiff has been injured in his business and property and has suffered lost earnings, profits and business opportunities and incurred incidental and consequential damages.

WHEREFORE, plaintiff demands judgment against the defendants, jointly and severally, for compensatory damages in the amount of $1,500,000.00 and punitive damages in the amount of $3,000,000.00 and his costs in this action.

Trial by jury of all issues so triable is hereby demanded.

Paull Anderson, by counsel.

Thirty days after the complaint was filed, the defendants' lawyers submitted timely Answers denying all of the allegations. Johnson had retained Abingdon lawyer Frederick A. Rowlett to represent him and the Foundation while Mezvinsky retained his own counsel, Abingdon lawyer, Daniel K. Read, Jr.

The case was assigned to Senior Federal District Judge Glen M. Williams.

Mezvinsky and Johnson immediately filed separate, similar Motions to have the case dismissed "for the plaintiff's failure to state a judiciable claim."

On December 22, 1994, Judge Williams issued an order denying both motions.

Both sides filed their Interrogatories and Requests for Production of Documents. Burkholder provided timely and complete Answers to the defendants' lawyers; however, the defendants refused to provide the required information and documents. Burkholder filed a Motion to Compel the defendants to provide the required answers.

Judge Williams then assigned the case to his Magistrate Judge, Cynthia D. Kinser.

Magistrate Judge Kinser conducted a hearing on Anderson's Motion on August 11, 1995, then issued an order compelling the defendants to comply with the discovery rules and to provide the required information and documentation.

Undaunted, the defendants continued to brashly defy the court's orders and violate the Rules, insisting that they could not provide the information ordered by the court and required by the Rules because "to do so would incriminate the defendants."

In June of 1996, the previous effort to threaten, intimidate and coerce Paull Anderson to terminate his Kentucky litigation, with the anonymous phone threats to "burn you out," again raised their sinister presence in an even more brash and escalated effort to further intimidate him to abandon his Virginia lawsuit. The bizarre attempt to intimidate and coerce the Virginian arrived in the form of anonymous, threatening letters that were brazenly sent through the US Mail not only to Anderson, his family, and his lawyers, but even to Judge Williams. And once again, Anderson and his lawyers viewed the anonymous, threatening letters as especially menacing in light of the dire warning by Garvin Wells that Nick Johnson had "mob connections and is not adverse to using violence to get what he wants." The development also greatly disturbed Judge Williams and the federal law enforcement authorities who took precautions to insure that the threats did not lead to any overt actions to force a premature end to Anderson's lawsuit or result in harm to Anderson or his family.

Meanwhile, the lawsuit progressed uninterrupted as the defendants submitted sworn statements of facts which the plaintiff quickly refuted with new contradictory evidence whereupon the defendants then changed and reversed their previous sworn statements. Their utter refusal to comply with the discovery rules and the court's orders mirrored the same pattern of "contumacious misconduct" practiced by the defendants' cronies in the Kentucky case.

Mezvinsky's lawyer suddenly devised a way to distance his client from Johnson, the Indian Foundation, and the Virginia case. Attorney Read moved to have his client dismissed from the Virginia case based upon the legal technicality that Mezvinsky had never actually set foot in the Commonwealth of Virginia during the illegal acts. The motion was granted and Mezvinsky was dismissed as a defendant, leaving Johnson and the Foundation holding the bag in the Virginia case.

Attorney Rowlett soon became exasperated with Johnson's adamant refusal to comply with the discovery rules and court orders and he moved to withdraw as counsel. On November 15, 1995, Judge Williams granted Rowlett's request. After considerable searching about, Johnson finally found another lawyer to represent him and his Indian Foundation. On January 10, 1996, Abingdon attorney, Barry L. Proctor made his appearance as counsel for the defendants.

Burkholder filed another Motion to Compel.

On May 1, 1995, Judge Williams issued his order imposing a stiff monetary sanction against the defendants as a punishment for refusing to comply with the court's previous order and the discovery rules. The order also compelled the defendants to provide the previously required discovery information and documentation within fifteen days and threatened that a Rule 37 default judgment would issue upon further defiance of the court's order.

Once again, the recalcitrant defendants refused to provide the ordered discovery information and documentation in further defiance of the court's orders.

Attorney Burkholder filed a third Motion to Compel requesting the Court impose the extreme Rule 37 sanction.

The defendants' adamant refusal to comply with the Federal Rules of Civil Procedure and his repeated orders finally forced Judge Williams to impose the extreme sanction. On June 11, 1996, he issued his order sustaining a default judgment against the defendants and soundly denounced their reprehensible misbehavior:

> **In addition to the refusal of defendants to comply with discovery orders, the court finds the numerous instances in which defendants have changed their sworn testimony to be quite disturbing. The court has already observed nearly a half dozen significant instances where defendants have sworn under oath to a fact, or set of facts, and then have changed their testimony when confronted with new evidence submitted by the plaintiff.**

> **Defendants have also made the same basic motion to dismiss for failure to state a claim no less than three times. This motion has been denied every time. Furthermore, defendants**

have often stated that plaintiff's case is spurious and without merit. However, the same defendants assert that forcing them to disclose discoverable information would incriminate them.

Furthermore, the court finds that the discovery provided by defendants at this time is incomplete and unquestionably inadequate. Moreover, the court is concerned by the manner in which defendants frequently alter their factual assertions and legal positions. These alterations are particularly disturbing when the court considers that to date, discovery has largely been a one-way street.

Furthermore, the court will also consider holding Johnson in criminal contempt.

Defendants have refused repeatedly to obey this court's orders and have engaged in blatant and inexcusable abuses of the discovery process.

Accordingly, the court now grants plaintiff's renewed motion for a default judgment pursuant to Rule 37 of the Federal Rules of Civil Procedure.

Therefore, plaintiff's total damage award for attorney's fees and damages sustained from the racketeering violations equals $3,862,126.40. Furthermore, the plaintiff is awarded $1,000,000. in punitive damages. Defendants are jointly and severally liable for this judgment for which execution will issue.

Interest shall accrue at the statutory rate from the date of this judgment.

The defendants appealed Judge Williams' ruling and judgment.

In August of 1999, the United States Court of Appeals for the Fourth Circuit upheld the default judgment and a reduced damages award to Anderson in the amount of $1.5 million, which concluded the Virginia litigation with legal, *res judicata*, finality.

CHAPTER IV

SNAKEHUNTING: TENNESSEE

WASHINGTON COUNTY LAW COURT,
Johnson City, Tennessee
Paull Anderson v. Edward M. Mezvinsky

US FEDERAL DISTRICT COURT,
Greenville, Tennessee
Paull Anderson v. Samuel F. Grigsby, Sr.

The ruling in the Virginia case, dismissing Mezvinsky from that litigation on a legal technicality, did not deter Anderson's quest for justice and his determination to hold Mezvinsky accountable for his illegal acts. Anderson and Burkholder conferred and decided that Burkholder's firm would file a companion lawsuit against Mezvinsky in Tennessee. The Tennessee suit would be similar to the one he had avoided in Virginia and be filed in Washington County Law Court at Johnson City, Tennessee, where Mezvinsky had set foot during the illegal acts.

In January of 1995, Burkholder joined with another lawyer in his law firm, John Kieffer, who was licensed to practice in Tennessee, to file a Complaint against Mezvinsky in the Law Court at Johnson City alleging the same civil RICO racketeering, fraud, conspiracy, and breach of contract charges, as in the Virginia case.

Soon after Anderson's Tennessee lawsuit was filed against Mezvinsky that lawsuit and the two companion

Virginia and Kentucky lawsuits against his cronies began to attract the attention of reporters. Paull Anderson and his lawyers began receiving phone calls from reporters in Tennessee, Virginia, Pennsylvania, North Carolina, New York, and Washington, DC, seeking comments and information to facilitate reports and stories they were developing.

Although Anderson and his lawyers were somewhat restricted about what they could divulge concerning the ongoing Tennessee litigation they tried to be cooperative and accommodate the reporters as much as possible, especially concerning public information and documents that had been filed in all three cases. Their cooperation resulted in the reciprocal sharing of information by the reporters with Anderson and his counsel that included information, documents, and leads to other significant sources of relevant materials that subsequently proved of great value to Anderson's case preparations. It also greatly helped Anderson uncover much of the information and materials that the defendants had suppressed throughout the discovery process in the Kentucky and Virginia cases.

These reporters included Bob Moore, of the Morristown, Tennessee *Citizen Tribune*, Betty Bell, of the Gallatin, Tennessee, *News-Examiner*, and reporters Rochelle Carter, Ann Paine and Jennifer Peebles of the Nashville *Tennessean*. They diligently investigated and exposed the suspicious *bona fides* and illegal activities of Johnson and Mezvinsky, and their scam Indian Foundation. They uncovered vital information and leads that proved valuable in establishing *prima facie* documentation supporting the racketeering and fraud charges in Anderson's lawsuits.

Bob Moore dug up factual Oklahoma background information and documentation about the Indian Foundation that refuted Johnson's representations and exposed Johnson's criminal history. Moore's startling revelations included relevant, breaking news concerning a local Morristown, Tennessee bank employee and embezzler, Mary B. Brady. He exposed Brady's long criminal history of embezzling as a bank officer while she also held an executive level position with the Indian Foundation.

Moore's carefully researched articles closely followed the rapidly developing details of Brady's "half-million-dollar embezzlement from the accounts of eight elderly bank clients, including widows and widowers, whose trust she had and abused with abandon, while the question of where the money went remains a mystery." Moore reported that Brady was "a former assistant vice president" at Samuel F. Grigsby's Bank of East Tennessee during her four-and-a-half-year embezzling spree. He described how "she used BOET cashier's checks to transfer the money into a personal account at nearby Jefferson Savings and Loan where the money did not stay there long." Moore reported details of "Brady's $26,000 per year executive position with the Indian Foundation."

Moore noted US Federal District Court Judge Thomas G. Hull's expressed concern, at Brady's sentencing hearing, that the Indian Foundation was loaning Brady a half-million dollars to make restitution for the money she had embezzled. Judge Hull and the prosecuting US Attorney, Guy Blackwell, were greatly troubled about what they had learned about the career criminal, Johnson, and his sham Indian Foundation and Brady's role in the Kentucky land scam. They were concerned about the circuitous bank loan to Brady, from bank president, Grigsby, through the Foundation where it was washed and made to appear as a Foundation loan to one of its officers to cover restitution to avoid a lengthy term of imprisonment.

Neither Judge Hull nor US Attorney Blackwell liked what they saw and the judge placed his concern into the record:

> **I am not convinced this is a proper investment for this Foundation to make. I've got a bad feeling on this one. You ought to investigate it.**

US Attorney Blackwell nodded in agreement and emphatically replied that "It's an endless den of snakes!"

Rochelle Carter further exposed the details behind the Brady embezzlement and Foundation "loan" and how "the Foundation's Kentucky charter was revoked after no annual reports were filed and it lost its tax exempt status for giving special treatment to employees or insiders, according to the IRS spokesman in Atlanta, Eric Roberts."

Betty Bell exposed the facts concerning Johnson's con game claims about "creating a school for American Indians through Project New Hope" and how "funding for the construction and operation would come from rights on a Kentucky coal mine, part of which was a donation by an elderly North Carolina woman." She also reported checking into several native American Indian organizations Johnson claimed to have helped only to find that they all disclaimed any knowledge of Johnson, his Foundation, and his claims that they had received any such help or contributions.

The Virginian's lawsuits also began to interest the authorities. In April of 1995, Anderson agreed to supply the Northern Virginia office of the Criminal Investigation Division of the IRS with materials and information exposing the illegal actions of the interstate network of crooks: Johnson, Mezvinsky, Godley, the Wades, and the Indian Foundation. In subsequent meetings and discussions with IRS agents, Paul Herbert, Mike McElroy, and Roger Wilson, Anderson provided additional, crucial information and documentary evidence. He subsequently met with and provided important information to Virginia and Tennessee FBI special agents Thomas Snapp, S.A. Kidder, R. Loar, Tim Burke, and to US Attorneys Guy Blackwell, Carl K. Kirkpatrick, Gary S. Humble, and Randy Ramseyer.

Meanwhile, the Tennessee litigation moved along its own convoluted and bizarre course in the Law Court at Johnson City. The case was initially assigned to the well-known, highly-experienced circuit judge, W.M. May, who had a sterling reputation for being an excellent, no-nonsense and scrupulously fair jurist. However, early on in the case, that judge became ill and the case was reassigned to Chancellor George Richard Johnson.

The reassignment did not sit well with Anderson and his lawyers because Chancellor Johnson did not enjoy the same stellar reputation as Judge May and had not even rated the distinction and office as a circuit judge under Tennessee's apolitical system of elected judges. Anderson's inquiries within the Johnson City legal community were hardly reassuring. "When you see, first-hand, his cherry-red complexion and antics on the bench you will quickly understand why they call him 'Sauce Johnson,' " warned the voice from the clerk's office with a chuckle.

After a contentious discovery phase, the Mezvinsky case was finally scheduled to be tried before a jury in June of 1997. However, that trial suddenly ended in a mistrial, while Mezvinsky was on the witness stand testifying, after the trial judge learned that Nick Johnson had tainted the jury outside the courtroom, violated specific court orders, and raised brazen threats and intimidation in furtherance of the prior threatening phone calls and anonymous threatening letters. Johnson was jailed for tainting the jury and Mary Brady was jailed for violating court orders. The trial judge then issued a court order promulgating an investigation by both the FBI and the US postal authorities.

Despite the bizarre turn of events, Anderson's lawyers had managed to place into evidence in the Mezvinsky mistrial much of the same voluminous documentary evidence from both the companion Virginia and Kentucky civil cases.

The subsequent retrial commenced in March of 1998 and proved no less bizarre. Mezvinsky suddenly reversed his earlier trial testimony, swearing that he was neither the chairman of the Foundation nor had he participated in its activities. He further declared that he was the chairman and had participated—but only because he had also been victimized and conned by Johnson. The trial judge suddenly reversed his previous rulings, creating huge problems that seriously impaired and crippled the prosecution strategy of Anderson's lawyers. One of the crucial rulings prevented Anderson's lawyers from following the trail of racketeering cash from the Foundation bank accounts through Mezvinsky's shell companies in Pennsylvania and the District of Columbia. Anderson's lawyers found the trial judge's actions baffling—totally without legal basis, and highly prejudicial.

Following the cash trail was crucial. Anderson had obtained copies of bank-to-bank wire transfers showing hundreds of thousands of dollars of fraud proceeds going into the bank account of Mezvinsky's scam Indian Foundation. Anderson also had the documentation from Harber confirming the transfer, from Harber to Mezvinsky, of another $50,000. Anderson's lawyers needed to follow the tainted cash to ascertain their suspicions that it was further channeled, laundered and used to support the illegal activities of Mezvinsky and his cronies. However, the trial judge adamantly refused to allow Anderson's lawyers to follow the trail of that cash beyond the bank accounts of Mezvinsky's Indian Foundation and his two shell companies, Growth Holding and American Federal Insurance. Anderson knew how much his case depended upon following the money trail and he expressed his incredulity at the trial judge's actions to his attorney.

"I can't believe this judge, Chip. He knows how crucial it is for us to force Mezvinsky to give us that information. What would the Watergate investigators have done if they had been stopped from following the money trail from the burglars to President Nixon's office? We are pretty much in the same boat here. We need to show this jury where the money went, how it got there, and how it was eventually used for the racketeering and illegal activities of Mezvinsky and his corrupt associates."

Despite strong arguments from Anderson's lawyers, the trial judge refused to reconsider his decision prohibiting Anderson's lawyers from following the money trail.

The strange behavior of the trial judge continued as he then refused to allow Anderson's lawyers to call upon witnesses who had been allowed to testify during the first mistrial. These important witnesses included John Mousourakis, who had been defrauded out of more than $200,000 by Mezvinsky, Johnson, and Foundation vice president, William P. Campbell. The US Federal District Court in Chattanooga had convicted Johnson and Campbell of criminal acts for their actions relating to that fraud. Mousourakis' attorney, Frank Perry, was also suddenly barred from giving his important testimony, which had also been allowed at the first trial.

Anderson and his lawyers were extremely dismayed with Chancellor Johnson's actions and the damage he had done to their case. However, after each side had presented and rested their case, they felt better. Anderson's lawyers had called numerous witnesses to testify on his behalf and the large stack of documents entered into evidence had nearly all been placed into evidence by Anderson's legal team.

Despite the overwhelming case put up by the plaintiff, and the meager defense case, Anderson and his legal team knew that Chancellor Johnson's highly prejudicial actions had deprived them of entering several crucial evidentiary elements of their case.

However, the pattern of strange and illogical conduct by Chancellor Johnson had not concluded at that point. Still to come was a final, bizarre development that would absolutely astound Anderson, his legal team, and other lawyers who later learned about the event.

Throughout the trial, as each evidentiary document was admitted into evidence and then read into the trial record, it was marked with an exhibit number by the clerk, sitting beside the judge, and then placed into the stack piling up on the bench in front of Chancellor Johnson, at his fingertips. By the end of the trial testimony, the stack was some six inches high and nearly all of that documentary evidence had been presented and placed into the record by Anderson's legal team, and testified to by Anderson's numerous witnesses. During the defense's case, hardly any documentary evidence was placed into the record.

At the conclusion of the testimony phase of the trial, both sides rested their cases and Chancellor Johnson informed the lawyers that they should plan to deliver their closing arguments the next morning when the trial continued. Chancellor Johnson announced that he would carry the stack of documentary evidence that had been admitted into evidence home with him to review during the evening and return the evidence the next morning to have the evidence available for the jurors to carry with them to the jury room at the conclusion of the closing arguments and his charge to the jury.

The following morning, as Chancellor Johnson took the bench he placed the stack of evidence back in front of him, after which both sides made their closing arguments. Chancellor Johnson then gave a lengthy and complex charge to the jury and directed them to take the stack of evidence with them to the jury room where they were to deliberate. They were to consider that documentary evidence, the testimony of the witnesses, the closing arguments, and his charge. The jury members then left for the jury room, accompanied by the bailiff, carrying the stack of evidence. After a short deliberation, they returned to announce that they were unable to determine that the plaintiff had sufficiently proven his case as required by the instructions of Judge Johnson and they found in favor of the defendant.

Soon after the verdict, Anderson and his lawyers were shocked to learn that many of the documents placed into evidence that had been placed in the stack during the trial were not in the stack that went to the jury room with the jurors. The clerk's office and the official trial transcript confirmed that, amazingly, eight documents submitted by Anderson's lawyers and then admitted into evidence and placed into the record were "somehow lost" during the period that they were in Chancellor Johnson's exclusive custody.

The lost evidence represented nearly a third of the documentary evidence entered into the case—the most crucial and incriminating evidence. They had mysteriously disappeared between the time Chancellor Johnson took the stack home with him and the time he sent the stack off to the jury room with the jurors. When this startling fact was subsequently presented to him, Chancellor Johnson offered no explanations; he refused to even consider remedying the grave problem. He did not appear in the least concerned.

The end result of the strange and highly prejudicial actions of Chancellor Johnson proved disastrous to Anderson's case. The cumulative effect prevented Anderson from establishing the legal proof necessary to bind Mezvinsky to the liability and damages that his crony, Nick Johnson, and their sham Foundation, had been held accountable for by Senior Judge Glen Williams in the US Federal District Court across the state line in Abingdon, Virginia.

Mezvinsky was elated that he had thwarted justice in the Tennessee civil litigation and was free to continue his criminal career.

Anderson and his attorneys decided that further efforts at civil litigation against Mezvinsky in the Tennessee state courts, or even in the federal courts, would likely fail to end his criminal actions and Anderson decided to concentrate, instead, on encouraging and cooperating with the authorities to pursue closing Mezvinsky down through criminal prosecution. Anderson refocused his efforts by assisting the authorities who were building collateral criminal cases against the interstate network of career criminals.

Eventually, the Virginian's Ahab-like pursuit of justice would prove instrumental in bringing the corrupt defendants and their crooked associates to justice. They were punished with prison sentences, disbarments and bankruptcies. This marked the end of their scam Indian Foundation.

A year later, Paull Anderson was forced to initiate another civil lawsuit in Tennessee after he learned that Margaret Godley, the Wades, Johnson, and Mary Brady were involved in the efforts of Sam Grigsby, Sr. to peddle the bogus Kentucky land title to Texan, Dr. William McKnight, for $28 million using the updated "bait package" they had used six years earlier to defraud Anderson. Grigsby had the previous Skelly-Loy Report, extolling the vast, valuable mineral resources and timber on the Kentucky tract, revised with much higher values; a similarly deceptive title insurance policy, increased to $100 million, was added; James Wade provided a "lawyer's letter" on his firm's letterhead attesting to the "good title." Assurance of a "good survey" was added to complete the updated lure.

The brazen conspirators had not been deterred in the least by the previous six years of litigation in the courts of Kentucky, Virginia, and Tennessee; they openly defied and ignored the rulings, judgments and authority of the federal courts that had decisively held the Godley title to be "null, void and worthless." Instead, they had lined up their latest victim and raised the stakes of their fraud to $28 million—a far cry from the $3 million they had earlier tried to steal from the Virginian.

The Virginian decided to pursue a civil action solely against the major operative in the scheme, Sam Grigsby, and to file it in the Federal District Court in Tennessee where jurisdiction would lie as a diversity of interest case because Grigsby was a citizen of Tennessee and Anderson of Virginia. Anderson's complaint echoed many of the same allegations, documentation and evidence used in his prior cases in Kentucky, Virginia and Tennessee and it presented many of the relevant rulings, both findings of fact and conclusions of law, from the Kentucky and Virginia cases that supported his allegations against Grigsby.

When Anderson's Abingdon, Virginia, process server, Robert Taylor, reported that Grigsby had threatened to kill him if he ever again tried to serve another paper on Grigsby or if Taylor ever came back to Morristown, Tennessee, Anderson suspected that his Tennessee lawsuit against Grigsby might reflect some of the same bizarre developments as his previous Tennessee litigation against Grigsby's crony, Edward Mezvinsky. Taylor gave Anderson an affidavit documenting the serious threat and it was subsequently added to the allegations in the complaint. However, a few days later, Anderson received a phone call from Grigsby, in what appeared to be a friendly and cordial manner, requesting that they meet "to settle this legal matter to avoid wasting money on lawyers."

Anderson accepted Grigsby's invitation and, a few days later, drove to Morristown to meet with Grigsby in the nearly deserted parking lot of the Manly Baptist Church. Grigsby awaited him, parked in the edge of the parking lot farthest from the church building. Anderson pulled up behind Grigsby's car and both men got out of their cars. Grigsby walked over to Anderson's vehicle to glance in to insure it was empty and handed Anderson a small flight bag he was carrying with a curt "Check it out."

The Virginian unzipped the bag and ran a hand through the stacks of neatly banded hundred-dollar bills.

"There's two hundred thousand now and there will be another two hundred thousand after you withdraw that lawsuit and we complete the sale of the Godley stock that we've lined up. I want you out of my life and business affairs from now on." The banker's tone and hard-lined facial expression was all business and not in the least cordial.

Anderson slowly zipped up the bag and maintained Grigsby's eye contact for a long minute before responding in a relaxed but firm tone.

"Sorry to disappoint you, Sam, but I no can do for several reasons. If I went along with your proposition and accepted this down payment I would have complicity in your deal to peddle Godley's worthless title—and especially since I have full knowledge that the courts have held it to be null and void as a matter of law. Then, I would be complicit in the very type of activity I've been trying to stop. I would be making a mockery of my own principles and integrity."

Anderson paused to hand the bag back to Grigsby, smiled at him, and continued. "Oh—one other incidental likelihood that I am sure never crossed your devious mind, Sam, is the fact that once I took this money and impaled myself on that hook you would never pay me one cent more, let alone another two hundred thousand. And you would rest assured that there would be nothing I could ever do to force you to keep your word."

Grigsby's grip on the handles of the bag tightened as his knuckles whitened and his facial expression reflected his seething but well-controlled anger. "It will please me to watch my lawyers destroy you in the courtroom—in our courtroom."

"Maybe so, Sam, but I recall your cronies, Johnson and the Wades, giving me the same warning when I filed my complaints against them in Virginia and Kentucky. And we all know how those cases ended. I will continue to take my chances in the courts—even in your Tennessee courtroom. And rest assured that I will continue to do whatever it takes to prevent you and your cronies from peddling your worthless Kentucky land title to anyone else."

Anderson abruptly turned away and returned to his car. He waited for Grigsby to drive away, and waited for another few minutes, carefully observing the area around him—insuring that there was no suspicious activity, before easing away from the parking lot and heading back to Bristol.

Grigsby wasted no time in hiring one of the most prestigious and expensive law firms in the area to represent him. They filed a timely response, denying all of the allegations in the complaint. Anderson fired off a lengthy list of interrogatories demanding relevant, discoverable information and the discovery process commenced.

When other creditors began to move against Grigsby, he suddenly moved to thwart their advances, and Anderson's efforts with the civil case, by filing for Chapter 11 protection in the Federal Bankruptcy Court in Knoxville. The shrewd move surprised both Anderson and the creditors and it legally stayed all of their civil actions against the banker. The Virginian soon learned that Grigsby's slick ploy was also intended to "wash" the bogus Godley title through the bankruptcy court and thereby attribute legitimacy and value to it, based upon the declaration of its value as a Grigsby asset in Grigsby's bankruptcy petition.

The Virginian immediately filed a motion with the bankruptcy court to foil the ploy, requesting the court issue an order forcing Grigsby to inform any and all potential purchasers of the worthless Kentucky land title of the binding and final decisions by the federal courts holding that the title was legally null and void. Grigsby was furious when the order came down thwarting the final effort by him and his cronies to peddle their sham title for twenty-eight million dollars.

However, Grigsby's bankruptcy action eventually allowed him to avoid his obligations to his many creditors, including Paull Anderson.

In the early morning of November 22, 2007, Thanksgiving Day, Sam Grigsby, Sr. died and at high noon on November 24, 2007, those attending his funeral service exited Manly Baptist Church and left in a funeral procession for nearby Jernigan Cemetery. No one paid any attention to the car parked in the most remote area of the church parking lot, or the driver who had quietly sat there throughout the church service, when it fell in at the end of the funeral cortege. The driver remained in his vehicle throughout the graveside service and only after all of the mourners had left the cemetery did he leave his vehicle to visit Grigsby's final resting place. He stood silently for some minutes reviewing his past memories of the deceased and before turning to walk away, said softly, "Such are the plans of mice and men, Sam. Guess you won't get to see your lawyers destroy me in your courtroom after all."

CHAPTER V

THE SNAKES: HOWARD N. JOHNSON

Howard Nicholas Johnson came from humble beginnings in the hardscrabble coalfields of eastern Kentucky. After a stint in the army he became involved in local politics.

A neighbor described Johnson as "a natural politician and con man who would lie when the truth would better serve him. He had a real mean streak and was ruthless when money was at stake."

Johnson found Kentucky's bare-knuckled backroom politics to his liking; he maneuvered himself into a two-year term in the Kentucky House of Representatives, followed by four years in the State Senate. He also positioned himself on the Harlan County Draft Board during the Korean Conflict but was subsequently forced to resign as a result of his highly controversial policies concerning special waivers and extensions to people in his community in return for cash-stuffed envelopes. He also made enemies trying to enhance his own political interests by promoting radical legislation to persecute "Kentucky Commies." His growing political, financial and family problems eventually necessitated his move to Florida where he wheeled and dealed, using several Daytona Beach investment firms as fronts.

In 1973, Johnson was convicted of major mail and securities fraud that occurred in New Orleans. It involved hundreds of thousands of dollars and the fraudulent sale of securities—stock of Television

Productions International Corporation. The SEC (Securities and Exchange Commission) condemned these as major violations. The United States Federal District Court in Atlanta sentenced him to three years in federal prison. Johnson raised wild and totally unsupported claims that he had been the political scapegoat of an effort to persecute close friends and associates of President Nixon

Upon his release from federal prison in 1976, he immediately conned his young daughter, Lynn Johnson, and two Oklahoma acquaintances, Josephine LaMonte and L.G. Hawkins, to join him in incorporating the Foundation for the Advancement, Education and Employment of American Indians as a non-profit Oklahoma Corporation under the pretense that he would use the Indian Foundation to do good works for needy American Indian tribes across the United States.

The Foundation's Articles of Incorporation specified that its noble works would include "programs for education, scholarships, technical training, and all other educational programs legally permissible to enhance the education and knowledge of the American Indian; to provide funds for the physical rehabilitation, mental rehabilitation and any other type of medical aid within its means for disabled or afflicted American Indians; to provide funds and assistance for on the job training for untrained and unskilled American Indians; to provide funds and develop programs for the assistance and aid of American Indians that are victims of natural disasters; to provide religious scholarships for American Indians engaged in or seeking further education in recognized Indian religions or beliefs; and to promote and establish facilities that will aid the employment of Indians or produce profits for the purpose of accomplishing the aims and purposes of this Foundation."

In fact, Johnson had created the Foundation purely as an effective façade to legitimize and facilitate his ongoing fraudulent and criminal activities.

The sworn statement of Johnson's then-confidant, and later—victim, Garvin Wells, of Lincoln, Alabama, afforded an accurate insight into some of Johnson's scam activities at that point in his criminal career. Wells related how he had met Johnson in 1976 at Monteagle, Tennessee. Johnson was operating behind the fronts of three engineering and mining companies, Dixie Mining and Engineering Company, Stoner Mountain Coal Company and the McHenry Land & Mining Company. He conned Wells into providing financial support and soliciting clients interested in investing in the coal businesses. Wells subsequently loaned Johnson large sums for operational expenses but Johnson kept putting off repaying the loans and compensating Wells for his services with endless excuses that the funds were tied up or that just as soon as the next deal closed, Wells would be reimbursed and compensated.

Wells narrated how Johnson's deals usually involved coal mines scams in Kentucky. Johnson assured those conned that he had high-level contacts in Washington, DC who could provide mine reclamation numbers and certifications that were otherwise unobtainable. Wells described how Johnson used those assurances to glean large fees and investment capital from the investors who subsequently never received what they had been promised. Instead, they were further pressured with additional requests for even more money to obtain the promised approvals and documentation. Wells eventually realized that Johnson "was a crook" who had victimized him and many others.

Wells described how Johnson had scammed Wells' business associates out of thousands of dollars. The victims included a Georgian, Victoria S. Howard, who lost more than $30,000, and a Gadsden, Alabama, detective, James H. Williams, who was cheated out of $15,000. Wells related how Johnson routinely used as bait a 1,729 acre tract in Grundy County, Tennessee, that he purported to own. In his concerted efforts to scam investment capital, he claimed it possessed large, valuable mineral deposits.

Wells explained how Johnson also used a 24,700 acre tract in eastern Kentucky as similar bait. He had hooked up with two other con men, Hugh N. Rakes, of Floyd, Virginia, and Marvin R. Godley, of Charlotte, North Carolina, to perpetrate the Kentucky property scam using Godley's bogus title to the property. Rakes eventually fell out with Godley over the Kentucky land scam operation and denounced Johnson and Godley for being "common thieves that don't have enough brains between them to zip up their fly, let alone pull off any classy sting." Hugh Rakes was a legendary con artist with a long record of highly sophisticated and very lucrative con games, and a reputation for intolerance of his less competent peers.

Wells described how Johnson bragged about using his Indian Foundation scam to line his pockets, "This is a great moneymaker, because if somebody donates $100,000 to the Foundation, we may eventually give two percent to the Indians, but we put ninety-eight percent in our pocket off the top." Johnson tried to lure Wells into participating in the Indian Foundation scam, promising him, "You can make a ton of money out of this thing."

Wells recounted Johnson telling him, while sitting at the Holiday Inn in McCalla, Alabama, how he had cut a deal with a Glen O'Neal, of Birmingham, Alabama, to sell him an interest in the Foundation. The deal involved three condominiums in Florida that Johnson had acquired through the Foundation and was disposing of for his own benefit. Johnson had also bragged about his scams in both Carolinas.

Wells described how he had received a call from Johnson, in 1992, bragging about lining up a "new mark" in Bristol, Virginia, named Paull Anderson who had already "been stung for a few thousand and should be good for lots more" and who had "brought in good donations." That disclosure eventually led Wells to search out Anderson's phone number and leave a vague, warning message on his answering machine. However, by the time Anderson managed to sit down with Wells and learn of Johnson's corrupt history, he had already been victimized.

The information provided in the sworn statement of Garvin Wells left both Paull Anderson and his lawyer, Christen Burkholder, grateful for the inside information and leads Wells provided which proved vital in their civil litigation.

However, his final statement and warning had left them wary of the fight ahead. "Don't underestimate Nick Johnson and keep in mind that he has mob connections and he's not adverse to using violence to get what he wants."

One of the most important bits of information gleaned from Wells was the name of Glen O'Neal and his connection to the Indian Foundation. Anderson tracked down O'Neal's current address and contacted him. He found O'Neal to be very cooperative in providing information about the Foundation and adamant in his assurances that he was the legitimate national president, not Johnson, and that the Foundation had not received any significant contributions. He stated that he had filed the Foundation's IRS returns, which verified that no donations had been received, and he would provide copies to prove the point. Shortly thereafter, Anderson received copies of the Foundation's IRS Form 990 EZ tax returns filed for the years 1991-1994.

Anderson found the 990 tax returns especially interesting not only because they had been submitted and signed by O'Neal, as president, but because they claimed that the Foundation had reported no income or donations during the years 1991-1994. They contradicted the copies of IRS Form 8283 and deeds of conveyance, signed by Johnson as president, for those same years. Johnson's bogus forms purported to demonstrate that the Foundation had received income and donations of cash and property worth millions of dollars.

In 1991, Johnson and Mezvinsky began to more fully exploit the use of the Indian Foundation in their scams. This was possible because of Mezvinsky's stellar credentials and his prominent, wealthy and powerful friends and associates.

When Dr. Walter Harber's Riverview Farm came into play as a possible donation, Johnson recognized the need for Mezvinsky's credibility and Mezvinsky recognized the prospects for quick, big bucks. Johnson stepped back into the shadows and Mezvinsky assumed center stage, as "chairman of the board," to facilitate the donation. Mezvinsky tightly orchestrated Harber's schmoozing for the next six months. In September of 1992, the property conveyed and Mezvinsky pocketed a quick $50,000. Harber received an IRS Form 8283, signed by Chairman Mezvinsky, verifying a tax deduction value of $2.8 million.

Meanwhile, Johnson had been busy on a side deal scamming a Ringgold, Georgia, couple out of their valuable real estate. In that instance, Johnson brought in two of his cronies to facilitate the scam: Bill Campbell, a former FBI special agent, geologist, and "Vice President" of the Indian Foundation, and Malcolm Crosland, a non-practicing lawyer with a drinking problem. Johnson had used Crossland's "Juris Doctor" credentials as the "Foundation in-house counsel." Johnson cleverly brandished both men's former credentials, as "former FBI special agent" and "attorney," to enhance his Foundation's façade of legitimacy.

When Johnson learned that John and Donna Mousourakis needed tax deductions and were sitting on some valuable Chattanooga property, he manipulated the assistance of Campbell and Crosland to effect the scam. After impressing the Mousourakises with the Foundation literature and the gilt-edged credentials and biographies of its chairman, vice president and in-house counsel,

Johnson had Crosland draft a highly favorable "property appraisal and inspection" report. Crosland's report was drawn on impressive letterhead that flashed his "D.J., LLB, BA" in bold face above his assurance that the total property value was $210,000. Johnson then assured the Mousourakises that he would provide a "letter ruling from the IRS" for the value of the property in "retroactive, carry-back tax benefits." Johnson also promised that in the interim, after the property was donated to the Foundation, it would not be sold or conveyed by the Foundation so that if, for any reason, the anticipated tax benefits were not received by the Mousourakises, the property would be returned to them. The Mousourakises received a IRS Form 8283, signed by "Foundation Director/Special Counsel" Malcolm Crosland, verifying a tax deduction value of $220,000.

However, soon after the property was conveyed to the Foundation, Johnson sold it off. After he failed to provide the promised IRS letter ruling and the Mousourakises learned of the scam, they sued Johnson, Campbell and the Foundation in US Federal District Court in Chattanooga. During that litigation period, Johnson and Campbell perjured themselves in attempts to cover up their illegal actions. Consequently, the Mousourakises received a judgment against them for $220,000, Campbell was indicted for perjury, and Johnson was indicted for perjury and conspiracy. Campbell pled guilty and, in 1995, Johnson was tried, convicted and sentenced to two years in federal prison.

Meanwhile, Johnson had been busy promoting the sale of Margaret Godley's bogus title to Dr. Harber in November of 1992. That effort to peddle Godley's bogus title later led to the defrauding of Anderson of $15,000 in April of 1993, followed by the scamming of John Wolcott of $50,000 three months later. Finally, in September of 1993, Godley conveyed the bogus title to the Foundation in return for $3 million in cash and an IRS Form 8283, signed by "Foundation president, Johnson," verifying her tax deduction value of $3 million. Johnson then arranged for all of the Godley, Inc. shares, and the bogus title, to convey to his crony, bank president, Samuel F. Grigsby, Sr., of Morristown, Tennessee, for which the Foundation received no consideration.

Soon after that, Johnson and Grigsby arranged to sell those same shares and bogus title to the Wolford brothers of Louisa, Kentucky for $28 million, and then again, four years later, to Dr. William McKnight for another $28 million. Nevertheless, both scams were foiled by Anderson's legal efforts which exposed the attempts to peddle Godley's "null and void, worthless" title.

In December of 1993, Johnson was also busy bringing in other major donations to his sham Indian Foundation. He conned the Graham family out of a valuable parcel of their Sullivan County, Tennessee property in return for an IRS Form 8283, signed by "President H.N. Johnson," verifying a tax deduction value of $360,000. Two weeks later, the same parcel was conveyed by the Foundation to Blake W. Carter for consideration declared on the transfer deed to be $360,000.

That same month, Johnson also scored big when he was able to con country and western legend, Tanya Tucker, into donating her palatial mansion, on the banks of the Tennessee River in Gallatin, Tennessee, to the Indian Foundation under the pretense it would be used as a school for disadvantaged Indian children. Johnson signed an IRS Form 8283 for her, verifying a tax deduction value of $1,057,968.09. He then promptly moved into the mansion as his personal residence.

Johnson started off 1994 with the carefully prearranged conveyance, by quitclaim deed, of the Unisys industrial property donation to the Foundation by Sam and Flora Mae Grigsby on January 14th. Johnson handed Grigsby an IRS 8283 verifying a tax deduction value of $1.3 million. A mere hour later, the Foundation conveyed the same property, by warranty deed, to the Exide Corporation for $3.5 million. Two million, two hundred thousand dollars of that purchase price went to repay the two bank loans Grigsby had taken out to purchase the property from the Unisys Corporation eight months earlier. Johnson and Grigsby had also arranged for the $1.3 million profit to revert back to Grigsby as a "loan" by the Foundation, in return for a promissory note by Grigsby in favor of the Foundation. Thus, the Indian Foundation ended up with nothing but a worthless, sham, promissory note that Johnson later claimed as a Foundation asset in a "Limited Financial Statement' filed during the sentencing proceedings for bank embezzler and Foundation executive, Mary B. Brady. Grigsby never paid off the promissory note, but he did arrange to wire transfer $150,000 to the Indian Foundation bank account. Ever the opportunistic con man, Johnson promptly skimmed off the $150,000 for his own use and deleted the deposit from the Foundation's bank records.

Later in the year, Johnson and Mezvinsky hooked up with corrupt real estate con artist, Robert Krilich, to perpetrate a gambling casino scam in the Nashville area using the Indian Foundation as the front and Mezvinsky's powerful Washington connections to grease the federal BIA and IRS approvals. Johnson and Mezvinsky structured an ingenious scheme to fleece millions through a bogus bond float that would end up double-crossing Krilich. However, Krilich eventually caught on, turned the tables on Johnson and Mezvinsky, and stole millions before he was finally caught and convicted of fifteen counts of bank fraud and racketeering. He was shipped off to a federal prison near Chicago.

In December of 1994, Johnson conned two Virginians, Larrie Kline and Joseph A. Muia, into donating their valuable parcel of real estate in Rockingham County, Virginia, to the Indian Foundation.

Although the 990 IRS Forms submitted by "Foundation President Glen O'Neal" reflected "no donations or income" from 1991-1994, the 8283 forms handed out by "Foundation president, H.N. Johnson" and the recorded transfer/quitclaim deeds attested to the millions actually taken in by Johnson through his "Indian Foundation" scams. Although the IRS forms filed by O'Neal declared that "the Indian Foundation received no donations between 1992 and 1996," donors using the Foundation's tax identification number and 8283 verifications signed by Johnson had claimed seven million dollars in deductions for donations. In addition, Johnson had never actually filed any IRS form 8282, which must be filed with the IRS whenever a donated property has been sold. When this information was subsequently presented to O'Neal, he expressed "shock and disbelief."

Anderson obtained copies of the Foundation's bank records and statements, which confirmed that during those same years, hundreds of thousands of dollars had flowed through its account in the Bank of East Tennessee and Security Trust Bank, under Johnson's sole control. Those records contained copies of hundreds of cancelled checks drawn on those accounts and signed by Johnson. When Johnson was subsequently questioned under oath about those checks he admitted that he could not identify even one check that went to any Indian tribe or for their benefit. He was forced to admit that the checks went for his own needs and uses and to family members, including his son, daughters, and ex-wife. He refused to account for the huge amounts of cash that had disappeared.

In 1995, the Mary B. Brady embezzlement scandal became public and US Attorney Guy W. Blackwell and Federal District Court Judge Thomas Hull began to inquire into Johnson, the Indian Foundation and its secretary, Brady. Brady was caught embezzling half-a-million from Grigsby's Bank of East Tennessee and Johnson had offered to make her a Foundation loan to make restitution to avoid a prison sentence.

Serious questions were raised about the *bona fides* of both Johnson and his Foundation. How could a non-profit corporation justify such a loan? Where did the loan money come from? The press took an interest that grew as they dug up more and more information about Johnson's criminal history, the suspicious activities involving his Indian Foundation, and Anderson's racketeering lawsuits in Virginia, Kentucky and Tennessee.

US Attorney Blackwell's subpoenas to Johnson and the Indian Foundation produced interesting results. Johnson's "Limited Verified Financial Statement," of June 15, 1995, claimed that he had total assets of $560,000. Attached was a "Promissory Note" for $60,000 dated August 11, 1994, by Mary Brady in favor of Johnson and which was secured by her home in nearby Morristown, Tennessee. A purported Foundation debt to Johnson was monumentalized by an attached "To Whom It May Concern" statement, dated June 15, 1995, and signed by one James W. Connors as "Secretary to the Board" certifying that "the Foundation owes its President, H. Nicholas Johnson, a minimum of $500,000 for his past services to the Foundation if and when he formerly requests same." This contradicted Johnson's prior sworn statement that he had never been, or could be, compensated by the Foundation for his services.

The "Limited Verified Financial Statement" submitted by the Foundation, dated June 15, 1995, also signed by Connors, listed the debt to Johnson as its sole liability and as its sole asset an attached promissory note in favor of the Foundation by Sam F. Grigsby, Sr., dated January 14, 1994, in the amount of $1,331,787.96. This represented a "loan" back to Grigsby of the profit from the sale by the Foundation of the Unisys property to Exide for $3.5 million, although the property had been earlier "donated" to the Foundation by Grigsby. The promissory note's attached "Payments & Transaction Record" indicated that on June 16, 1995, a payment had been made against the note in the amount of $472,188.36. This payment confirmed that the money the Foundation had used to make the loan to Brady had actually originated from Grigsby who channeled it through the scam Indian Foundation. Essentially, the president of the Bank of East Tennessee was surreptitiously loaning the embezzler employee of his bank, and the scam Foundation, nearly a half-million dollars. Those funds had been channeled through the sham, non-profit, Indian Foundation to allow Brady to make restitution to the Bank of East Tennessee to avoid a prison term. This convoluted and suspicious transaction provoked further concern by both US Attorney Blackwell and Judge Hull.

At her September 25, 1995 sentencing hearing, Mary Brady and her lawyer admitted that she was playing an "essential role" in the Foundation's attempts to peddle the bogus Godley title to the Wolford brothers for $28 million and manipulating the related books and legal documents involved in the scam. She also revealed that she routinely did private work on the side for bank president, Grigsby. As more and more of the sordid details of Brady's criminal activities and the Foundation's, Johnson's and Grigsby's involvement in loaning and channeling her restitution money developed, US Attorney Blackwell and Judge Hull grew more disturbed.

Judge Hull seriously questioned the propriety of the embezzler, Brady getting restitution money from a tax-exempt, non-profit organization and said he did not know if paying off an employee's half-million dollar embezzling debt "is a proper investment for this Foundation to make."

Blackwell agreed and warned Judge Hull about the sordid facts concerning Brady, Johnson and their Foundation. Blackwell also expressed deep concern over related, disturbing documents he had just received which left him "Not at all willing to accept the reasoning and rationale behind it because of the way these transactions were set up."

After hearing further disturbing details, Judge Hull shook his head somberly and advised Blackwell, "I've got a bad feeling on this one. You ought to investigate it."

Blackwell nodded in agreement. "It's an endless den of snakes."

At the same time Johnson was trying to contain the Mary Brady problem before Judge Hull in Federal District Court in Greenville, Tennessee, he was also tied up with the Mousourakis lawsuit against the Foundation in Federal District Court in Chattanooga, Tennessee, before Federal District Judge James H. Jarvis. After learning that Johnson had conned them out of their property in 1992, John and Donna Mousourakis sued the Foundation to recover their property.

During the 1995 Mousourakis litigation, Judge Jarvis learned that both Johnson and Campbell had submitted false sworn testimony concerning crucial material issues of fact. John Mousourakis produced tape recordings that proved Johnson and Campbell were intentionally lying to the court. Judge Jarvis subsequently entered judgment in favor of the Mousourakises, against the Foundation, for $210,000 and he instructed the US Attorney to pursue perjury and conspiracy charges against Johnson and Campbell.

The final months of 1995 proved no less problematic for Johnson as adverse developments in the Virginia racketeering case continued to mount. The lawyer representing Johnson and the Foundation, Fred Rowlett, withdrew from the case in response to his client's adamant refusal to comply with the Rules. Johnson's replacement counsel, Barry Proctor, was likewise unable to make his client cooperate with the court's orders and rules. In early 1996, Judge Williams expressed his emphatic displeasure with the defendant's egregious misconduct and threatened to apply the extreme default judgment sanction if the abusive and defiant behavior persisted. Johnson refused to relent.

In June of 1996, Senior District Court Judge Glen Williams refused to further tolerate the defendant's continuing, contumacious misconduct. He ordered that the defendants suffer default judgment and awarded Anderson a total of $4.8 million in damages.

Barry Proctor immediately withdrew from the case and Johnson filed a *pro se* notice of intention to appeal the judgment. Sam Grigsby then arranged to have one of his lawyers, Tom Dillard, enter the case to appeal Judge Williams' judgment to the US Court of Appeals for the Fourth Circuit.

Meanwhile, in June of 1997, Johnson's Foundation crony and former US Congressman Ed Mezvinsky had his hands full defending himself from Anderson's lawsuit in the Law Court at Johnson City, Tennessee, against charges of conspiracy, fraud and civil RICO racketeering. Johnson eventually tainted and halted that trial by tampering with the jury. This resulted in Johnson receiving a jail sentence. When Mary Brady also interfered with the trial procedure and violated a Court order, she was also jailed.

In 1998, the Appeals Court sent Anderson's Virginia case back to Judge Williams to reconsider the damages award. After Judge Williams lowered the damages award to $1.5 million the Appeals Court fully affirmed the judgment in August of 1999, bringing that litigation to a final conclusion.

Meanwhile, Johnson was in the middle of the latest scheme to peddle the bogus Godley title for twenty-eight million dollars, as evidenced by the documents submitted in the Grigsby bankruptcy case.

In early 2000, Sam Grigsby petitioned for Chapter 11 protection before the US Bankruptcy Court in Knoxville, Tennessee. He sought relief from the millions he owed his creditors. Chief among them was the Christ Is Our Savior (C.I.O.S.) organization in Texas which had loaned Grigsby the three million dollars to pay Godley for her bogus title. She had partially sold and partially donated this to the Foundation, which the Foundation had later conveyed to Grigsby, through Johnson, for no consideration.

Anderson contested Grigsby's bankruptcy ploy and filed a Motion to Dismiss Debtor's Petition for Fraud and Deception Upon the Court and Creditors. The Motion contained document exhibits that revealed the latest scheme to peddle the bogus Godley title to Dr. William McKnight.

Exhibit B to Anderson's Motion appeared to expose and document the scheme:

"Sale and Purchase Agreement: Dated June 25, 1999, evidencing a sale by and between SAMUEL F. GRIGSY, SR. (HEREINAFTER THE "Seller") owner and agent for stock of GODLEY, INC., a Kentucky corporation, (hereinafter the "Corporation"), and Prince Arnaldo Petrucci and Dr. William M. McKnight, Agents for the Buyers (hereinafter the "Buyers")

WHEREAS, the Seller and the Buyers have reached an understanding with regard to the sale and purchase of the following...

One thousand (1,000) shares, representing 100% of the outstanding corporate stock, (hereinafter the "Stock") of GODLEY, INC. owner of approximately Eighteen Thousand (18,000) acres, fee simple, as per new survey certified on October 4, 1996 by Licensed Surveyor Luke Hatfield, Johnson Engineering, Inc., the property located in Knott, Breathitt and Polk Counties, Kentucky, (hereinafter the "Property").

The Purchase Price to be paid by the Buyers to the Seller shall be TWENTY EIGHT MILLION US DOLLARS ($28,000,000).

Buyers expressly acknowledge that neither Seller nor any representative, thereof makes, or has made representation, covenant or warranty, as to the Stock, Corporation or Property not set forth herein and Buyers' decision to enter into and close the Agreement will be based upon Buyers' own 'due diligence' and not based on any representation, covenant or warranty of Seller or representative thereof, not set forth herein and the Buyers' shall take title to the Stock, the Corporation and the Property AS IS and WHERE IS.

Signed, AS TO THE SELLERS, Samuel F. Grigsby, Sr., 101 East Main St., Suite 301, Morristown, Tennessee 37814, and AS TO THE BUYERS, by Prince Arnaldo Petrucci, 1259 Windsor Drive, Gallatin, Tennessee 37066, and Dr. William M. McKnight, Global Ministries, Inc., 7310 Breda Drive, Baytown, Texas 77521."

Anderson's Motion noted that "the address listed for Prince Arnaldo Petrucci is the same address as Johnson's residence at the Tanya Tucker mansion and which served as the Foundation Headquarters, confirming that the scheme involved Johnson and suggesting that the 'Prince' was likely bogus and fictitious." The Motion also documented that "the brash seller is trying to peddle, for $28 million, what has been held to be a 'null and void, worthless title, as a matter of fact and law,' by two US Federal District Court Judges and the US Court of Appeals for the Sixth Circuit and which echoed the previous, similar scheme perpetrated four years earlier by Johnson, Godley, and the Wades to defraud the Wolford brothers."

Exhibit D to Anderson's Motion purported to be a letter, dated July 15, 1999, on the letterhead of Economic Finance Trust, 3411 Garth Road PMB 137, Baytown, Texas 77521, Tel: (281) 839-1234 Fax: (281) 839-1199, to Mr. Sam F. Grigsby, from Dr. William M. McKnight, President:

> *"Dear Sir:*
>
> *This letter is to confirm our intentions to purchase the Kentucky Coal Properties in the amount of $28,000,000 USD.*
>
> *You will receive a Letter of Credit in that amount on Tuesday, the 20th of July from one of the top American banks issued by C. David Hallman and Group. We would like to be in closing within at least 60 days.*
>
> *Please confirm by fax if this is agreeable with you and I will immediately put you in contact with C. David Hallman in order for you to receive the Letter of Credit."*

<u>Exhibit E</u> to Anderson's Motion was a document that purported to be a:

> "Memorandum To: Mr. Sam F. Grigsby, Sr.,
> From: Prince Arnaldo Petrucci,
> Date: July 23, 1999,
> In Re: Kentucky Coal Property.
>
> *Please accept my apology for our delay in closing our purchase of the coal property.*
> *We are now scheduled to receive the 28 Million Dollar Letter of Credit in New York City on Wednesday July 28, 1999, and we will be able to secure the funds for you on or before Friday, July 30, 1999."*

The signature purported to be that of Prince Arnaldo Petrucci; however, it bore no likeness whatsoever to the purported Petrucci signature on the Sales Agreement.

Exhibit F to Anderson's Motion was a statement by Grigsby:

"On Monday, April 23rd, I met with a group of investors in California. Also in the meeting were two investment bankers who agreed to finance the purchase of the Kentucky and New Mexico properties. I am under restraints from the purchasers not to divulge details of the acquisition other than to state that there is a down payment sufficient to cover the indebtedness to C.I.O.S. and those debts listed with the Chapter 11 Bankruptcy Court. The down payment contractually is to be made within 30 days from the 23rd of April or sooner, possibly as near by as the 5th of May. The funds will be wired directly by the purchaser to C.I.O.S. and to Bob Bailey who represents me in the Bankruptcy proceedings. The confidentiality involved is because of considerable competition involved for the purchase of both the properties.
This 26th day of April, 2001.
S/Samuel F. Grigsby, Sr."

Anderson's Motion also cited the rulings by Judges Wilhoit, Hood, and the Sixth Circuit that the DeGroot patents and Godley title was "null, void and worthless."

Bankruptcy Court Judge Richard Stair, Jr. subsequently held a hearing on Anderson's Motion.

After carefully considering Anderson's convincing oral arguments, supported by his overwhelming supportive documentation, Judge Stair solidly denounced the ploy to peddle the bogus title during the bankruptcy proceeding and issued his order forcing disclosure of the actual, bogus nature of the Godley title to all future prospective purchasers:

Any solicitation package submitted to a prospective purchaser by the Debtor in an effort to sell the collateral securing the Class 12 claim of C.I.O.S. is to be accompanied by three unpublished opinions issued by the United States District Court for the Eastern District of Kentucky and by an unpublished opinion issued by the United States Court of Appeals for the Sixth Circuit. Specifically, any solicitation shall include the Summary Judgment and Opinion and Order issued on March 20, 1992, by the Honorable Henry R. Wilhoit, Jr., in Civil Action No. 84-53 styled Bessie Berry v. Cyprus Coal Company; the opinion of the Sixth Circuit in Case No. 92-5543 filed March 19, 1993, affirming Judge Wilhoit styled Bessie Berry v. Cyprus Coal Company; the Memorandum Opinion and Order filed December 1, 1995, by the Honorable Joseph M. Hood in Civil Action No. 94-111 styled Paull Anderson v. Julius Jennings Wade, Jr., et al.; and the revised Memorandum Opinion and Order issued by

the Honorable Joseph M. Hood, on June 14, 2000, in Civil Action No. 94-111.

Fortunately, Anderson's timely Motion had thwarted the most recent 1999-2001 scheme to peddle the worthless Godley title for twenty-eight million dollars.

Meanwhile, in 1999, Johnson's crony and fellow Foundation officer, William P. Campbell, Jr., pled guilty to the perjury charge arising from the Mousourakis fraud. Johnson refused to plead out and he was subsequently tried by a jury and convicted of perjury and conspiracy. On February 14, 2000, US Federal District Chief Judge, R. Allan Edgar sentenced Johnson to a prison term.

In 2002, Johnson's crony, Armen Showalter, was a key operative in an innovative new entity based upon their usual format of criminal fraud. The Universal General Corporation was created as a Delaware company under the pretense that it would provide investors with handsome profits from public-work projects in Africa. Showalter occupied a key position on the Board of Directors that also listed New York banker James Sargent and the Chancellor of the Anglican Diocese of the Seychelles islands, Bernard Georges, esq., as Board Members to enhance the shell corporation's façade of legitimacy. UGC operated out of banker Sam F. Grigsby, Sr.'s downtown location in Morristown, Tennessee where bank embezzler Mary Brady served as corporate secretary for both UGC and the Indian Foundation while working out of Grigsby's office.

Showalter quickly lined up California software programmer Timothy Carlson and defrauded him out of

$250,000 with the promise of an excellent return on his investment in a short time. When the profit failed to materialize the scamsters attempted to further deceive Carlson with a litany of excuses that the project had been delayed by The Patriot Act and that UGC officials were facilitating matters working with Donald Rumsfeld, Alan Greenspan, and President Bush's brother Neil.

Eventually Carlson took his growing concerns to Morristown lawyer, Erica Greene, and their efforts to recover Carlson's money were met with further deceitful assurances of multi-million dollar projects and complex, high-level transactions involving major banks. Attorney Greene's diligent investigation led her to contact Paull Anderson who provided information about the entire network of crooks. She filed a civil action against UGC and documented how the seemingly outrageous claims and assurances by the fraudsters appeared creditable based upon the façade of legitimacy of those involved. "They talk the talk. They've got the right suits and they run in the right circles. They were fairly sophisticated."

The first court ruling in the litigation held that the UGC had been "created for the purpose of giving 'the appearance to lenders and victim investors that they are dealing with a legitimate enterprise.'" Later, U.S. District Judge Ronnie Greer granted Carlson judgment against UGC for the $250,000 he had been defrauded, $250,000 in interest, and $500,000 in punitive damages. Attorney Greene noted that it was money her client would never collect but that Timothy Carlson's consolation was that he had made the crooks "squirm," extracted his "pound of flesh," and forced them to be held accountable before the bar of justice.

In May of 2002, while Johnson was still in prison, Foundation "Secretary/Director" Malcolm Crosland, filed a Chapter 11 Petition on behalf of the Indian Foundation in the Bankruptcy Court at Nashville. Anderson immediately challenged the veracity of the statements made in the petition, contended that the filing was intended to further defraud the creditors and to deceive the Court, and requested the Bankruptcy Court to appoint a Chapter 11 Trustee to investigate the matter. On January 21, 2003, Bankruptcy Court Judge George C. Paine appointed Nashville lawyer John C. McLemore to serve as Chapter 11 Trustee and ordered him to conduct an investigation.

McLemore began investigating the sordid affairs of Johnson and his cronies and their sham "Indian Foundation." McLemore also immediately initiated actions to liquidate the only discernible Foundation asset, the Tanya Tucker mansion in Gallatin, Tennessee. It had served as Johnson's private residence and the Foundation headquarters and been allowed to fall into serious disrepair. On April 5, 2003, the mansion was sold at public auction. The sales proceeds were distributed to pay the auctioneer's commission and related sales expenses, the Bank of Carthage's first position mortgage note, the fees and expenses of Trustee McLemore and Edwin M. Walker, the Trustee's "legal counsel" and partner in their law firm, and the paltry balance was distributed among the remaining creditors who received little or none of what they were owed.

In the summer of 2004, Trustee McLemore was contacted by a lawyer on behalf of his client in Johnson City, Tennessee, who was actively pursuing the purchase of a fifteen percent interest in an apartment building located in Elizabethton, Tennessee. The client had been approached by a Howard N. Johnson who had offered to sell his "Foundation's fifteen percent interest in Lynnwood Apartments for a quick, cash deal." In conducting a title search for his client, the lawyer had learned about the Indian Foundation bankruptcy case which prompted him to contact the Trustee.

McLemore soon learned that Johnson was trying to surreptitiously sell off a fifteen percent interest in the Lynnwood Apartments that the Indian Foundation had acquired in 1994 through a donation from a Dr. Slagle. The entire complex was valued at $1.6 million and the Foundation's interest appeared to be worth some $220,000. The documentation also revealed that the Foundation's interest had been generating annual income of $24,000 which Johnson had been siphoning off for his own uses. The asset had not been declared in the petition for bankruptcy. Furthermore, Johnson had been using its income illegally for his private, unreported uses and then attempted to surreptitiously sell it off for his private gain. This clearly evidenced a distinct pattern of additional illegal acts to further defraud the bankruptcy court and the creditors. The incident also emphasized the resourcefulness and tenacity of Johnson who was still actively pursuing his criminal career from his remote, federal prison cell in Kentucky

As soon as Anderson learned about the situation from the Trustee's legal counsel, Attorney Walker, he began to investigate the bizarre development. He strongly encouraged Trustee McLemore and Walker to swiftly bring the matter before the bankruptcy court and the US Attorney's office for appropriate legal action.

The bankruptcy court action subsequently ended Johnson's Indian Foundation scams. Although the Virginian found some satisfaction in knowing that his long and arduous efforts had finally resulted in closing down Johnson's Indian Foundation crimes, he had no illusions. He recognized that he had simply cut off one of the heads of the malevolent Medusa and as long as the incorrigible career criminal was alive, his remaining heads would be conniving and conning the unwary.

CHAPTER VI

THE SNAKES: EDWARD M. MEZVINSKY

Edward Maurice Mezvinsky was born in 1937 and grew up in a prosperous family in Ames, Iowa. His father owned a Midwest supermarket chain, Fruit & Grocery. After receiving his B.A. degree, Mezvinsky went on to take a Masters in political science, from the University of Iowa. He then earned a J.D. degree from the elite Boalt Hall Law School at the University of California. He returned to Iowa to operate the family business, married and had four daughters. He became active in politics, serving as a legislative aide to Iowa Representative, Neil Smith. He then exploited that position and the considerable influence of his family and friends to gain a seat as an Iowa State Representative in 1969. He went on to gain a seat in the US House of Representatives, which he occupied from 1973 through 1977.

Mezvinsky found the Washington, DC, hothouse of political power, ruthless deceit and insatiable greed stimulating, challenging, and much to his liking. The environment was fertile grounds for him to develop his natural penchant and talents to deceive and manipulate. He lived up to his nickname, of "Rat Claw," and became a well-accomplished con man and master of deceit that served him well in the Washington circles. He exploited contacts and opportunities to con his way in and out of deals and situations that earned him the fast and easy big bucks. He became highly skilled at ruthlessly fleecing his victims with the "smooth con" that left his hapless victims more disappointed than angry with him for their losses, convinced that their losses were the result of bad luck and bad timing, and hardly the fault of the charming, friendly, and sincere Congressman.

Mezvinsky maneuvered himself onto the powerful Committee to Impeach President Richard M. Nixon. He reveled in the national spotlight like a snake basking in the high noon sun. This enhanced his stature and capital among the Democratic power brokers. He gained a position on the prestigious UN Commission on Human Rights and exploited those contacts on an international scale as he began to develop the tangential image of a powerful, wealthy, international businessman with high-level political influence and connections in Washington.

Along the way, he ditched his first wife to devote his total energy toward his relentless, obsessive, political pursuits. In 1975 he met and married his second wife, Marjorie Margolies—a Philadelphia "blue blood" who had earned her B.A. from the University of Pennsylvania in 1963 and gained recognition as an Emmy Award-winning NBC television reporter. In 1976, Mezvinsky lost his Iowa re-election bid to James A. Leach and the Mczvinskys then moved to his wife's Main Line base in the posh area of Philadelphia's "Mansion Row."

In 1980, Mezvinsky lost a primary bid for a US Senate seat to fellow Democrat and former Pittsburgh Mayor, Pete Flaherty. The next year, he became chairman of the Pennsylvania Democratic Committee where he reigned for five contentious years, after which he launched his final, unsuccessful bid for public office as Pennsylvania's Attorney General.

Publicly, Ed Mezvinsky continued to carefully maintain and enhance his well-tended façade as a highly successful lawyer and wealthy, international wheeler-dealer businessman with powerful Washington connections. He maintained a plush corner office at the prestigious Philadelphia law firm of Blank, Rome, Comisky & McCauley, zipped around town in a flashy Jaguar, and extensively traveled the world.

Meanwhile, Mezvinsky's shadow life continued to flourish as his alter ego, the highly polished con man, looked for fresh conquests. His criminal exploits became a lucrative source of huge ill-gotten gains that exceeded thirteen million dollars over the following two decades; his pattern of frauds and Ponzi schemes became more brazen and sophisticated. His "smooth con" left his hapless victims strung out and totally unaware they had been defrauded.

The Mezvinskys' increasingly expensive lifestyle, hobnobbing with the rich, famous and politically powerful, necessitated a growing need for capital to not only sustain the lavish lifestyle, but also to supply new funds to periodically placate the victims at the lower levels of the rising pyramids of ongoing Ponzi schemes.

Mezvinsky maintained meticulous records and documentation of his expanding web of deceit and fraud at his home office, which allowed him to keep tight control of the numerous ongoing illegal schemes. He became adept at readily fabricating any necessary false documentation to maintain the deceptions. When necessary, he enlisted the aid of a master forger in London to produce sophisticated bank, stock and bond documents to facilitate his frauds, allowing Mezvinsky to readily deceive and fleece both banks and individuals out of millions.

He systematically, ruthlessly defrauded even quite sophisticated targets, including large banking institutions: Jefferson Bank, Second National Federal Savings Bank, CoreStates Bank, First Union Bank, and Bank Hapoalim. He also routinely fleeced local contractors, tradesmen, service providers, and small businessmen where he lived.

He stole $500,000 from Virginia businessman, David Sonders, with the con line that he was closing a business deal on the Ivory Coast of Africa and needed some short-term cash until his fifty million dollars in profit, which was waiting in a Spanish bank, was released. False documentation and altered bank statements helped facilitate the scam.

Mezvinsky ruthlessly exploited the friends of his wife and her family to facilitate his frauds and criminal activities. He ripped off a client of his son-in-law for a million dollars on phony oil wells and scammed real estate developer Ron Rubin, out of $50,000. He had Marjorie co-sign the one million, one hundred thousand dollar loan contract that defrauded Milford, Pennsylvania, businessman, Richard Snyder.

The Mezvinskys were sued by Penn State in an attempt to recover tuition expenses for their daughter, Holly. They were pursued by their local utility company, PECO, which tried to recover some of the $13,000 it had been defrauded.

He routinely funneled and washed large sums of cash into and through the accounts of his wife and their son, Marc. Mezvinsky used several accounts in Pennsylvania,

Iowa, the Ivory Coast and the Caribbean to shuffle funds. A $55,000 check, scammed from Maryland businesswoman, Patricia Stein, and endorsed by both Mezvinskys went into their private account.

In 1991, Mezvinsky hooked up with the career criminal Nick Johnson, a con man who was exploiting his sham Indian Foundation to support his lifestyle. Mezvinsky recognized the opportunity to exploit Johnson and the potential of the bogus Indian Foundation for his own avaricious purposes. Mezvinsky quickly took control as the chairman of the board and began to greatly expand the scope of the Indian Foundation scams and other illegal activities.

Mezvinsky immediately assumed control of the Tennessee scam to defraud Dr. Walter Harber of his Riverview Farm. Mezvinsky arranged for Harber to donate the farm to the Indian Foundation in return for a bogus IRS tax deduction certification by the Foundation asserting its highly inflated value to be $2.8 million. Mezvinsky also conned Harber into personally loaning him $50,000 that he never intended to repay. Finally, in November of 1992, Mezvinsky, Johnson, Margaret Godley and the Wades, attempted to set up Harber to be defrauded out of several million dollars through Godley's Kentucky land title scam.

In April of 1993, after their plans to defraud Dr. Harber fell apart, Mezvinsky and Johnson lined up Paull Anderson to be the next victim of the Kentucky land fraud. When the effort to scam Anderson failed, netting Godley and the Wades only $15,000, another victim was quickly lined up. In July of 1993, the thieves sold a $25,000 option to purchase Godley's bogus land to

Texan, John Wolcott, They then conned him into purchasing an extension of that option for another $25,000.

Two months later, the cadre of thieves suddenly arranged for Godley to transfer the bogus title to the Indian Foundation in return for three million in cash and a three million IRS tax deduction. That deal relied upon the key participation of prominent, wealthy, Morristown, Tennessee bank president, Samuel F. Grigsby, Sr., to provide the surety to insure the purchase. The transfer would effectively "wash" Godley's bogus title through the Indian Foundation conveyance to lend it an appearance of legitimacy to facilitate the conning of their next intended victims, the Wolford brothers of Louisa, Kentucky, out of $28 million.

By 1994, Mezvinsky's public façade and power base was at its zenith; he was not greatly concerned about the civil RICO racketeering, fraud, conspiracy lawsuit that Anderson had filed against him, Johnson and their Indian Foundation that April. The experienced Philadelphia lawyer was well aware that criminal RICO racketeering cases are extremely difficult to successfully prosecute by even the most competent of lawyers. The Virginia farmer would have little or no chance of prevailing in an even more difficult civil RICO racketeering action. Notwithstanding, Mezvinsky decided to take no chances and established his tightly controlled strategy with Johnson at the onset of the Virginia litigation and insured that his cronies in the companion Kentucky litigation followed the same strategy.

The defendants in both cases resolved to stonewall every attempt by Anderson to gather information and evidence he was entitled to during the discovery phase of the case to deny him what he needed to prevail at trial.

From the onset of the Virginia case, Mezvinsky and Johnson adamantly defied and refused to comply with the Federal Rules of Civil Procedure and orders of both Magistrate Judge Cynthia Kinser, who was conducting the discovery phase of the case, and presiding Senior Federal District Court Judge Glen Williams. The defendant's brazen intentions were made clear early into the discovery process with their declaration, in answer to Anderson's interrogatories, that they "could not comply with the required answers and production of required materials because to do so would force the defendants to disclose incriminating evidence."

The strategy was also intended to delay and obstruct the progress and due process in both cases, forcing Anderson to contend with mounting legal and attorney fees in the Virginia case while taxing his time, resources and energies in the Kentucky case where he was proceeding *pro se*. They fully expected to wear him down so he would be forced to abandon the arduous, protracted, expensive litigation.

Although the strategy did succeed in delaying and obstructing the discovery and progress in both cases, it also proved to be a flawed and counter-productive strategy for the defendants. Anderson's resolve never wavered and the courts in both Virginia and Kentucky soon made it clear that the defendants' flagrant defiance of the Rules and court orders would not be tolerated.

A year into the Virginia case, the stonewalling strategy began to crack under the increasing pressure from Magistrate Judge Kinser to force the defendants' compliance with the discovery rules and her orders. After a no-nonsense warning, she imposed monetary sanctions against them. Judge Williams then issued a stern warning that continued defiance could result in the ultimate sanction, a Rule 37 default judgment against the defendants.

Mezvinsky quickly moved to remove himself as a defendant in the Virginia case by exploiting a legal technicality and the fact that he had never physically set foot in Virginia during the illegal acts. Mezvinsky's slick, self-serving maneuver removed him as a defendant in the Virginia case, which left Johnson and the Indian Foundation with sole liability. Needless to say, this greatly displeased Johnson.

Attorney Burkholder wasted no time refiling another complaint, similar to the Virginia complaint, against Mezvinsky in the Tennessee Law Court at Johnson City, Tennessee. Mezvinsky had set foot in Tennessee on numerous occasions during the perpetrating of the pattern of fraudulent and illegal acts. That lawsuit began to encounter many of the same legal obstacles the defendants were using in the Virginia and Kentucky cases as Mezvinsky once again maneuvered to deny Anderson recovery for his damages. As that lawsuit dragged on, Mezvinsky greatly expanded his criminal activities in the US and abroad.

As Mezvinsky watched his political prospects diminish, he convinced his wife to enter the local political arena where she could exploit the considerable influence and connections of her formidable circle of family and friends. In 1992, he guided her successful campaign to become the first Democrat in seventy-six years to be elected to the US Congress from the heavily-Republican Montgomery County.

However, a year later, she suddenly ruined her chances for re-election by reneging on her promise to her Republican constituents and casting the deciding vote in favor of President Clinton's Budget Reconciliation Act. While her treachery to her constituents cost her office, the carefully calculated ploy gained her great favor with the Democratic power brokers and enhanced her personal relationship with Bill and Hillary Clinton, which she had been aggressively seeking. The Mezvinskys were well satisfied with the net result.

The power-hungry couple immediately began to exploit Marjorie's political IOUs with the Democratic powers and the Clintons to expand their network of wealthy and influential contacts. They hobnobbed with the rich, famous and political "in crowd." Gloria Steinem, Katie Couric and Hillary Clinton became Marjorie's buddies and Ed Mezvinsky became friends with IRS commissioners. The Mezvinskys spent lavish vacations at the Arizona spa, Canyon Ranch, and Renaissance Weekends at Hilton Head with the Clinton crowd. They pushed their son, Marc, to maintain a relationship with his classmate, Chelsea Clinton, at Stanford College.

Meanwhile, Marjorie Mezvinsky did her utmost to polish their image of wealth and power. As deputy director of the US delegation to the United Nations' Fourth World Conference on Women, in 1995, she invited her clique of friends to accompany her and Hillary Clinton on a junket to China. She maneuvered an appointment to head the Women's Campaign Fund and traveled the country, hosting posh fundraisers, giving cocktail speeches, and expanding her network of influential contacts. She parlayed that position into her own offshoot—Women's Campaign International—to further exploit international political prospects. She traveled to India, Kazakistan and Bosnia to enhance her image and power base. In Pennsylvania, she feverishly organized her planned run for the Lieutenant Governorship as a prelude to her shot at the US Senate.

As Marjorie Mezvinsky's political career blossomed, her husband's criminal career began to implode, crashing down around him. The criminal accusations raised against Mezvinsky and his cronies in Anderson's lawsuits and the information and documentation provided by Anderson to the authorities had caught their attention. They began to look into the Mezvinskys' financial affairs.

In early 1998, Mezvinsky's bankers began to take notice of computer-generated "Suspicious Activity Report" warnings that Edward Mezvinsky was engaged in "structuring"—in violation of federal laws. The federally-mandated reports allow the government to identify the fraudulent and money-laundering practices of trying to hide the large movements of cash to avoid the law requiring cash transactions of $10,000 or more to be reported through a properly filed "currency transaction report." Violators try to hide their large cash movements through a series of cash movements, each of which is slightly less than the $10,000 trigger amount. They avoid filing any currency transaction reports, and then hope that nobody notices. In Mezvinsky's case, bank records eventually confirmed that between 1995 and 2000, alone, he made more than 8,000 transactions spread over at least twenty-seven accounts involving at least ten banks, which included at least 165 withdrawals of either $9,800 or $9,900 to thwart the law.

After the "structuring" red flags went up in the banks, the cracks in Mezvinsky's criminal career quickly began to spread throughout the complex network of fraudulent pyramid schemes and activities he had carefully crafted over the decades. The bank auditors and investigators quickly brought the matter to the attention of the office of the Philadelphia US Attorney.

Meanwhile, Paull Anderson's lawsuits against Godley, the Wades, Nick Johnson, Ed Mezvinsky and their sham Indian Foundation continued to fuel investigations by both the authorities and prominent news reporters in the Philadelphia and Washington, DC, communities where the Mezvinsky's had promoted and maintained their high-profile shell games.

In response to their requests, Anderson provided both the authorities and the investigative reporters with important information and documentation about the Mezvinskys and Ed Mezvinsky's well-hidden criminal career. Ace investigative reporters, Sabrina Rubin Erdely and Dr. Ralph Vigoda, for the *Philadelphia Inquirer*, engaged in a thorough investigation to uncover and expose the sordid facts behind Ed and Marjorie Margolies-Mezvinskys' public façades. The distinguished Washington, DC, political reporters, John Kruger and Matthew Rees, also began uncovering and exposing the Mezvinskys' skeletons and running the sordid facts in the capitol's prominent political newspapers and magazines, *The Hill, Regardie's Power* and *The Business of Greater Washington.*

In 1998, US Attorney Patrick L. Meehan, his diligent Assistant US Attorney, Robert A. Zauzmer, and the FBI began an extensive investigation. They subpoenaed bank records and raided Mezvinshy's home office, where they confiscated eighty large boxes where he had kept meticulously detailed records of his criminal activities. They identified and conducted probing interviews of many of Mezvinsky's victims. Their documentation and *prima facie* evidence soon became so extensive and overwhelming that the authorities decided to simply use 1980 as a cutoff date for prosecution purposes. The records from the previous two decades of Mezvinsky's lengthy criminal career were more than sufficient to insure his conviction.

During the next three years, the authorities investigated, documented and exposed the sordid facts evidencing Mezvinsky's long and convoluted criminal career. The FBI and IRS uncovered solid evidence that, since 1995 alone, Mezvinsky had deposited more that $13.3 million into his many "stash" accounts.

In 1999, Virginia businessman, David G. Sonders, brought suit to recover the $500,000 he had been defrauded of by Mezvinsky. A month later, Sonders' powerhouse Alexandria, Virginia, lawyer, Philip J. Hirschkop, obtained a court order freezing Mezvinsky's bank accounts.

Sonders, Hirschkop, attorney Len Goldburger, and other attorneys representing many of Mezvinsky's victims subsequently contacted Paull Anderson, seeking his help. He supplied them with copies of documents from his extensive files to use in their legal actions against Mezvinsky. Anderson was pleased to cooperate—to finally have other victims join in his ongoing seven-year battle to close down Mezvinsky, his corrupt cronies-in-crime, and their scam Indian Foundation.

Related documentation surfaced, tying Mezvinsky to dealings involving huge deposits of African iron ore and the brutal dictator of Uganda, Idi Amin.

In January of 2000, the Mezvinskys filed for bankruptcy, listing debts in excess of $7 million and no appreciable assets.

In March of 2001, Mezvinsky was indicted and charged with sixty-six specific counts of fraud amounting to more than ten million dollars. Three more charges were later added.

On the following day, Mezvinsky indicated the defense he would raise by filing a bizarre lawsuit in the Philadelphia Common Pleas Court alleging that the drug, Lariam, had contributed to his mental problems and caused his criminal behavior. Listed as defendants in his lawsuit was the maker of Lariam, the Swiss pharmaceutical, Roche Holding, the physician who had prescribed the drug, and the pharmacy that had sold it to him. Mezvinsky claimed that his prior use of the anti-malarial drug, during his trips to Africa, had exacerbated his bi-polar disorder and mental state which affected and resulted in his criminal actions.

In his complaint against Roche, Mezvinsky individually listed his many victims and the millions of dollars he had bilked from them. He then brazenly demanded that Roche compensate him with those millions for his damages. Ironically, in his Complaint, listed among the many creditors that he admitted owing and having defrauded was "Paull Anderson for an unknown amount." Although Mezvinsky had repeatedly testified and stated under oath during the Virginia and Tennessee cases that, "I don't owe Paull Anderson any money," when it later suited him, he reversed his testimony and admitted that Paull Anderson was indeed among the list of his many creditors and fraud victims. Another creditor Mezvinsky listed was the law firm that had represented him in the Tennessee case: "Wilson, Worley and Gamble for the amount of $13,365.88." This confirmed that, in addition to cheating Dan Read, the lawyer who had represented him in the Virginia case and who had subsequently sued Mezvinsky, he had also cheated his lawyer from the Tennessee case.

On July 5, 2001, Mezvinsky's lawyer notified the Federal District Court Judge scheduled to preside at the Mezvinsky trial, the Hon. Stewart Dalzell, that Mezvinsky would plead innocent by reason of insanity to the fraud charges.

"It is the defense position that due to Mr. Mezvinsky's mental illness, he did not appreciate the wrongfulness of his conduct and consequently, was legally insane." The lawyer further contended that Mezvinsky's mental problems were exacerbated by the use of the anti-malaria drug Lariam, which he took on many business trips to Africa.

US Attorney Zauzmer dismissed the move as a "red herring ploy—just an invention he's recently come up with to defend against these criminal charges."

In August of 2001, the Mezvinsky bankruptcy petition was heard by US Bankruptcy Judge Diane Weiss Sigmund who refused to accept Marjorie Mezvinsky's claim that she was entitled to the discharge of millions in debts. Judge Sigmund issued a blistering thirty-six page opinion that rejected Mezvinsky's claim that she was ignorant of the family financial situation and problems. The judge also sharply rebuked the former Congresswoman for failing to account for significant assets she had claimed to have had just a few years ago, but which had since disappeared. She also excoriated Mrs. Mezvinsky for failing to answer deposition questions posed to her about her assets. Judge Sigmund held that:

> **I can only conclude that her continued ignorance and/or lack of understanding of the facts...is a matter of choice. To the extent that this explanation could ever be found sufficient...it certainly would not be found to do so here. When she filed for bankruptcy relief and invoked the protection of this Court, she forfeited the right to remain ignorant of the disposition of her assets.**

Two weeks later, the Mezvinskys' string of bad luck continued when the authorities learned that barely five months after his indictment, and despite being out on bail, Mezvinsky was up to his old tricks with a host of new scams.

After arranging bail, Mezvinsky had quickly lined up Patricia Stein, a Maryland businesswoman, for a fleecing. Stein was seeking minority-owned status for her New York company, M&S Steel Fabricators and Erectors, Inc. He conned her into believing he could readily obtain the certification through the close friendship and influence that he and his wife had with Bill and Hillary Clinton and Hillary's influence, as a New York senator. To further impress Stein and to facilitate the scam, Mezvinsky arranged a meeting with Stein in the New York office of Senator Clinton. Mezvinsky instructed Stein to make out her check, for $55,000, to both himself and his wife, "the congresswoman." Mezvinsky quickly used some of Stein's money to send an associate to Africa to pursue one of the ongoing oil scheme scams. He never gave Stein anything more than lies for her money.

Mezvinsky had also snuck away, without properly notifying the Court, according to the terms of his bail, on a clandestine trip to Las Vegas to try to con a prominent Chinese family into paying him $60,000 to obtain green cards for some of their relatives. At that meeting, Mezvinsky played up his wife's trip to China, emphasizing that "the Congresswoman had taken the trip with her good friend, First Lady Hillary Clinton, as part of the delegation representing the president of the United States," to facilitate the con.

Upon his return to Philadelphia, Mezvinsky attempted to draw money from his account on a $98,000 counterfeit check deposited in the Bala Cynwyd Allegiance Bank. The bogus check appeared to come from France and it had been delivered to the bank in a shipping envelope by an overnight courier company. A suspicious bank officer had notified the authorities.

When US Attorney Zauzmer got wind of Mezvinsky's latest activities and scams, he asked Judge Dalzell to revoke Mezvinsky's bond for violating the terms of his release under bail. At the subsequent hearing, on January 14, 2002, Zauzmer documented the recent episodes of Mezvinsky's "new criminal conduct."

"Nothing has changed. He's using the same playbook he used all along, committing the same types of frauds. This was his life for ten years, and he's still doing it while he's on bail," argued Zauzmer.

Mezvinsky's lawyer, Thomas Bergstrom, was hard-pressed to try to conjure up any reasonable explanation or justification for Mezvinsky's latest activities and lamely suggested that perhaps his client "had no knowledge this was a counterfeit check."

Judge Dalzell considered locking Mezvinsky up until his trial but then opted to tighten up Mezvinsky's house arrest conditions. He ordered Mezvinsky to wear an electronic ankle bracelet to closely monitor his movements, to report all deposits over $5,000 to the court, and sternly warned Mezvinsky that the court would not tolerate any further misconduct. Three more fraud charges were added to the long list awaiting trial.

On March 16, 2002, a hearing commenced in the Federal District Court to present expert medical testimony and evidence to resolve whether there was any legitimate basis to Mezvinsky's claim that he could not be held legally responsible for his illegal actions because the drug Lariam had impaired his mental state and affected his specific intent to commit crimes. US Attorney Zauzmer assembled a group of top medical experts to head off the mental-health defense from being used at Mezvinsky's approaching criminal trial. Dr. Hans Lobel gave exhaustive testimony concerning malaria research. Dr. Ruben Gur then presented a detailed seminar on brain function. Finally, the eminent forensic psychiatrist, Dr. Robert Sadoff, debunked the claim that a mental disability had affected Mezvinsky's capacity to form the intent to commit deception.

Noting that Mezvinsky was a frequent world traveler, a highly successful politician and attorney, and one who routinely and simultaneously handled many complex activities, Sardoff concluded, "It would be folly to think he had the capacity to do all sorts of things he was doing but not have the capacity to form the intent to defraud."

Mezvinsky's lawyer brought in psychiatrist Dr. Gary Sachs to try to rebut the strong prosecution witnesses. However, that testimony backfired when Dr. Sachs admitted that a person with the mental problem claimed by Mezvinsky could still be capable of lying and deception. At the conclusion of the hearing, Judge Dalzell ruled against the use of the mental disability defense by Mezvinsky at his criminal trial.

During the hearing, Thomas A. Bergstrom, who had been appointed in August of 2001 to represent Mezvinsky, suddenly requested permission to withdraw as counsel noting an "irreversible breakdown" in the relationship with his client. US Attorney Zauzmer complained that the move was an obvious "manipulative effort by the defendant to prolong the proceedings, and the delays are fraudulent and a waste of the government's resources."

Judge Dalzell agreed and warned Mezvinsky that "We're not going to play musical chairs here." He noted that the court "found you the best criminal defense lawyer in the district." After a strong warning that no more delays would be tolerated, Judge Dalzell appointed a distinguished lawyer and psychologist, Dr. Bryant Welch, to represent Mezvinsky and set a new trial date for the following October session.

In late August of 2002, Mezvinsky pulled out his final delaying tactic, informing Judge Dalzell that he wanted to switch to an insanity defense. After Dalzell denied the request, it left Mezvinsky with no plausible defense.

On September 27, 2002, on the eve of his scheduled jury trial, Mezvinsky's lawyer notified the court that his client had decided to plead guilty to all sixty-nine charges against him to avoid a trial.

By this time, the Mezvinskys' numerous serious problems, with their bankruptcy, Lariam lawsuit, and the mounting criminal case jeopardy, were taking a growing toll on their circle of family and influential friends. Marjorie Mezvinsky's elderly mother, Mildred, suddenly passed away and there was talk that the stress on her from the legal and publicity nightmare could have hastened her demise. Marjorie Mezvinsky's brother-in-law, a prominent New York lawyer, was so angry that one of his clients had been ripped off for one million dollars in one of Ed Mezvinsky's phony oil well scams that he refused to attend Mildred's funeral to avoid facing the crook.

The fact that Mezvinsky had included his "good buddy" and personal physician, Brad Fenton, as one of the defendants being sued in Mezvinsky's Lariam lawsuit had wrecked their previous friendship. It had also seriously impacted upon the previously close friendship between Brad Fenton's wife, Marie Savard, and Marjorie Mezvinsky.

Marie Savard, also a physician, was incredulous when informed that her husband had been sued. "When Brad brought home the complaint and showed me her name, her signature, which I was so familiar with, I felt absolutely sick. I am outraged that my precious, so-called best friend is doing this." Savard had been Marjorie's biggest and most loyal supporter throughout her political career and a constant shoulder to lean on after Marjorie's mother died in April of 2000. Two years later, Marie Savard and Marjorie Mezvinsky were totally estranged. "I feel so totally used!" Savard fumed.

The Mezvinsky's lawsuit against one of their closest confidants and Marjorie's "best buddy" shocked their circle of friends and political cronies, and created an ugly buzz in the Philadelphia and DC social circles. Snippy comments began to circulate.

One friend found "totally ludicrous" Marjorie's claim that she had been completely blindsided and unaware of the financial problems. "It's hard to not know something's up when the bank's trying to evict you," she opined with raised eyebrows and a smirk. She also noted that in the year prior to filing for bankruptcy, Marjorie had been named in several lawsuits demanding payment; she had co-signed on the Mezvinskys' huge loans.

As the Mezvinskys' problems escalated and Ed faced the certain prospect of a lengthy prison term, their network of "dear friends" rapidly diminished. Friends noticed big changes in Marjorie. Once the glib-tongued and energetic extrovert, social butterfly and publicity hound, she became more withdrawn and deeply morose over the magnitude of their problems. Her demeanor hardened, her quick wit took on a sharp edge, and she made morbid jokes about their disastrous financial situation. When faced with a well-intentioned, "How are you doing?" greeting, she caustically snapped back, "Oh, I'm great! How else should I be?"

Despite her threatened and uncertain future, Marjorie Margolies Mezvinsky tried to maintain some presence of mind and stability by becoming as active as possible in the Women's Campaign International organization, an organization she co-founded in 1998, to promote woman's rights around the world. She took every opportunity to travel on organization matters and arranged to teach two courses at the University of Pennsylvania's Fels Center of Government—to receive a vital, steady paycheck. Ironically, she had been forced to go to the university with hat in hand seeking some form of employment, after the university had earlier been forced to sue her and her husband for failing to pay undergraduate tuition for one of their daughters.

All of Marjorie Margolies Mezvinsky's large circle of family erstwhile friends, and political cronies would readily express often dissimilar opinions as to the many and complex effects of the criminal actions of Edward Mezvinsky upon his family and wife. However, they all seemed to agree that the most devastating and lasting effect upon his wife was that he had shattered her hopes and dreams along with her promising political future. They knew she would never forget, never mind forgive him for involving her in his criminal manipulations.

On December 17, 2002, US Attorneys Patrick L. Meehan and Robert A. Zauzmer submitted a lengthy "Government Sentencing Memorandum" to Judge Dalzell which documented Mezvinsky's extensive criminal history. The Sentencing Memorandum was part of the pre-sentencing process which followed Mezvinsky's sudden guilty plea to all charges on the eve of his scheduled jury trial on September 27, 2002. The ninety-eight page Sentencing Memorandum supplemented a previously submitted 133-page "Guilty Plea Memorandum" and a "Pre-Sentence Report."

The memorandums and report debunked Mezvinsky's cowardly effort to escape accountability after he was caught, by claiming his criminal career resulted from mental illness or medications, and laid bare an astounding, complex, web of ruthless criminal activities that exposed the dual Jekyll and Hyde countenances of Edward M. Mezvinsky:

> *What the evidence truly reveals is that Mezvinsky is, and always has been, a con man. He has deliberately and consistently engaged in deceit to serve his own ends for a period of decades. During the period of time which the government investigated, from 1980 on, it did not identify any significant business venture in which he engaged which did not involve fraudulent representation.*
>
> *The government's most thorough knowledge of Mezvinsky's affairs extends back only to 1980 because, in conducting a search of Mezvinsky's home on January 27, 2000, it elected to remove*

only documents dated in 1980 and later. Mezvinsky was a remarkable record keeper, who seemingly kept and filed every financial document he created or received. Faced with a mountain of materials in his home, the government elected to stop at 1980. As is turns out, the evidence which was seized is more than sufficient to demonstrate Mezvinsky's decades-long habit of fraud.

Mezvinsky's conduct during the 1990's, which form the basis of the indictment, was not a new development. To the contrary, he had exhibited exactly the same behavior for years, without being caught. Remarkably, the 24 fraudulent schemes described in the superseding indictment comprise only a portion of the fraudulent conduct of which the government is aware. His propensity to deceit is simply a matter of character, and defeats any assertion that the crimes of conviction were the product of mental illness. When the authorities finally caught up with him, in 2000, the judicial system became his problem, and Mezvinsky then tried to deceive it with a spurious claim of mental illness. This Memorandum documents some of Mezvinsky's deceit.

Acquaintances in Iowa, from which he moved in 1979 after losing his Congressional seat, report that he left a number of debts and broken promises in his wake. He picked right up in Pennsylvania. In 1981, he undertook a venture to ship grain from Iowa through the port of

Camden, New Jersey. The effort collapsed in inexperience and disorganization, but not before a freighter which Mezvinsky'a enterprise had commissioned arrived, spent time waiting at the dock, and then was compelled to leave empty. Mezvinsky's fraud bilked the investors and the shipping line and left the Philadelphia Port Corporation out $77,000.

In subsequent litigation by the shipping company, Mezvinsky attempted to evade liability by falsely claiming that he was merely an investor in the project. After a trial, United States District Judge John Gerry did not believe his testimony. 'At this point, credibility of witnesses becomes critical. The court simply does not believe much of the testimony of Mezvinsky. Mezvinsky was consistently reluctant to answer questions, and his answers were evasive and frequently beside the point.' Hellenic Lines, Ltd. V. Commodities Bagging and Shipping, 611 F.Supp. 665, 681 (D.N.J. 1985).

When the matter was raised by the press during Mezvinsky's 1988 campaign for state attorney general, Mezvinsky resorted to more falsehoods. He told the Philadelphia Daily News that he did not directly manage the project, but was only an investor. 'I have not only been successful financially,' Mezvinsky said, 'but I've been able to conduct myself as a manager in terms of certain investments that I've taken a part in. That particular investment, I didn't take a part in.' 'Attorney General Candidates Scrap

Debate' Philadelphia Daily News, Oct. 22, 1988. His entire premise was false; Mezvinsky was never 'successful financially' in any endeavor.

Even while the shipping debacle was in progress, Mezvinsky was using false information about his efforts to obtain loans from banks. This was identical to conduct he repeated many times later, some of which is charged in the superseding indictment. Documents found in his home show that in 1982 and 1983 he prepared statements which claimed millions of dollars of activity and value in the enterprise, which did not exist.

The pattern continued throughout the 1980's. Mezvinsky attempted another commodities venture in Spain, which resulted only in a $217,000 judgment against him and his partners which was never paid. Yet a false claim of significant value in the enterprise continued to appear on his financial statements for years. For example, in February and December of 1988, Mezvinsky's accountant, Steven Getzow, wrote to investors that any investment in Grain Bagging and Shipping 'had no current or future value as of December 31, 1986.'

Notwithstanding, Mezvinsky sent a letter to one of his lenders, First Valley Bank, claiming a value in commodities firms of $200,000 in Grain Bagging and Shipping Ltd. and $250,000 in Soygasa, Soja de Galicia S.A. He sent a similar letter on June 21, 1988, long after Getzow had attested that an investment in Grain Bagging was *worthless: the only change was that he reduced the value of Grain Bagging to $100,000. First Valley extended credit to Mezvinsky on this basis, then had to pursue him for years to gain repayment (which came from other frauds). (The false statements to First Valley are also notable for the spurious claim that a shell entity held by Mezvinsky, 'Growth Holdings Enterprises, Inc.,' was worth $2 million during this period.)*

Throughout this period, Mezvinsky reported to banks that his ownership of Grain Bagging and other related entities was worth hundreds of thousands of dollars.

Indeed, Getzow told the government that in the late 1980's – before the first false financial statement charged in the indictment was submitted – he told Mezvinsky that he would no longer prepare financial statements for Mezvinsky because Mezvinsky could not justify the values he claimed for the companies he held. Mezvinsky simply undertook preparing the statements himself, using Getzow's format. The essence of the false statements to Jefferson Bank, Second National Federal Savings Bank, and CoreStates Bank, in the 1990's, to which Mezvinsky pled guilty, is that Mezvinsky continued to substantially inflate his worth with spurious claims of large value in companies he owned.

Mezvinsky used these methods during the 1980's for the same reasons he used them in the 1990's – he was always in debt and needed ever-

increasing loans to get by. Whenever a lender noticed something untoward, Mezvinsky used the same excuse he repeated in many of the schemes charged in the indictment, of blaming Getzow, his accountant. For instance, in the early 1980's Mezvinsky drafted a form letter to send to lenders who questioned his late payments on loans from PSFS and Bank Hapoalim, falsely stating that such delinquencies occurred because these matters were handled by his accountant, who occasionally was out of town and some payments 'must have fallen through the cracks.' But at that time as at all others, only Mezvinsky personally handled all of his accounts. That letter was located in a file Mezvinsky maintained regarding a $450,000 mortgage he received from Meridian Mortgage Corp. in 1986. This loan was used in part to pay off the $100,000 loan owed to Bank Hapoalim, based on a 1983 extension of credit. This demonstrates that Mezvinsky's practice of living off ever-increasing debt and fraud, and making whatever false statements were needed to persist, began years before the events of the 1990's.

Besides this routine submission of false statements to banks, Mezvinsky engaged in many fraudulent episodes which have not been charged only because of the passage of the statute of limitations. In part:

In 1987, he entered a partnership to repair medical equipment called InSurg. He and his partner obtained a line of credit for

$125,000, but Mezvinsky, without telling his partner, drew the entire line and spent the money for his own purposes. While Mezvinsky repaid this money over the next eight years, plus an $80,000 judgment which the partner obtained against Mezvinsky, it was too late to save the company, which failed in 1989.

Also in 1987, Mezvinsky received a short-term $100,000 loan from Henri Landwirth, who then spent over eight years trying to collect it. At one point, in 1992, Mezvinsky used as an excuse for failing to meet a payment schedule that there had been a fire at the Mezvinsky home. Even though the insurance company by that point had paid for nearly all of the damage, Mezvinsky falsely wrote: 'Because the insurance payments for repairs to our home have not been forthcoming, I would appreciate it if we could continue the payment plan as currently in existence since our cash flow has been sorely hampered.' (This lie is similar to that charged in the indictment which cost First Union Bank $1 million.)

In September 1989, Mezvinsky and InSurg borrowed $24,000 from Harold Small of Blue Bell, Pennsylvania, promising to repay the money in three months. Small had to make repeated demands before he was finally repaid part of the money; along the way, Mezvinsky used the accountant excuse and many others which he repeated in his later *affairs. Mezvinsky never did repay the Small loan.*

Mezvinsky borrowed $25,000 from his dentist, Jacob Kriger, in 1990, agreeing to pay it back in one year. Mezvinsky made small payments throughout the early 1990's, always accompanied by a note stating that there were delays in Africa transactions which would be resolved soon and allow repayment. Kriger wrote on August 21, 1995: 'I am hurt and very disappointed in your lack of consideration and regard for a friend that helped you without question in your time of need.'

On May 28, 1991, Mezvinsky attended the closing of a bank loan at the office of the closing agent, Robert Cook. The loan was made by Second National Federal Savings Bank to Mezvinsky based on false information provided by Mezvinsky. Mezvinsky was required to contribute a check in the amount of $52,290.82. Mezvinsky brought that check to the closing, but then upon leaving surreptitiously picked it up and took it with him. Cook was required to use his personal money to close the transaction, and then began to send plaintive communications to Mezvinsky seeking the money. Finally, on the eve of election day in November 1992, when Mezvinsky's wife sought a seat in Congress, Cook threatened to inform the press if Edward Mezvinsky did not pay the debt.

In 1993, Mezvinsky obtained a $275,000 loan from Lou Paolino, on the pretense that Mezvinsky would hold the money in a cash bond needed by an insurance company Mezvinsky owned (which was really defunct). Mezvinsky promised that he would not touch the money, but in truth he simply spent it. For the next seven years, Mezvinsky constantly promised that the repayment was imminent, but nothing was ever repaid. As recently as late 1999, Mezvinsky continued to say that the money was tied up in the insurance company and could not be released, yet was safe as long as it was there. In fact, the insurance company had been liquidated in 1996 by a government regulator and went out of existence.

In December 1993, Stewart Resnick, a businessman, lent $100,000 to Mezvinsky, who said he needed short-term financing while awaiting money from an investment in Nigeria. The loan was only to be for a few weeks. Over future years, Mezvinsky gave various excuses for failing to pay the money back, until Resnick stopped calling because he found it too embarrassing. Nothing was ever repaid.

Mezvinsky engaged in a significant embezzlement of client funds in 1994. This involved Agro-Resources International, Inc., which retained Mezvinsky to assist in resolving a real estate dispute in Costa Rica, *and at one point transferred $375,000 to Mezvinsky's escrow account, representing nearly all of the company's liquid assets. Mezvinsky promptly spent the money, and then ignored requests for its return. At one point, in October 1994, to justify his withholding of the money, he sent the company's lawyer a fraudulent bill which falsely stated that Mezvinsky was owed more in legal fees than the amount he supposedly held in escrow.*

On December 21, 1994, attorney Kenneth Jacobsen, who had lent $500,000 to Mezvinsky and not been repaid wrote:

'I have been unable to meet business obligations, have missed investment opportunities, and been personally humiliated by my inability to honor commitments which I made based on my expectation (and your promise) that you would honor your commitments to me. Make no mistake about it. There has been no "misunderstanding" about our arrangement. Rather, there has been nothing but lies and broken promises which have persisted for more than a year. My only regret is that I did not recognize sooner that I was being manipulated and defrauded by people in whom I had reposed my personal trust and confidence.

Resorting to civil remedies are not enough to redress the damage which you have done to me, although rest assured that those will be aggressively pursued. As a lawyer, you also know that your actions also constitute, at a minimum, wire fraud and obtaining money under false pretenses.'

A number of similar frauds (similar to the Jacobsen fraud) appear in the indictment as well, the most recent being the Stein matter which occurred in late 2001 after the original indictment was returned (in that matter Mezvinsky, while on bail, defrauded Mrs. Stein out of $75,000 using the New York office of his close friend, US Senator Hillary Rodham Clinton).

Mezvinsky obtained $500,000 in 1995 from Dr. Douglas Colkitt, promising to invest the money in a specific venture in Kentucky (in collusion with the disbarred lawyers Julius and James Wade and their client Margaret Godley relating to the defrauding of Paull Anderson). Instead, Mezvinsky just spent it. Mezvinsky stated that he was trying to acquire property and then lease mineral rights to a coal company, with a potential return of tens of millions of dollars (the same 'bait package' of lies and bogus documentation used to defraud Anderson and others). Trusting Mezvinsky, Colkitt did not inquire again about the project until 1999. At that time, Mezvinsky said that the project was proceeding slowly due to permit decisions that had long been awaiting approval by either federal or state bureaucrats. Mezvinsky stated that there were complicated problems to resolve, including title disputes and environmental regulations, but that he had the legal and political skills to make the project viable. In truth, Mezvinsky was not pursuing any such project, and had spent the $500,000 as soon as he received it in 1995, on personal and business expenses. Colkitt was never repaid.

Mezvinsky also used false statements to gain money in other uncharged ventures, which he repaid only with new frauds. For example, in connection with the 1997 fraud on Mellon Bank, Mezvinsky forestalled payment of a $400,000 debt to Michael Hanks in 1997 with elaborate ficticious documents which purported to address a loan to be given to Mezvinsky from an insurance company. Similarly, Mezvinsky obtained over $300,000 from Norman and Elizabeth Tener, their life savings, in 1996, on the false pretense that their investment would be secured by the stock of a Mezvinsky entity which was in fact valueless.

The government also found copious evidence that Mezvinsky for decades acted dishonestly toward utility companies, service providers, contractors, and anyone else to whom he owed a personal debt. These matters tend to involve much smaller sums, but are as illuminating as any other evidence in this case in revealing Mezvinsky's true character and predilection to *deceit. In these matters, he routinely cheated small businessmen and other workers. Many examples of this conduct emerged from the January 1992 fire which took place at the Mezvinsky residence. After that fire, the insurer paid $403,740.14 to the mortgage holder, Howard Savings, of which $348,623.96 was placed in an escrow account pending the completion of repairs. During the rest of 1992, the Mezvinskys completed repairs and provided evidence to Howard, and all of the money was released from the escrow account. But Mezvinsky did not use the money to pay the contractors who did the work on his house, and instead spent it on his personal and business ventures. He was pursued for years by a host of contractors, repeatedly asserting false defenses to payment. As an example: Weaver & Witwer, a small company which did heating and air conditioning work in the house charged $15,396.71; Mezvinsky refused to pay, making up a story about non-existent litigation concerning the mortgage to the house and never paid Weaver & Witwer a dime for its work.*

Along the same lines, on occasions separated by ten years, Mezvinsky sent nearly identical letters to escape responsibility for thousands of dollars in credit card charges, falsely claiming that the cards were lost before the charges were incurred.

Mezvinsky also did not pay his electric bills for years. In 1994, PECO sought over $10,000 in *back charges, which Mezvinsky 'disputed.' He settled and paid a small portion of that debt, then proceeded to run up another unpaid $13,800 in electric bills before filing for bankruptcy in January 2000 and listing this debt, which has never been paid.*

And on top of all of this—a 20-year record including the failed commodities ventures, the uncharged lies to banks, the fraud involving InSurg, the Robert Cook affair, the huge thefts from Paolino and Colkitt, the many lies in connection with loans and client funds, and the habitual cheating of contractors and creditors - Mezvinsky stands convicted of 24 schemes causing $10 million in loss. The notion that any of this is the product of the use of an anti-malaria drug is an insult to the intelligence of this Court.

Simply put, Mezvinsky has shown for decades that he is a person of dishonest character who has a complete lack of caring for others' financial needs. This is neatly illustrated by a pair of letters he wrote months apart in 1997. In the Hanks matter, Mezvinsky was receiving increasingly threatening demands for payment. For instance, Hanks wrote on November 24, 1997: 'I strongly advise you to wire the $230,000 that is due to our investors. If this is not accomplished, I can assure you that the repercussions will be severe.' Mezvinsky responded: 'You are upset, as am I, but hard line and vindictive positions are not justified and clearly counterproductive in this particular *situation.' At the same time, Mezvinsky himself was trying to collect a debt allegedly owed to him by a person named Tom Keeter. Mezvinsky had been trying to get Keeter, a resident of Tulsa, Oklahoma, to 'invest' $500,000 in connection with an oil deal, and 'loaned' Keeter $1,000 to help pay taxes. When Keeter did not immediately repay, Mezvinsky sent several nasty demand letters, at the same time he was fending off Hanks. In one, on July 11, 1997, barely three months after the purported loan to Keeter, Mezvinsky wrote that '[m]y patience has worn thin...I do not intend to continue calling you for what I believe is your ethical and legal responsibility...I do not wish to explain this situation to your wife and business associates.'*

As this incident depicts, Mezvinsky occasionally resorted to nastiness when necessary to get his way. Another example lies in his attorney's correspondence with counsel for Dr. Jason Theodosakis, trying to withstand Theodosakis' rightful demands for the return of the more than $600,000 which Mezvinsky stole from him. (Records found in his home show that Mezvinsky carefully edited and often drafted every letter his attorney, Mark Pearlstein, sent) On December 4, 1998, Pearlstein sent a letter to Theodosakis' counsel, adhering to the maxim that the best defense is a good offense. He wrote: 'Your suggestion that the monies which GHE, Inc. [Mezvinsky's shell company] is holding for itself and Dr. Theodosakis pursuant to the Rexall *and Affinity matters was missing or misapplied was taken in a very negative way by Mr. Mezvinsky, who believes that this suggestion by you and/or your client is libelous. You should know that he has inquired of me regarding legal action as to that matter. In Pennsylvania, such statements receive a qualified immunity only if made within the context of ongoing litigation.'* *The letter continued with thinly veiled threats to expose certain alleged conduct of Dr. Theodosakis if the matter was not resolved without litigation and through payment of additional compensation to Mezvinsky – even though Mezvinsky could only have learned of such information in his privileged role as Theodosakis' attorney.*

Mezvinsky's crimes were most complicated and time consuming affairs. Of the 24 schemes detailed in the superseding indictment, most existed simultaneously, and persisted for years. This required Mezvinsky to keep track of multiple false stories at the same time, and he never slipped once. Here is a sampling of examples:

He was continuously assuring Jefferson Bank, to whom he owed $1 million, that he would collect the money from sums owed him by the Nigerian government.

He persisted in elaborate falsehoods to First Union National Bank regarding the fictitious account of unpaid insurance money which he said justified his failure to pay his million-dollar mortgage.

He engaged in regular conversations and correspondence, at least monthly, with Ronne Tener, to assure her that he was investing funds on her behalf and to persuade her to give him more.

He persevered in a running dispute with Dr. Jason Theodosakis for years to attempt to falsely justify Mezvinsky's theft of book and other royalties which were due Theodosakis.

He had regular discussions with Dr. Martin Weich and his associate, Jay Oppemheim, regarding an alleged effort to sell a "bug-band" bracelet in Africa, justifying Mezvinsky's collection of money from Weich.

He regularly described an oil deal to Lloyd Miller and Miller's attorney, Ken Maiman, to justify and persist in the fraudulent collection of $1 million from Miller.

He engaged in elaborate negotiations and drafting of contracts for years with Frank Greenberg on the pretense that they were endeavoring to create a joint venture for investment in coins, all as a cover for Mezvinsky's true goal of receiving and keeping Greenberg's $700,000.

He made regular misrepresentations to Joe Klieber and others that he was pursuing litigation on behalf of a Las Vegas man, as a pretense for receiving hundreds of thousands of dollars from Klieber and another victim.

Clearly, these were not simple affairs. Notably, in the most common fraud, in which he told victims that he needed money on deposit in his trust account that would not be moved, Mezvinsky told each a benign and false explanation of his need for the money, each version being different and carefully tailored for the particular interest and sensibility of the victim. He also went to considerable lengths to assure the "investors" of the safety of their money, for instance providing them with signature cards to sign to suggest that each had independent control of his account. He gave others forged bank statements, created at a master forger's printing shop in London, to further the false statement that the depositor's money remained safe.

In all of the frauds, Mezvinsky demonstrated a most sophisticated feel, typical of the best con men, of telling a victim what the victim wanted to hear. For instance, he told A.C. Mercurio, who was trying to gather money for vast investment deals, that Mezvinsky's success in the matter for which he needed a trust account deposit would produce $50-60 million to invest. He told Richard Snyder, who has a charitable bent, that after success in his project, Mezvinsky would donate $1 million in proceeds to the charitable causes which Snyder and his associates favored. He told Greenberg, a coin dealer, that Mezvinsky would produce millions of dollars from foreign investors for investment in coins, and allow

Greenberg to buy a building instead of rent space for his business.

Further, it must be kept in mind that these were not imbecilic or gullible people he was defrauding. By and large, the victims are men and women of accomplishment and means, who had been successful in their endeavors, who were simply taken by a con man of great skill and persuasive power – each gave him sums up to $1.2 million.

Mezvinsky was also quite sensitive to the consequences of his conduct, illustrating his complete awareness of the wrongfulness of his actions. Witnesses recount that the surest way to get Mezvinsky to repay some of the money he had taken would be to threaten to make a complaint to the press, particularly during one of his wife's election campaigns. Mezvinsky's wife, Marjorie Magolies-Mezvinsky, ran successfully for the US Congress in 1992. She lost races for Congress in 1994 and for Pennsylvania lieutenant governor in 1998, and was in the midst of a campaign for the 2000 Democratic nomination for the US Senate when compelled to withdraw in January 2000 due to exposure of her husband's affairs.

Mezvinsky was also quite selective in choosing victims. The notion that he took money from "family and friends", a myth he told doctors is untrue. It appears that none of the victims was close to Mezvinsky; he purposely ranged far and wide, throughout the United States and abroad, entreating wealthy people he encountered, while limiting his fraudulent efforts at home. Though the Mezvinsky's had many rich local acquaintances, none appears on the list of victims.

For example, one of Mezvinsky's friends was Professor Edward Shils of the Wharton School at the University of Pennsylvania, who later spoke to Mezvinsky's doctors on his behalf. Few people would be in a better position to make contact with prominent or wealthy entrepreneurs, world leaders, and industrialist. Yet Mezvisnky never came to Shils with any business deal or asked him for money.

Similarly, Mezvinsky never disturbed any of the substantial amounts of money raised by his wife for any of her political campaigns, or approached any of her major contributors. In other words, this was not a person suffering from a grandiose notion of impending success innocently asking others for investments; this was a person deliberately choosing people to defraud and victimize.

At the same time that all of this was going on, Mezvinsky ran all of the affairs of his family. That required, in part, keeping at bay dozens of creditors. Also, simultaneously, he pursued all of the Nigerian investments which required constant correspondence and attention, and which ranged from mineral investments to oil transactions to his infamous black money schemes.

In order to do all of this – take and keep dozens of people's money, pay his bills, and pursue his investments – Mezvinsky, during just the five-year period from 1995 through 1999, conducted over 8,000 transactions involving 27 different bank accounts at ten different banks on a daily basis in an orderly and logical manner, without assistance from anyone. In furtherance of this Herculean effort, he kept copious notes, regularly listing the dozens to whom he owed money and had defrauded and the amounts involved. On a daily basis, he juggled which debts to pay and which to defer, how to get new funds, and how to transfer funds in order to have money available without his criminal conduct being detected.

The offenses which appear at the tail end of the indictment—the CTR violations, the false statements to postal inspectors, the tax violations, and the post indictment fraud—are extremely significant and demonstrate beyond any doubt that Mezvinsky's conduct was not the fault of mental illness, but pure criminality nature of Mezvinsky's criminal conduct.

The evidence clearly shows that Mezvinsky believed that all his affairs were illegal. There is no other way to explain his astonishing record of cash withdrawals. Amidst his thousands of bank transactions between 1995 and 1999, alone, there were 165 cash withdrawals in the precise amount of $9,500, $9,800, or $9,900, for the evident purpose of amassing cash while avoiding the requirement of a report to the government which is triggered at amounts of $10,000 and *above. On many days, Mezvinsky went to multiple banks on the same day in order to structure cash withdrawals in the tens of thousands of dollars. Similarly, on numerous occasions, instead of wiring funds as needed while he was traveling overseas, he would have his maid or handyman take cash to a supermarket in increments of $9,900 to be sent by Western Union to Mezvinsky or his designees. He knew he was engaged in illegal conduct and was determined to prevent a report being filed with the US Treasury documenting a cash withdrawal of more than $10,000 and he was amassing cash which has never been located. The same criminal intent explains his filing of false tax returns giving no true account of his affairs.*

This is also confirmed by the false statement to postal inspectors to which Mezvinsky pled guilty regarding a $55,000 wire he had sent two months earlier to a known recipient of funds related to Nigerian fraud, at a bank in Massachusetts. The wire in truth involved Mezvinsky's payment of a fee connected to a black money scam and the funds he wired came from Mezvinsky's fraud on Richard Snyder. The primary inspector truthfully explained to Mezvinsky that he was trying to help Mezvinsky and that other people were victims of a scam and the inspectors were trying to find out what was happening. Mezvinsky lied to the inspectors by having his attorney provide a false story that the *payment was an advance Mezvinsky had made on behalf of an African legal client.*

The ample record in this case paints a clear picture of a person of great stature and potential, who has repeatedly chosen to act deceitfully toward others without care for the substantial harm he has routinely imposed. The instigation of this criminal prosecution saw Mezvinsky act true to form, perpetrating falsehoods, at great expense to this Court and others, in a fraudulent attempt to escape liability for his conduct. That effort continues to this day.

In sum, all of Mezvinsky's affairs evince conniving, impressive organization, significant intelligence and recall, and a steady determination to pursue financial advantage through illegal conduct. It would be simply impossible for a person suffering from a severe mental illness to carry this off for even a week, let alone years.

The Sentencing Guidelines, prescribing an imprisonment range of 108-135 months for the nearly $10 million loss caused by Mezvinsky, squarely apply to this conduct. There is no basis for any reduction. Moreover, the record of the defendant's mendacious conduct in this case would support a sentence at the upper end of the guideline range.

Prior to his appearance at the sentencing hearing, Mezvinsky dropped his baseless civil lawsuit against Roche Pharmaceutical, his physician and the pharmacy that had sold him Lariam. In the end, that con had not worked.

However, at his sentencing hearing, on January 9, 2003, Mezvinsky effected perhaps his most unique con performance in his criminal career. Standing before Judge Dalzell, he suddenly, tearfully, feigned deep remorse for his crimes, stating that, "I made mistakes. I'm remorseful. My life was meant to be committed to the human condition. And here I've hurt people. It's hard to believe I did these things."

Judge Dalzell noted that Mezvinsky's remorse came "a little late in the game," but nevertheless, afforded Mezvinsky some credit in his sentencing because the consummate con man had finally admitted some responsibility. He sentenced the sixty-six-year-old Mezvinsky to pay $9.5 million in restitution to his victims and to serve six years and eight months in federal prison to be followed by five years of supervised release.

As the sentencing hearing concluded, Mezvinsky flashed a huge smile of bravado and disdain for the legal system and the prison time he faced at the Eglin Air Force Base Incarceration Unit in Florida. He brazenly said, "I plan to work on a nice tan, do some tennis, and get in top physical shape at the Eglin Country Club."

One of Mezvinsky's victims, Richard Snyder, had been bilked out of a million dollars. He attended the sentencing hearing, but was unimpressed with the Mezvinsky performance and contrition, seeing it as it was—another con. He opined that, "He has a fine-tuned instinct for the vulnerabilities of others. That very instinct makes him a highly-skilled con artist. He is still a liar, a cheat, a thief."

Another spectator simply shook his head and noted that, "Right to the end, Mezvinsky is still the inveterate con man with his latest con game on the judge. He will always be a predator and menace to society. He will be back at it after he gets out of prison."

On February 10, 2003, the former US congressman, former lawyer, former head of the Pennsylvania Democratic Committee, former candidate for the US Senate, former candidate for the Offices of the Pennsylvania Attorney General and the Pennsylvania Lieutenant Governor, close friend and confidant of President Bill Clinton and First Lady Hillary Clinton, and former globetrotting member of the international rich and famous jet setters turned himself in to the US Bureau of Prisons Camp at Eglin Air Force Base, Florida, to become Prisoner Number 55040-066. In a lengthy prison interview with reporter Mike Kilen, of the *Des Moines Register*, the incorrigible Mezvinsky continued to whine and tearfully blame medications for his despicable, criminal career. Meanwhile, Mezvinsky's brother, Norton, a college professor, remained deeply troubled that "Ed hasn't shed his obsessions."

In the summer of 2005, Ed Mezvinsky's future prospects improved after his son, Marc, twenty-seven, successfully moved into a romantic relationship with the then-twenty-five-year-old daughter of Ed and Marjorie's good old friends, Bill and Hillary Clinton. Although Marc had a reputation as "a laid-back goofball" among his fellow employees at Goldman Sachs, he demonstrated some of Ed's "smooth moves and slick style" by out-maneuvering Chelsea's previous lover, Ian Klaus, and keeping the heat on her with his romantic pursuit.

If Marc hooked up with Chelsea and Hillary had succeeded in her fierce quest to become the first woman president, it would surely have resulted in a presidential pardon for Ed Mezvinsky. This would have presented him with the golden opportunity to resume his criminal career on a grand and lucrative scale—possibly in concert with the "First Brother," Roger Clinton, who had established a reputation for his slick exploits, peddling presidential pardons during Bill Clinton's presidency.

The Yiddish tabloid, *Forward*, lauded the conquest by "Chelsea's Jewish Beau" as a natural result of their past relationship as Stanford classmates. *Forward* proudly trumpeted Marc's father as the "former US Congressman" and conveniently omitted any mention of the despicable facts regarding the con man's extensive criminal career. Meanwhile, Marc and Chelsea continued to enjoy the paparazzi limelight, playing up their public romance on the international stage and in the world press tabloids. Their steamy relationship was included in the ABC television network's "20/20" special, "Scams," which aired on December 8, 2006, and documented Edward Mezvinsky's major role in the infamous Nigerian "oil and black money frauds" that had been defrauding victims worldwide.

While Ed and Marjorie Mezvinsky were likely delighted by their son's growing attachment to Chelsea Clinton, and the benefits and influence it might bring to the Mezvinskys, the Clintons appeared to be deeply troubled by the developments. The February, 2006, issue of a major national newspaper reported "Bill and Hillary's outrage" when they learned that Marc Mezvinsky had jetted off with their daughter for a "secret honeymoon" to the Indian lake city of Udairpur. The report documented how the couple "...nestled in at the luxurious $3,000 per night Royal Villa at the fabled Oberoi Rajvilas Hotel and spent most of their time in their room sleeping off the jet lag. This was the secret code Marc used when they wanted more private time in their room. From there, they traveled to the luxurious, thirty acre, Hotel Udaivalis in Udaipur to settle in at their plush $2,500 per night presidential suite that included a private hot tub and pool where they rubbed each other's back and legs and shared some sensual treatments together. They looked like they were on a honeymoon."

While reporters wondered whether Bill Clinton was giving some serious thought to what it would mean to add Ed Mezvinsky's dirty linen to the pile he had stashed in the Clinton family closet during his sordid terms in the Arkansas Governor's Mansion and the White House, Ed Mezvinsky's many victims back in the United States wondered if Ed's son was spending some of the stolen money his father had surreptitiously stashed away—that the authorities had been unable to track down.

In 2007, while Ed Mezvinsky was still serving his prison sentence, Marjorie dumped him in a quiet divorce proceeding that added a final, personal insult to his public injury and humiliation.

In December of 2009, Ed Mezvinsky gloated as his future prospects brightened after Secretary of State Hillary Clinton announced the engagement and coming June wedding plans of daughter Chelsea to Marc

Mezvinsky. Reporters Joseph Rhee and Drew Sandholm wondered if "the disgraced father of the groom might consider ducking out before the reception." One of Ed's many victims wondered "how long it will take the inveterate and incorrigible con man to manipulate Hillary into wangling a presidential pardon from Obama that allows Mezvinsky to resume his criminal career."

The postscript on this snake's criminal career has yet to be written.

CHAPTER VII

THE SNAKES: MARGARET L. GODLEY

Margaret L. Pfleeger was born in 1914 into a respectable middle class family in Limon, Colorado. After graduating from Limon High School she enrolled in Colorado State Teachers College and met and married Marvin R. Godley. Times were difficult in the dust bowl during their early years together and in 1935 they moved to Charlotte, North Carolina. There they started the Godley Auction Company and reared three sons, James B. Godley, John C. Godley, and Frank H. Godley.

Margaret was far more energetic and ambitious than her husband and she became the controlling force in their auction company and other business activities which later included real estate, farming and rental properties. She constantly prodded her husband to meet her growing thirst for wealth and status among the social elites of Charlotte. Meanwhile, she carefully promoted a public image of respectability by becoming active in the local Thomasboro Presbyterian Church and later the Pleasant Grove Presbyterian Church, the Women's Club, and other community civic groups. She publicly radiated Southern charm and Christian virtue, with reassuring hugs and warm smiles and her most sincere assurances that she was "always ready to do the Lord's work and share His goodness with every soul." Each Sunday she sat in the Amen corner of her church while during the week her alter ego controlled her ruthless activities as an incorrigible thief and hypocritical scoundrel.

All the while, she relentlessly prodded and guided her husband to ruthlessly exploit any and every way possible to make money, especially the "fast money" deals and opportunities that paid off handsomely—even if they required illegal activities.

Along their way, Margaret developed a close friendship with one of her husband's "business associates" from Virginia. From the moment she first met the handsome Hugh Rakes, she was taken with the accomplished con man. She greatly admired his unique, natural talent that her husband lacked—to make the fast and easy money. She appreciated Rakes' smooth and charming demeanor, glib tongue, quick mind, fast lifestyle, and ability to recognize and execute a "score" with daring bravado and open contempt for the victims and authorities that he was beating. She relentlessly pushed her husband to try to emulate Rakes while accepting the fact that Mr. Godley could never hold a candle to the far more talented and successful Virginia con artist.

Hugh Rakes recognized in Margaret Godley a kindred, larcenous soul that shared his intense energy and insatiable thirst for both the satisfaction and the easy money rewards that came from "beating a mark with the smooth con." Hugh Rakes did not hesitate to denigrate M.R. Godley while extolling the talents of his wife:

M.R is a millstone around Margaret's neck. She always was better at scamming a buck than the millstone and they succeeded because of her. M.R. was pretty thick between the ears and never could master the art of the smooth con. He's just a crude, in-your-face thief. Margaret understands the genius and fine touch it takes to raise a crude con job to the level of the smooth con, where the mark never even knows he's been scammed. She can easily size up and set up a whole operation, looking way down the road, and planning for all the possibilities. M.R. is dumb as a flat rock but has sense enough to do it her way. She has all the brains of that pair. But she also is ruthless and treacherous to the core. She once made a very enticing proposition to me that had me thinking for a spell, until I realized that if she was treacherous enough to be proposing doing such a number on her own husband then down the road she would not hesitate to do the same to me when it suited her. So I backed away from her proposition and from that day forward regarded her as "the black widow" to remind me of her ruthless capacity. And I never did leave myself exposed to where she could do a number on me. I can vouch that there is one cunning and cold blooded bitch under that Southern charm and big smile who will not hesitate for a heartbeat to cut you and gut you if you get between her and a score. She loved to run her mouth about her big scores and the last time she rang me up it was mainly to reminisce and brag about how she had set up the scams to beat Ron Manning and his two business partners, and then others, out of millions with her bogus Kentucky land title and how she would leave Grigsby and the Wades holding the bag.

Hugh Namon Rakes had grown up in the rough and tumble Shooting Creek area of Franklin County, Virginia, along the border with North Carolina. His fearless nature, attraction to the fast buck, and reckless abandon behind the steering wheel quickly caught the attention of the largest moonshine distributor in the nearby Floyd County. Rakes' wild, criminal career got off to a blazing fast start at fifteen years of age as he made "speed runs" carrying loads of "white lightening" from the stills in the Blue Ridge Mountains of Virginia up into the hollows of West Virginia and down into the flat Piedmont of North Carolina.

Rakes lived up to his nickname and legend as "the wild man, who never lost a load." One favorite story the mountaineers told was how he forged his mother's signature on a thousand dollar bank note, bought several hundred gallons of "top stuff" with the paper, loaded it up on a wagon with his Winchester beside him, and made a non-stop run over impossible logging roads to avoid the law and deliver the goods to Christiansburg where he sold it for a five hundred dollar profit—all in a day's work.

In 1935, the operation Rakes drove for was busted after another moonshiner, two counties away, decided to eliminate his competition and tipped off the federal agents. They swooped down, smashed everything in sight, put everyone in shackles and filled up the local jail in the middle of a raging storm. Among those arrested was a former Virginia general assemblyman and the grand-nephew of Robert E. Lee. Charges were also brought against several deputy sheriffs for taking payoffs and protecting the operation, allowing it to flourish along the East Coast.

Although Hugh Rakes and his cousin, Amos, were central figures in the operation's distribution network, they quickly put some cash money in the right hands and escaped indictment. Undaunted, Rakes resolved to aid his less fortunate comrades. He persuaded his brother, Ed, to participate in an intricate scheme to bribe jurors and entrap Carter Lee, the Commonwealth's attorney, to force him to compromise the case. The brothers clandestinely met with out-of-state family members of three jurors at a local inn and laid down some bribe money. One dark night they picked the lock at the Commonwealth attorney's office and planted a listening device.

The sensational trial of the thirteen defendants drew spectators and reporters from several states and after long and heated deliberations resulted in nine prison and thirteen probationary sentences, and large fines. During the deliberations, Judge John Paul learned of Rakes' jury-tampering activities; he and his confederates were sentenced to two years in prison and a thousand dollar fine.

While in prison, Rakes worked at the dairy and learned all about that business. Upon his release, he immediately put that knowledge to use, building up a large dairy operation and buying up farms with leveraged money supported with huge mortgages and "creative financial arrangements." He was soon purchasing some of the finest farms in Virginia, including the magnificent 1,200 acre Court Manor breeding farm for some of Virginia's finest horse bloodlines. When he converted it into a dairy operation, the horse world was stunned and appalled. By the end of the Second World War he had amassed a string of fourteen huge dairy farm operations in Virginia and ten in Wisconsin. His farms had been major producers of milk in both states during the war and Hugh Rakes was on a roll.

In 1946, his unorthodox, creative financial arrangements began to attract closer scrutiny after problems developed in the main institution of his myriad transactions, Farmers and Merchants State Bank of Fredericksburg. The FBI specialist auditors and examiners spent the next year trying to unravel the intricacies of Rakes' complex and ingenious check-kiting operation that had provided the underwriting capital subsidizing his dairy empire. In March of 1947, Rakes, his wife, Lillian, and eight others were charged with aiding and abetting or committing bank fraud. Bank vice president, William Reeves Gardner faced the most charges for cashing some half-million dollars worth of Rakes' checks, although there had been insufficient funds to cover the checks.

The trial was even more sensational than Rakes' earlier one and lasted fifty-three days. Rakes called in all his markers. This produced a stellar cast of character witnesses that included Governor William Tuck, Virginia Judge Herbert B. Gregory, Representative and later Governor J. Lindsey Almond, as well as two of Virginia's most distinguished circuit court judges. Rakes employed a trick bag of tactics to delay and disrupt the trial.

The trial was disrupted when Rakes feigned a sudden heart attack, and again when he claimed to suffer a severe case of the flu. Rakes' attorney, J.B. Morgan, suddenly had a severe respiratory attack. However, the astute presiding judge, J. Waties Waring, refused to be manipulated into declaring the mistrial Rakes was trying to pull off and the case eventually went to the jury. Nine of the defendants were convicted, with Rakes receiving the most severe penalty. On July 16, 1948, Rakes was sentenced to four years in a federal prison. Meanwhile, his dairy empire was placed in receivership and Farmers and Merchants State Bank failed.

Upon his release from federal prison, he unsuccessfully tried to manipulate a pardon from President Harry Truman. He immediately began looking around for a new game and decided to get into the timberlands business, where he could exploit some of the tricks he had learned earlier in acquiring his farm operations.

Rakes learned of a 3,000 acre tract of decent timberland in the East Dismal Swamp area on the North Carolina East Coast. He convinced the owner to grant him deeded right to the property for some $11.00 per acre, supported by a promissory note. He then contacted an old buddy crop-duster, Curtis Turner, and convinced him to help put together a crew of timber jacks to work mainly on shares and commission.

A month later, Rakes, Turner, and their hardy crew were working long days dropping, bucking, pawing, dragging, loading and shipping timber. The work was difficult and dangerous, but on Sundays the crew got loaded on moonshine at the camp or went to the nearby town of Roper for whiskey and women. Rakes inflated his production and sales records at the two banks he was dealing with and created an inflated equity profile that greatly enlarged his borrowing limitations and credit line. During that period, he made some serious money on a quick turnover sale of a large tract adjoining the Great Dismal Swamp, to a co-op of Mormon farmers. Three years into the timber operation, Rakes pulled out and began pursuing other promising timberland and real estate projects.

The next several years were very profitable and successful for Hugh Rakes as he moved from one real estate and timber deal to another, often involving more illegal than legal maneuvering; however, he kept ahead of his disgruntled victims who never had quite enough evidence to support an indictment and bring the law down on him. Successfully walking along that razor's edge suited Hugh Rakes; he knew he was on a solid roll, and he became bolder with each successful game.

While conning a sophisticated investor from Washington into taking out a $100,000 loan to buy Natural Bridge, Rakes was simultaneously trying to arrange another huge loan deal with a consortium of investors to underwrite his sale to them of a huge section of the Great Smoky Mountains National Park. The National Park scam reached the US Forest Service authorities and they stopped it before Rakes could close on it. He avoided prosecution on that by the skin of his teeth and a handful of money into the right hands.

In the sixties, Rakes was preparing the groundwork for a promising land scam in Eastern Kentucky when he ran into the Godleys. He was immediately attracted to

Margaret, whom he recognized and later described as "a kindred soul chained to a millstone husband. We just connected and she was the reason I ended up having anything to do with him. We got along real good right from the start and basically ignored the millstone."

Rakes acquainted the Godleys with the stage he was in, "baiting the trap," preparing his latest scam. He was "working up" a packet of land patents and deeds that went back to 1870 and claimed title to thousands of acres of mineral-rich and timber-laden property stretching across three counties in eastern Kentucky. Although the legal ownership of the same property was rightfully vested in another legitimate set of patents going back to the same date of recording, Rakes would "work up" his DeGroot patents to give them the sufficient appearance of legitimacy and legal ownership of the property to con some hapless "mark" into purchasing them. The Godleys jumped at the opportunity to hook up with the legendary, sophisticated con man and to join in his latest, and most promising con game.

Margaret Godley was even more delighted in the new relationship with the handsome thief. She saw Rakes as a dashing, cavalier, brilliant con man that dwarfed her pitifully endowed husband. Although Margaret Godley was well past the "sparking days," and a mother, she found herself swept up with her physical attraction to Rakes, which was intensified by her admiration for his bold style and money-making genius. Rakes sensed their common chemistry as kindred spirits and he facilitated her discreet advances and efforts to develop their own private, personal relationship—that successfully escaped detection by "the millstone."

By the spring of 1971, the DeGroot patents scam preparations were well underway and Rakes brought in an amenable land surveyor to add the final, crucial touch to the lipstick he was applying to his pig. Hugh Rakes paid surveyor Harvey Atkinson handsomely to follow him around, verifying the physical points, metes and bounds that Rakes identified and pointed out based upon an old map he carried that supposedly depicted the DeGroot patents tracts. After a similar, perfunctory tour of 119 individual patents covering the 23,800 acre tract, Atkinson returned to his office to work up the documentation Rakes desired declaring that the tract described in the DeGroot patents could actually be located on the ground.

Later, Rakes and the Godleys began carefully assembling the entire "bait package" necessary to "sucker" their hapless victims. The first element was a Skelly-Loy Report, commissioned to scientifically and commercially document and extol the vast mineral and timber resources on the huge tract. It fully documented the vast coal, oil and gas reserves combined with an impressive timber cruise. The resultant report cast the estimated value of the natural resources "very conservatively over 100 million dollars." The second key element was the Atkinson documentation which had been made to appear as a *bona fide* surveyor's report confirming the huge size of the tract and the validity of the 119 DeGroot patents supporting title to the property. The third and fourth key elements required help from a dishonest lawyer: a title insurance document that looked solid on its face but was carefully crafted to contain well-hidden exceptions to providing any real clear title coverage and a convincing letter from the same lawyer vouching that the title was good.

The Godleys insisted they knew a corrupt lawyer, from their Charlotte area, who would fit the bill perfectly. Julius Jennings "Jake" Wade, Jr. jumped at the opportunity to participate in the scam and to provide the necessary legal presence and cover for the "bait package." Jake Wade began contributing to the Kentucky land scam preparations and he would later bring the talents and efforts of his energetic, lawyer/son, "Jimmy" Wade, into the scam.

In 1977, the Godleys suddenly made a power move to doublecross Hugh Rakes and nullify his claim and stake in the DeGroot Patents. The falling out turned bitter and soon ended up in a civil suit before the US Federal District Court in Pikeville, Kentucky. In 1978, that Court ruled, quieting the title against Rakes, thereby giving Godley sole, clear claim to the DeGroot patents.

In 1988, the Godleys lined up a $4 million sale of their worthless DeGroot patents to a Clyde W. Galloway. However, Galloway's later suspicions about the integrity of the DeGroot patents led him to default on the promissory note securing the sale. That forced a subsequent public auction foreclosure sale of the DeGroot patents on the steps of the Knott County Courthouse in Hindman, Kentucky, on May 16, 1988. The Godleys were the last and highest bidders and thereafter received a limited warranty deed conveying the DeGroot patents title from the Court. The Godleys and the Wades then exploited that warranty deed by deviously portraying it as a court document that validated their good title and legitimate claim to the property.

Next, the Godleys and Wades arranged to convey portions of the patents to the New Brush Creek Mining Company to further launder the worthless DeGroot Patents and enhance its appearance as a valuable and good title to the property that they could convey.

Finally, the Godleys and Wades decided to move against the actual owners of the property, the Cyprus Coal Company, as a strategic ploy to enhance their scam. They convinced two squatters, Bessie Berry and Ezra C. Adair, who had been living on the property for years, to join them in moving to claim ownership to the property based upon the squatters' rights and the DeGroot patents. The Berry, Adair, Godley faction initiated litigation against Cyprus in the federal district court at Pikeville, Kentucky, claiming Cyprus was trespassing on their property.

Cyprus had maintained a large coal mining operation on some of the acreage within the DeGroot patents area for the previous eighteen years and maintained that its patents were the only legitimate ones vesting clear title to the acreage. Cyprus regarded the lawsuit as frivolous and the civil action dragged on throughout the 1980's.

Meanwhile, the Godleys had established the Godley Land and Auction Company as a cover and façade to operate behind and which provided cover from lawsuits brought against them. One of the major legal actions against the Godleys during this period resulted from the sale of their bogus title to Lexington, Kentucky businessman Ronald Manning, and two of his business associates which netted the Godleys several million dollars from the scam. Unfortunately, the victims were unable to recover their losses.

During this period, Marvin R. Godley died and Margaret smoothly assumed full control of the Godley family operations, which included the Godley Land and Auction Company, farm operations, rental properties, real estate holdings and the Kentucky land scam. She became president and sole stockholder of Godley, Inc., the shell Kentucky Corporation which provided the vehicle to peddle the bogus title to the Kentucky acreage and whose only asset was the DeGroot patents.

She immediately modified the con line used to promote the Kentucky land scam. The revised con line pitched that "the owner is a little, old widow lady in dire need of cash to cover her dear, departed husband's business losses."

In December of 1990, Cyprus Coal Company suddenly built a fire under the long simmering litigation with a motion for summary judgment to have its title held to be valid and the DeGroot patents declared legally null and void. The move put the case on the fast track and it was assigned to the newly-appointed federal district court judge, Henry R. Wilhoit, Jr., who ran a no-nonsense, highly efficient courtroom at Pikeville. Judge Wilhoit quickly brought in his highly competent magistrate judge, Joseph M. Hood, to move the case along to proofs at an evidentiary hearing.

Cyprus Coal Company supported its position by bringing in the expert testimony of two distinguished surveyors.

Robert W. Ray, a professional surveyor licensed in Kentucky, testified that he "reviewed the 119 DeGroot patents and then tried to locate them on the ground, using generally accepted methods, procedures and principles of surveying, without success." His opinion was that "the 119 DeGroot patents cannot be located on the ground, no matter what method is used."

David K. Blythe was a professional surveyor licensed in Kentucky and a retired dean and former faculty member of the University of Kentucky College of Engineering, where he taught surveying and photogrammetry. He fully supported Blythe's methods and expert conclusion.

Finally, Cyprus produced their deposition of Harvey Adkinson and his admissions that not only had he not actually completely surveyed any of the DeGroot patents, he had no idea who had made the map that Rakes had produced. His work product was based upon the accuracy of the location of the patents as depicted on the map, and he had no underlying factual basis for the conclusive statements in his affidavit giving the DeGroot patents validity to title on the ground.

On March 19, 1992, Judge Wilhoit ruled that the DeGroot patents were "null and void." His judgment was appealed, and on March 19, 1993, the Court of Appeals for the Sixth Circuit fully affirmed his ruling and the judgment.

Meanwhile, Margaret Godley had solicited the assistance of one of the Godleys' long time criminal associates, H. Nickolas Johnson, to identify and cultivate some promising, new "marks" to fleece with their bogus Kentucky land title scam.

By November of 1992, Godley and Johnson had lined up Dr. Walter Harber, of Johnson City, Tennessee.

Johnson carefully plied the "bait package," extolling the "great opportunity to take advantage of the little, old, widow lady's predicament, to make some serious money." Johnson was also trying, at the same time, to con Harber into donating his Riverview Tree Farm to Johnson's scam Indian Foundation.

When the prospects for conning Harber faded, Godley, the Wades and Johnson redirected their efforts toward Paull Anderson and his business associates. It mattered not that the Court of Appeals for the Sixth Circuit had, less than a month earlier, affirmed Judge Wilhoit's ruling that the DeGroot patents were "null and void." The brazen career thieves had no qualms about further defying the laws and court rulings. That scam quickly netted Godley and the Wades $15,000 but it was foiled before they could fleece Anderson out of the three million as planned.

A month after the Anderson scam soured, Godley and the Wades had a Texan, John Wolcott, lined up as their next victim. In July and August of 1993, Wolcott was quickly fleeced out of $25,000 for a worthless option, and then another $25,000 for an extension of that option to purchase Godley's bogus title.

The following month, the cadre of career thieves transferred half of the Godley stock to Johnson's and Mezvinsky's sham American Indian Foundation for $3,000,000 in cash. The other half of her stock was acquired for a half-million-dollar tax deduction. Four months later, Johnson arranged for those same shares of Godley, Inc. stock, which had been purchased by and donated to the Indian Foundation, to be surreptitiously transferred from the Foundation to his personal ownership—for no consideration.

A month later, those shares were transferred from Johnson to his crony and Bank of East Tennessee president, Sam F. Grigsby, Sr.—again, for no consideration.

Each conveyance of those worthless shares of Godley, Inc. stock had been cleverly devised and intended to further launder them and enhance the façade and scam that they constituted good title to the Kentucky property. It set the stage—for the Kentucky land scam sights to be raised to the $28 million mark and for the subsequent attempts to victimize the Wolford brothers and later Dr. William McKnight.

Margaret Godley and her cronies scoffed at the judgment that Judge Hood awarded Paull Anderson and again at the ruling from the US Court of Appeals for the Sixth Circuit fully affirming that judgment. Godley and the Wades knew that Anderson would have to enforce that judgment in their North Carolina state courts—before their juice judges—where all the cards would be stacked in their favor. She threatened and mocked the Virginian and his judgment in a mean-spirited phone call where she bragged that the judgment could never be enforced in Charlotte because "We control the judges in this city. You bring your judgment to Charlotte and I will personally place it on your tombstone."

Although the Virginian never forgot or took lightly her caustic warning it did not deter him from vigorously pursuing the enforcement of his judgment before the North Carolina courts.

On January 16, 2007, Margaret Godley died and some time later a single black rose wrapped in a sheaf of papers and tied with a black ribbon was placed on her gravesite. The papers were copies of a judgment issued by a Kentucky federal district court in May of 2000 in a case where Margaret L. Godley was one of the defendants.

CHAPTER VIII

THE SNAKES: JULIUS J. WADE, JR.
and JAMES H. WADE

Julius Jennings "Jake" Wade, Jr. was born in Greensboro, North Carolina in 1928. He grew up in a respectable middle class family and his father was a highly-respected and competent sports editor for the *Charlotte Observer*. Wade Sr. relentlessly pushed his son, who was a small boy, to do well in sports at an early age and emphasized the importance of winning. As the son grew, he became a tenacious competitor in all that he did and he learned to make up for his lack of natural athletic and scholastic abilities with a fierce, competitive spirit that would often set him apart as "angry to win at any cost."

After Dilworth Elementary School and A.G. Junior High, his father packed him off to Darlington High School, a no-nonsense boarding school for boys in Rome, Georgia. He went on to take an undergraduate degree at Davidson College in 1950. In 1956 Wade graduated from the law school at the University of North Carolina at Chapel Hill and in 1956 he was admitted to the North Carolina bar.

Soon after passing the N.C. bar, Jake Wade found a job with the Charlotte law firm of Robert Potter, who went on to become a US district judge. In 1971, Wade and his friend, Cart Carmichael, joined up to open their own law office. Carmichael was a talented young lawyer who added prestige to the practice, while Jake Wade, a far less capable lawyer, became known as a "junk yard bulldog" and gravitated to representing insurance companies, land speculators, and fellow lawyers with legal problems.

Along the way, Jake Wade married Sarah Hunter and they had two sons, Julius Jennings Wade III and James Hunter Wade, and a daughter, Amelia H. Wade (Worley). The law practice thrived and the Wades soon moved into a stately, expensive home in the exclusive Myers Park area of Charlotte's "old money families." The Wades strived to emulate their wealthy neighbors and to be accepted into their high society.

The Wades acquired an impressive "ski home" in the winter resort of Sugar Mountain near Boone, North Carolina, and they created a "family compound" at trendy Wrightsville Beach, North Carolina. Jake Wade became active in the upper echelons of the Republican Party and with civic groups. He sat on the boards for the North Carolina School for the Deaf, the Charlotte Council on Alcoholism, and the Florence Crittendon Home for pregnant girls. At one time he chaired the Ethics Committee of his county bar association.

During the 1980's, Wade became increasingly involved with the Kentucky land fraud schemes of Marvin and Margaret Godley, forcing him to devote more and more time and energy to the attendant litigation that developed around the Kentucky land scams. Wade found himself enmeshed in burgeoning lawsuits, title problems, bankruptcies, and ever-increasing legal work in the Kentucky courts that forced him to neglect his responsibilities to the North Carolina law practice and its clients. His work for the practice became increasingly sloppy; he missed deadlines, and he routinely failed to deliver for other lawyers and to uphold his responsibilities to his partner, Cart Carmichael. Wade's interest was intensely focused on the Godley scams and the promise of fast millions.

During that period, Wade was a key operative in the Godley's Kentucky land scheme that eventually scammed Kentucky businessman, Ron Manning, and his associates out of several million dollars using the bogus DeGroot patents title.

In 1986, Wade convinced Carmichael to join him on a bank loan for $100,000 to underwrite Jake Wade's growing expenses in the Kentucky case and to offset their ever-diminishing cash flow from the law practice. In 1988 Wade conned Carmichael into borrowing an additional $33,000. A few months later, Carmichael informed his partner that he had had enough of the Wade game, the lame excuses, and the lies and broken promises. The seventeen-year-old law practice ended on a sour note.

Meanwhile, Jake Wade's youngest son, James, had followed his father's footsteps and become a lawyer in 1987 after graduating from Campbell Law School in 1986. Along the way, he married Susan Quinn and they had three children, Malone E. Wade, Quinn O. Wade, and R. Carney Wade.

In 1991, Jake Wade partnered up with his son to open a new law practice. Wade borrowed $258,000 to set up lavish new law offices in the prestigious Fourth Street area of downtown Charlotte and announced the opening of Wade and Wade, Attorneys at Law.

James Wade proved to be a willing understudy who shared his father's greed and lust for the lavish life style and expensive material possessions of Charlotte's wealthy clique. He also readily adopted his father's criminal behavior. James was soon fully enmeshed in the Godley Kentucky land scams and he quickly picked up on his father's lucrative side practice of surreptitiously stealing from client trust accounts. James also dutifully emulated his father's example of carefully maintaining a false front of respectability in his community and among the Wades' growing circle of wealthy and influential friends and associates.

As the criminal activities of the father/son team of Wade and Wade increased, they became more adept at using their law licenses to steal, manipulate their influential friends and associates, and to exploit their strong ties within the corrupt, "good old boy" network of North Carolina lawyers.

The scope of Jake Wade's illegal activities for only the two year period of 1992-1993 was astounding.

In early 1992, Jake Wade brazenly stole assets from the estate of former Family Dollar employee, William J. Sturdivant, of Charlotte, after he died of cancer. Sturdivant had appointed his "good friend and attorney," Jake Wade, to settle the estate which was worth in excess of $174,000 and included an expensive car, valuable jewelry, and a collection of very valuable silver coins. Wade simply converted those funds and assets to his own use along with a subsequent check from Merrill Lynch to the estate for $22,500. He covered up the thefts by weaving an intricate web of bold-faced lies to the beneficiary of Sturdivant's will, Ronald Gross, of Mertztown, Pennsylvania.

During the next several months, Wade continued to steal huge sums from client trust accounts while conning those clients with false assurances and documentation that their funds and assets were safely protected. In one instance, Wade stole $166,000 by forging names on three separate checks.

In August of 1992, Wade stole $25,000 from his client, Marguerite Pond, from the proceeds of the sale of her house. Wade surreptitiously diverted the First Union Mortgage Company check from the client's escrow account to his own devious uses.

In late 1992, Wade initially stole $3,775 from the checking account of deceased client Virginia Griffith and later another $48,930 from the money she had designated to go to her heirs.

By the end of that year, the government had slapped a lien on one of Jake Wade's homes for failing to pay his $82,944 tax bill. In the following April, of 1993, the tax authorities again pursued Wade trying to recover $19,630 he owed.

In April of 1993, the Wades met at their Charlotte law offices with Paull Anderson and his business associates intent on defrauding the Virginian out of three million dollars, using Godley's Kentucky land scam. As was mentioned earlier, the Wades and Godley stole $15,000 from Anderson, but his attorney, Chip Burkholder, discovered the scam in time to prevent his client's loss of the entire three million.

In July and August of 1993, the Wades and Godley, snared Texan, John Wolcott, in their Kentucky land fraud and fleeced him of $50,000 for a worthless option, and extension of that option, to purchase Godley's bogus title.

In August of 1993, Jake Wade fleeced a long-time client on his deathbed. Wade had been legal counsel for his longtime friends, Russell and Rowena Isidor. Two weeks before Russell's death, Wade conned him out of $30,000, which left Rowena shocked.

"He's been our lawyer for thirty years!" she exclaimed incredulously, after realizing how ruthlessly Wade had scammed her dying husband.

In September of 1993, the Wades and Godley arranged to transfer and launder their bogus title through the sham Foundation for the Advancement, Education and Employment of American Indians. They had their career criminal cronies, Foundation president, Howard N. Johnson, and Foundation chairman, Edward M. Mezvinsky, arrange a transfer in which Godley and the Wades received more than three million in cash and Godley obtained three million in IRS tax deductions credits. Their ploy then further laundered the bogus Godley title through the hands of Morristown, Tennessee banker, Sam F. Grigsby, Sr., where it was used to collateralize a multi-million dollar loan from Grigsby's bank for the Christ Is Our Savior (C.I.O.S.) religious organization.

These conveyances were intended to "put lipstick on that pig" to give the bogus title the deceiving appearance of having been legitimately conveyed for three million dollars, supporting the conclusion that it must have had that value and good title. The "lipstick" also included the updated "bait package" consisting of the revised Skelly

Loy Report, a new $100 million title insurance policy, the recent "good survey," and the most recent Wades' lawyers' letter assuring the good title. The same trap that had snared Ron Manning and his associates for several million, and nearly hooked Paull Anderson for three million dollars, had been reset with fresh bait to snare a twenty-eight million dollar victim.

The Wades and Godley subsequently attempted to peddle the bogus title to the Wolford brothers of Kentucky for twenty-eight million, and facilitated the subsequent efforts to peddle the bogus title to Dr. William McKnight of Texas for the same spurious amount. However, both frauds failed after Paull Anderson exposed the scams before the courts in Kentucky, Virginia, Pennsylvania, North Carolina and Tennessee.

Later, C.I.O.S. ended up losing their millions when the bogus nature of the title was revealed by Paull Anderson to the Tennessee bankruptcy court where Grigsby and the Indian Foundation filed bankruptcy petitions to defeat their creditors.

Paull Anderson's efforts and legal actions in the Kentucky federal district court against Margaret Godley and the Wades marked the beginning of their public exposure as crooks. In addition to his Kentucky lawsuit, Anderson filed complaints and provided incriminating documentation to the Federal Bureau of Investigation, the Criminal Investigation Division of the US Internal Revenue Service, and the North Carolina Bar Association. His relentless efforts to close down the corrupt activities of Godley, the Wades, and their criminal cronies, Edward Mezvinsky, Nick Johnson,

Mary Brady and Robert Krilich, finally began to reap positive results in the courts and to provoke the authorities into action.

The Virginian's efforts also encouraged other victims of the Wades, Godley, and their network of corrupt cronies to pursue justice.

By the fall of 1993, Anderson's efforts and the publicity and revelations of the Wades' brazen illegal activities had forced the N.C. Bar Association to take public action and they finally moved to seize all of Jake Wade's records and ordered him to stop handling any client funds.

The actions by Paull Anderson and the authorities also motivated the local banks into protective action. In November, Central Carolina Bank closed in on Jake Wade's home and office, starting foreclosure proceedings on its loans of $291,000.

The investigation revealed that, throughout his criminal career, Jake Wade had carefully maintained and polished his façade as a pillar of his community and one who could be trusted to serve as a role model for Charlotte's youngsters. Wade had carefully perpetrated that charade by exploiting and building upon the good name and reputation of his father who had established a solid reputation as a model citizen and respected sports editor of the *Charlotte Observer*. Jake Wade shrewdly capitalized upon his father's public persona as a sports enthusiast in the Charlotte community. Jake became involved coaching and refereeing local and church little league activities that allowed him to perpetuate the deception that he continued the family tradition as a sports-minded and respectable pillar of his church and community. He conned the little league parents into believing that he was an excellent role model and example of virtue, honesty and integrity.

Meanwhile, Wade had carefully concealed his criminal alter ego.

Wade's duplicity successfully deceived the Charlotte community, and even his closest friends, for many years. So well accomplished was his deception upon his church and community that even after Wade's extensive criminal career had been publicly exposed, his neighbors and associates expressed astonishment at the length and depth of their deception.

"I'm astonished. I just can't believe it," exclaimed Wade's childhood pal and fellow Charlotte lawyer, Jim Cobb. One of the little league team mothers, Barbara Thompson, was flabbergasted and could not understand Wade's criminal side and the "weird ways" of his two-faced façade.

Another long-time little league parent simply shook her head in disbelief and angrily admitted "He conned all of us for so long and tricked us into exposing our children to his corrupt influence."

Most of the Charlotte "good old boys" legal community quickly distanced themselves from their previously close friend and fellow lawyer who had suddenly become a public pariah. David Hanson, deputy counsel for the N.C. state bar, reflected the legal community's defensive posture. Hanson emphasized that his office had recently prosecuted other well-known and corrupt North Carolina lawyers, including Calvin Chesson, Peter Gerns, and Sidney Verbal. He stressed "There is nothing more serious than taking money from a client, and it justifies the most serious punishment." Other previously staunch "good old boy" buddies in the legal community, including Mecklenburg county district attorney Peter Gilchrist, simply declined comment and refused to denounce Wade's brazen criminality and long-running pretense of respectability.

As the subsequent investigation of the Wades' criminal activities developed, Jake Wade maneuvered to defeat and defy justice. He fabricated a web of lies to investigators who questioned him under oath and he tried to suborn perjury of others. Wade pressured Ronald Gross, the friend and heir of Wade's client, William J. Sturdivant, to give perjured testimony and lie under oath to the investigating authorities.

Meanwhile, the Wades' and Godley's efforts to steal millions through their Kentucky land fraud schemes continued relentlessly. Amazingly, one of Jake Wade's fellow lawyers and steadfast friends, Jim Carson, continued to defend the sham, arguing that "The (Kentucky) case he's been working on has come to fruition, and there's a pot of gold there."

However, despite such misleading statements and deceptive claims by Wade and his cadre of loyal "good old boy" lawyers, the authorities continued to piece together and document the extensive record of Jake Wade's criminal career.

On December 28, 1993, the North Carolina State Bar filed a detailed "Complaint," accusing Jake Wade of numerous, specific "criminal acts involving dishonesty, fraud, deceit...that reflect adversely on his honesty, trustworthiness or fitness as a lawyer." The Complaint also documented Wade's pattern of lies under oath to the authorities and his other criminal actions suborning perjury.

Jake Wade attempted to make light of the charges and to dismiss the ugly picture of his criminal career. "Everything is good and right, as it should be," he insisted. He tried to portray the charges against him as unwarranted and whined that he had simply "made a terrible mistake."

On March 11, 1994, Julius J. Wade, Jr. finally acknowledged the sordid truth of his criminal career by signing a "Consent to Disbarment" admission confirming that the "material facts upon which the Complaint, of the North Carolina StateBar Association, is predicated are true."

On March 18, 1994, the N.C. Bar Association issued an "Order of Disbarment" stripping Jake Wade of his license to practice law in North Carolina.

On June 28, 1994 Jake Wade pled guilty to the numerous criminal charges he faced before North Carolina Superior Court Judge Julia V. Jones in Mecklenburg County Superior Court. He was sentenced to a nine year suspended term, including three years of probation and 500 hours of community service. Judge Jones specifically noted that Wade "was not to be entrusted with people's money during his probation and that he not be in a position of trust for any work, volunteer services or paid employment."

Later, Jake Wade's son, James Hunter Wade, was also stripped of his license to practice law in North Carolina by the North Carolina State Bar Association in a separate procedure where the younger Wade pled guilty to criminal actions involving stealing huge sums from client trust accounts, etc.

The disbarment of the Wades reflected the shameful culmination and destruction of two once-promising legal careers. Jake Wade's downfall started when he hooked up with the Godleys and decided to use his law license and legal connections to facilitate his criminal activities and greed. He subsequently corrupted his son by leading him down the same path of destruction. Eventually both lawyers ended up selling their souls, fatally soiling their legal professions, and destroying their good names and reputations with an absolute finality that would taint and scar them and their families for the rest of their lives.

CHAPTER IX

SNAKEHANDLING: THE SNAKEPIT

MECKLENBURG COUNTY SUPERIOR COURT,
Charlotte, North Carolina
NORTH CAROLINA COURT OF APPEALS,
Raleigh, North Carolina
NORTH CAROLINA SUPREME COURT,
Raleigh, North Carolina
*Paull Anderson v. Margaret L. Godley, Julius J. Wade,
Jr., James H. Wade, Godley, Inc., Wade & Wade,
Attys. At Law*

Paull Anderson had pursued the Kentucky litigation against Godley and the Wades without trepidation, confident in the fact that the case was before the federal courts in Kentucky and Ohio where he could count on competent and fair-minded judges who would comply with the laws, the rules of civil procedure, and the controlling case law authority. He also knew that his constitutional rights to due process, equal justice, and fundamental fairness would be scrupulously protected by both the US Federal District Court in Pikeville, Kentucky, and the US Court of Appeals for the Sixth Circuit in Cincinnati, Ohio. Those courts and their distinguished judges had a well-established reputation for insuring that *pro se* litigants received a fair shake, with even-handed treatment and application of the laws to insure that justice prevailed.

On the other hand, the Virginia farmer had been emphatically forewarned of the diametrically opposite situation he would face when he tried to enforce his Kentucky federal court judgment in the North Carolina courts and especially in the Wades' home-town courts in Charlotte. A prominent attorney had laid it out in no uncertain terms:

> The litigation in the federal courts in Kentucky and Ohio has been the easy part. Those judges are top-notch and they treated you fairly. When you get to the North Carolina courts and the Charlotte snake pit you will be in the Wades' and Godley's backyard. You will be up against their good old boys and juice judges striking at you from all sides to protect one of their own.
>
> Your judgment is worth some seven hundred thousand dollars and with that much money at stake those crooks will be willing to spend some big bucks for a juice judge or two to help them beat you out of what they owe you. Later, you may have to handle more snakes in their state appeals courts.
>
> Your only real chance will be to try to get into federal court down there before a straight federal judge that will treat you fairly, but don't be surprised if the federal court action proves to be a fiasco and later the fourth circuit finesses from providing you any relief or justice.
>
> Hope and pray for just judges but expect and prepare for juice judges, and expect one of their juice judges to be presiding at the initial legal

process where the merits of the enforceability of your judgment are tested. If they can sufficiently prejudice and cripple your case at that point it will be easy for them to prevail on appeal. Like I said, it's a real snake pit. Lots of luck!

Similar, sobering warnings were offered by other lawyers long familiar with the notorious reputation of North Carolina's legal system.

The Virginian was also put on notice of the odds stacked against him in an ugly and threatening phone call from Margaret Godley. She cussed him out and made it very clear that his efforts to enforce his judgment in the Charlotte courts were doomed to failure. The Virginian attempted to respond in his most gentlemanly manner and to carefully explain an aspect of the situation she might not be fully aware of. "Any proceeds recovered from either the Kentucky or Virginia Judgments were long ago pledged to help reimburse my fellow victims of those frauds and to be distributed to my favorite charitable causes that help children, including Doctors Without Borders, Shriners Children's Hospital, St. Jude Children's Hospital, CASA, The Oprah Winfrey Foundation, and the Baptist Children's Homes of North Carolina—which is located close to your Charlotte area. I, personally, don't stand to recover anything more than the fifteen thousand dollars in cash that you and your cohorts stole from me. And, if you prefer, you can send the judgment money you owe me directly to those fine charitable causes and my fellow victims and take some credit for doing some good with that money you owe me."

"Screw you!" snapped Godley. "You aint getting your money back and those charities and your friends aint getting a cent of Godley money, not now and not ever. I'm sick and tired of reading your court writings about your fight for justice. You must be related to Oprah Winfrey who preaches the same crap on her TV show and also nauseates me. You two niggers belong together and can kiss my ass and go to hell together along with your charities. We control the judges in this city. You bring your judgment to Charlotte and I will personally place it on your tombstone."

Before the Virginian could begin to respond to Margaret Godley's disparaging tirade she hung up on him. He replayed the recording of the brief conversation and Godley's explicit warning and resolved to take her warning seriously but not let it deter his efforts to enforce his judgment in her North Carolina courts— although he had to face the reality that if she did control the judges in those courts his best efforts would likely prove futile.

Forearmed with the ominous forewarning, Paull Anderson entered the North Carolina snake pit. He simultaneously filed copies of his Kentucky federal court money judgment in the Charlotte and Wilmington, North Carolina, County Superior Courts. He knew that Godley had real estate holdings in the Charlotte area worth millions. The Wades had valuable real estate holdings in Charlotte, an expensive chalet in a nearby ski resort, and a posh family compound in the exclusive area of Wilmington Beach. On December 6, 2000, Paull Anderson filed a Motion to Enforce Foreign Judgment in the Mecklenburg County Superior Court at Charlotte.

A month after the motion was filed, a Charlotte attorney, Thomas M. Tillett, made his appearance in the case and filed a Response on behalf of Godley and the Wades. Tillett also filed a Motion to Suspend the Enforcement of the Judgment while the Kentucky Judgment was still on appeal before the Sixth Circuit Court of Appeals.

Anderson checked out Tillett's legal credentials in the Martindale-Hubbell lawyer directory, which indicated he was a solo practitioner with an unremarkable legal record. Further inquiries through two reliable North Carolina lawyers suggested that Mr. Tillett was "scratching out a living as a lawyer and trying to handle a drinking problem."

Anderson replied to the motion, contending that the defendants had failed to file a required copy of their proof brief with the Sixth Circuit in a timely manner, which left their appeal tenuous and their argument without merit. Notwithstanding, Anderson decided to simply await the formal ruling by the Sixth Circuit before proceeding further to enforce his foreign judgment in North Carolina.

Meanwhile, and despite Margaret Godley's caustic phone call and warning, the Virginian decided to make one final effort to resolve the litigation by appealing to the Godley and Wade family members with hopes they would be reasonable. Although those family members were not part of the ongoing litigation, they were in jeopardy of being sued by Anderson as alleged co-conspirators in the theft and defrauding of Anderson and for their involvement in the defendants' actions conveying assets to family members to further defraud

Anderson and to deny him access to assets necessary to collect on his judgment.

In May of 2002, Anderson wrote to the family members. Copies went to Margaret Godley's sons, Frank H. Godley, James B. Godley, and John C. Godley, and to her granddaughters, Cristal, Robin, Sandi, and Jennifer Godley. Copies went to Jake Wade's wife, Sarah H. Wade, and their children, Julius Jennings Wade, III, and Amelia H. Worley. Copies also went out to James Wade's wife, Susan Q. Wade, and their children, Malone E., Quinn O., and R. Carney Wade:

31 May 2002
Dear Ladies and Gentlemen:

For the past eight years I have been pursuing litigation in four companion civil RICO racketeering, fraud, conspiracy cases including the above styled case in which your family members, Jake and Jimmy Wade and Margaret Godley, are the defendants. The other three companion cases involve their cronies, H.N. Johnson, Edward Mezvinsky, Samuel Grigsby, and their scam "Indian Foundation." Except for the current ongoing criminal litigation against Mezvinsky in Philadelphia these cases have all recently concluded with the final ruling, Opinion and Mandate of the Sixth Circuit Court of Appeals affirming the Judgment of the District Court in my favor against your family members. Enclosed herewith please find copies of the Sixth Circuit's Opinion and Mandate along with other materials concerning said companion cases.

I am thusly now seeking to collect my judgment in the instant case either with or without the cooperation of your family members. I have commenced the domestication of that Judgment in North Carolina and am ready to levy, execute and foreclose as necessary and to subpoena them and each of you for judgment depositions to determine assets.

I also wish to inform you all that during the past year I have expended considerable time, effort and expenses preparing the Complaint in my companion case and cause of action re your complicity, etc. as co-conspirators, etc. and as supported by the findings of fact and law in the instant and companion cases, information and materials produced in said cases, and as expanded to include additional statutory violations. Attached herewith please find the caption page from said extensive Complaint.

I would also have you know that during the past year I made several bona fide overtures to defense counsel in the instant case to resolve this matter and the looming litigation against you all by simply paying the Judgment, in keeping with my policy of trying to avoid litigation but then advancing full bore once the effort fails. Indeed, prior to filing suit in the instant litigation, eight years ago, I similarly offered a fair and amicable solution and have repeatedly done so during the ensuing years; however, my efforts were always demeaned. Copies of that correspondence are attached herewith.

My efforts in that regard have included requests to your senior family members' counsel that this developing situation and my final overtures be brought to the attention of you family members facing the looming litigation; notwithstanding, I have reason to believe that you all have not been made aware of same, which has prompted me to submit this missive to you all directly.

Without commenting upon the particulars and merits of the Complaint I can simply assure you that they are very serious and whereas another collateral phase of related litigation will not phase me, and cause me no significant expenses since I proceed pro se, you all may wish to consider the certain effects upon each of you, the expenses, stress, worry, anxiety, time, energy and hardships that such arduous, protracted and difficult litigation involve and which include serious jeopardy of judgment damages liability and even the prospect of tangential criminal litigation.

I can only emphasize my policy and preference to always first attempt to amicably avoid litigation prior to loosing the dogs with hopes that you folks, contrary to the senior members of your family, will also be so inclined, as reasonable and fair minded people should be. I would, respectfully, urge you all to seek the advice of individual, competent counsel on this matter to protect each of your individual interests and to avoid the mistakes your senior family members made during the past eight years.

Please remember that this situation and your serious problems and exposure were not caused by me. I simply want what I am justly entitled to by law and the Orders of the Courts.

I shall hold the filing of said Complaint in abeyance for two (2) weeks henceforth with hopes to receive a positive, encouraging response from you folks and/or your counsel within the interim.

Meanwhile, in the Christian spirit, and bearing you all no personal ill will, I shall wish you all excellent health as I remain,

Sincerely,

Paull Anderson

The Virginian soon received a response to his letter from Frank Heaberlin, the last lawyer to represent the Wades in the Kentucky case. Heaberlin phoned Anderson to inform him that his clients had expressed intentions to honor and pay the judgment. Heaberlin requested a meeting with Anderson in Bristol, Virginia, to discuss the matter.

On June 26, 2002, Anderson met with Frank Heaberlin, Jake Wade and Margaret Godley's son, Frank, in Attorney Burkholder's Bristol, Virginia, law office. The meeting was very brief and its only productive result was that Anderson agreed to provide Heaberlin with the figure necessary to pay the judgment. The following day, Anderson, mailed off his calculations and supporting documents indicating that the current total amount due was some $775,000 which included statutory interest to date and recoverable costs for depositions, mailings, and other incidental expenses.

Heaberlin responded, suggesting a different figure based on a lower statutory rate of interest calculation but noted that his clients did not dispute the other recoverable costs Anderson had listed.

During the next several weeks Heaberlin engaged Anderson in a series of phone conversations where he began to edge away from his previous position, that his clients "are prepared to pay the judgment but require time to put the money together." Heaberlin suggested they consider a structured arrangement rather than a single payment. Then he suggested that the settlement involve a reduced amount rather than the full judgment figure. Finally, Heaberlin advanced his clients' preparedness to pay a significantly reduced amount in a structured format where they would make a small, initial payment and give a promissory note for the balance which was to be paid in incremental payments over a matter of years.

The Virginian informed Heaberlin that he was not prepared to participate in any such bad faith arrangement which backed away from the original settlement agreement and which left Anderson with a much reduced recovery figure, a token payment in hand, and an unsecured promissory note. Once Anderson accepted such an agreement and signed away his right to collect on his Kentucky Judgment, in return for the token payment and promissory note, he would be forced to chase the defendants to force them to honor their promissory note. That would require initiating another legal action in their home-town state court.

On August 15, 2002, Anderson informed Heaberlin that it was time to end his clients' subterfuge and deceit and he would proceed to move to enforce the judgment in the North Carolina courts.

On September 2, 2002, Anderson moved to enforce his Kentucky judgment in the Mecklenburg County Superior Court at Charlotte. The motion was originally set to be heard on October 14, and then continued to be heard on February 18, 2003.

Meanwhile, Jake Wade submitted a responsive memorandum contesting the enforcement of the judgment. Anderson replied, submitting his own memorandum which contained a plethora of controlling case law authority compelling enforcement of the judgment.

In late January of 2003, Anderson made several efforts to communicate with Mr. Tillett and found that he could not be reached at his law office.

On February 12, 2003, Anderson received a strange telefax from a Mr. Don Carroll, stating that Mr. Tillett was currently out of the state receiving medical treatment and that Carroll, on behalf of the North Carolina State Bar's Lawyer Assistance Program, would request the presiding judge continue the scheduled hearing of Anderson's motion until Mr. Tillett had completed his medical treatment. The fax indicated that a copy had been sent to Charlotte lawyer William K. Diehl, Jr., a partner in the Charlotte law firm of James, McElroy & Diehl, and who had apparently just stepped into the case representing Margaret Godley.

An hour later, Anderson responded with a fax to Carroll expressing his displeasure with, and suspicion of, the development. Anderson questioned the sudden intrusion by this unknown individual and its timing coming just a few days before the scheduled hearing:

Mr. Tillett has presented no affidavit and medical proof that he is unable to attend the hearing as a medical necessity and for that reason alone your actions are also highly suspect and improper. Mr. Tillett, and all of the defendants, have had notice of the hearing date for well over a month. The fact that Mr. Tillett appears to now be out of the state receiving medical attention verifies that his present medical problem did not arise in a medical emergency this morning and that he has had ample time, of at least some weeks, to bring in other counsel for the hearing. His dereliction is no meritorious reason to suffer additional obstruction and delay. The corrupt defendants have intentionally pursued such a course trying to obstruct and delay my due process and recovery for the past nine years and which has been thoroughly denounced and explicitly held to be reprehensible by the US District Court for the Eastern District of Kentucky and the Sixth Circuit Court of Appeals.

Mr. Diehl has had every reason to be fully prepared for the hearing and is expected to attend the hearing where he can readily and satisfactorily represent the interests of the defendants, which involve the same legal issues. Consequently, defendants Wades will suffer no prejudice if the defendants' co-counsel, Mr. Tillett, does not need to appear so long as Mr. Diehl is present to represent their interests.

This entire development smacks of another, most recent, predicate act in the ongoing RICO pattern of acts involving the defendants and/or in concert with others and/or conspirators to violate my civil and constitutional rights. Any request for a continuance is and will be vigorously opposed.

The development left Anderson extremely suspicious that he was witnessing the subterfuge and deceit he had been warned to expect in the Charlotte state court and from Jake Wades' lawyer cronies. He also wondered when Diehl had entered the case and why Godley's new lawyer had submitted no proper notice of appearance. Anderson checked Diehl out with Martindale-Hubbell and discerned nothing impressive in his legal background or accomplishments. A phone call to a knowledgeable, reliable North Carolina lawyer confirmed Anderson's suspicions that Diehl could be expected to be everything Anderson had been warned about. "If you are used to dealing with the Wades then Diehl should fit right in. Billy 'Bubba' Diehl is a real piece of work, a redneck legend in his own mind and about as narcissistic and obnoxious as they come."

On the following day, Anderson's concerns about his new adversaries were confirmed. He received a phone call from someone who identified himself as North Carolina Superior Court Judge Beverly Beal and who stated he was calling from his chambers in the presence of attorney John Arrowood, who was apparently a member of the law firm that had begun representing Margaret Godley. Judge Beal said that Arrowood had given him copies of the telefax from Carroll to Anderson and Anderson's response to Carroll. Beal said he had called to engage Anderson in a phone conference to discuss the matter of continuing the scheduled hearing of Anderson's motion.

The Virginian expressed his displeasure with the development and the fact that the judge and Arrowood had engaged in an *ex parte* conversation concerning the matter prior to phoning him, in addition to the fact that Anderson did not know Arrowood or that he was even involved in the case. Anderson also made it clear that he objected to Carroll's intervention in the case and to a continuance of the hearing and contended that the move was "an obvious, obstructionist, delay tactic by the Wades."

Judge Beal informed Anderson that attorney Tillett was "out of the state drying out, receiving treatment for his drinking problem; he is an alcoholic." He explained that Mr. Carroll had interceded on behalf of the North Carolina Bar Association's Lawyer Assistance Program which tries to help members of the bar with such problems. He opined that if the requested continuance were not granted the Wades could simply show up at the hearing without counsel, request a continuance to find replacement counsel, and the hearing would be continued to allow them to do so.

Judge Beal expressed some concern with Anderson's contentions that it all just looked like a repeat of the defendants' past strategy of delay tactics. Beal proposed that if Anderson would consent to a reasonable continuance his order would force the Wades to find replacement counsel within fifteen days and the rescheduled hearing date set for March 20 would not be continued if the Wades failed to find new counsel by that time. After Anderson and Arrowood agreed to the proposal, Beal directed Arrowood to draw up an order to that effect and the phone conference ended.

The following day Anderson received a faxed copy of Arrowood's proposed order and immediately responded by fax, to both Judge Beal and Arrowood, voicing his objections. Anderson noted that the proposed order failed to accurately reflect the phone conference particulars and what Anderson had agreed to. Anderson also objected to Arrowood's self-serving proposed order that denied Anderson a reasonable opportunity to investigate, develop, and present all of the important, relevant facts for consideration by Beal prior to making findings of fact and law. Anderson's response suggested explicit changes to Arrowood's proposed order to insure that it reflected only the explicit findings of fact and law that were consistent with what had expressly transpired and been agreed to during the phone conference.

Later that day, Paull Andersonn received a telefax from Diehl demeaning the integrity of the Kentucky judgment and berating him for daring to criticize Arrowood's behavior. Diehl demanded an immediate apology and promised "to fight you tooth and nail" to prevent Anderson from recovering the money stolen from him and his damages. Diehl was adamant that his client would never return the money stolen from the Virginian.

Anderson immediately responded to Diehl's harsh criticism with a letter to make it clear that he could not be intimidated by lawyers or such rhetoric. "Happy Valentine's Day. You are entitled to your opinion re Mr. Arrowood and mine will be based on cold, hard facts. Unfortunately, at this point, his actions over the very few days I have witnessed have not favorably impressed me with his veracity or integrity. You are also entitled to vent your opinions re the Kentucky litigation and its subsequent judgment; however, that case record and *res judicata* findings of fact and law by the federal district court and Sixth Circuit stand *res ipse loquitur* against your juvenile assertions. Meanwhile, do try to contain yourself; it is unhealthy to be so vexed. Try to have a stressless weekend and improve your health and mind."

Diehl and Arrowood had thrown down their gauntlet and the Virginia farmer had picked it up.

Diehl quickly replied to Anderson's letter with an even more caustic diatribe and insisted that the Virginian discontinue making any negative comments about his law partner or their client.

On March 20, 2003, Paull Anderson traveled to Charlotte, North Carolina, for the scheduled hearing in the Mecklenburg Superior Court of his motion to enforce his Kentucky judgment. He entered Courtroom 305, sat at the plaintiff's table, carefully removed the materials from his briefcase and placed them in an orderly fashion on the table before him. Then he looked over the courtroom with his peripheral vision.

Seated nearby, to his left at the defendant's table, were three lawyers for the defendants. Diehl and Arrowood were there representing Margaret Godley. Michael Schultze, from the Charlotte law firm of Cranford, Schultze & Tomchin, was there representing the Wades. Seated behind them, in the last row of the gallery, Anderson recognized Jake Wade and some elderly, heavily wrinkled, scowling woman. He surmised that this harridan was likely Margaret Godley.

The Virginian took a few minutes to more closely observe the defendants' lawyers.

He recalled the earlier description of William K. Diehl, Jr. and quickly concluded that Diehl had to be the one sitting at the end of the defense table nearest Anderson, some four feet distant. He was a short, squat, dumpy character in an ill-fitting, wrinkled, gray suit that hung on him like a WalMart special. He was slouched over a file folder that he was thumbing through. He wheezed with labored breathing. Diehl's flashy necktie was wrinkled and had a large poorly tied knot that hung off center and an inch beneath the button straining to hold his shirt together against the corpulent neck that bulged over the collar. He had a flabby, flushed face with an ingrained scowl that was accented by sagging jowls that drooped into the mass of neck blubber. His wispy, thinning, dingy gray hair was pulled back in a straggly pony tail contained by a rubber band. Anderson smiled to himself, thinking about the way Diehl had been characterized, by a veteran North Carolina lawyer as "a redneck legend in his own mind."

Arrowood most likely was the person sitting beside Diehl. He had carried in the file box and handed Diehl a folder, then busied himself reviewing copies of case law citations. Arrowood presented a stark contrast to Diehl in every aspect. John Arrowood fit the stereotype of a trim, polished, sophisticated Brahmin lawyer. His suit was obviously expensive, very well tailored, low key conservative with quiet, matching tie that precisely hung from a perfectly balanced, modest, Windsor knot. Arrowood had an unremarkably plain, poker face and a receding hairline of carefully groomed, thinning gray. Arrowood's chair posture was perfect and he appeared totally relaxed in familiar, friendly surroundings. He appeared more interested in checking out the Virginian with frequent, furtive glances than in the legal materials that the other two lawyers appeared engrossed in. When Arrowood noticed Anderson looking in his direction he momentarily caught Anderson's eye, smiled slightly, raised an eyebrow and slowly turned his attention to the materials before him.

Michael Schultze sat beside Arrowood and appeared oblivious to anything beyond the file that he was attentively bent over and poring through. Anderson found nothing remarkable or of interest in the younger lawyer other than his youthful appearance in contrast to that of the other two lawyers.

Moments later, Superior Court Judge Jesse Caldwell took the bench and quickly motioned Anderson to commence his oral argument.

Anderson carefully covered the major points of his argument, often referring to the large number of controlling case law authorities he had cited in his Memorandum that supported the enforcement of his foreign judgment.

The defendants' lawyers then argued against the enforcement of the judgment, focusing on the procedural technicality that it was not technically final because the US Court of Appeals for the Sixth Circuit had not yet issued its ruling affirming the Kentucky judgment. Under North Carolina law, the Kentucky foreign judgment could not be enforced until it was final. Judge Caldwell nodded in agreement with the defendants and summarily ruled, denying Anderson's motion without considering the merits of the judgment and the large body of controlling legal authority that compelled its enforcement. Caldwell had used the procedural issue as a way to avoid considering and adjudicating the merits of whether the judgment was enforceable in North Carolina.

In August of 2003, the Sixth Circuit issued its opinion fully affirming Judge Hood's judgment and $611,000 damages award. Anderson immediately submitted copies of the opinion and filed an updated Motion to Enforce Foreign Judgment. The Virginian once again filed a Motion to Enforce Foreign Judgment and scheduled it to be heard on December 10, 2003. On December 4, 2003, Anderson submitted a lengthy Memorandum in Support of Motion to Enforce Foreign Judgment. The Memorandum contained a plethora of controlling constitutional case law authority compelling the enforcement of his judgment. The defendants' lawyers submitted their own Notice of Defense and Motion for Relief from the judgment with very little case law authority supporting their contentions.

Judge Marvin K. Gray appeared at the scheduled hearing for Anderson's Motion. Gray was a seventy-two-year-old retired superior court judge from the Charlotte area who was friendly to the defendants and their lawyers and he had used his influence to intercede in the case. When Gray admitted he had not bothered to read the Memorandum brief that Anderson had sent to him a week earlier, the Virginian could see the handwriting on the wall and realized he was playing against a stacked deck. He was up against the defendants and their lawyers in their home-town courtroom, before their home-town juice judge that refused to even review the controlling case law authority in Anderson's Memorandum brief. Anderson knew the most he could accomplish would be to put as much as he could into the record to document and expose their game. He arose and stated his position:

> I emphasize the crucial importance of your Honor carefully reviewing my brief and my case citations and not depending on just what I say today. You know I'm not a lawyer and I'm doing the best I can but my brief is comprehensive and contains all the case authority. Those cases are everything; they go into detail. I rely on the case law authority that I have submitted in detail in my brief.

Judge Gray afforded the defendants' three lawyers ample opportunity to argue their positions and then ruled, arbitrarily denying Anderson's motion to enforce his foreign judgment:

The Plaintiff's action to have a foreign judgment enforced in North Carolina is

denied. It does not comply with the Rules of Civil Procedure, including Rule 60; it does not comply with Rule 1C-1703 of the General Statutes of North Carolina; it does not comply with Chapter 1D of the General Statutes of North Carolina; it is against the public policy of North Carolina, and it does not comply with other applicable Rules of Civil Procedure in North Carolina.

Gray directed the defense lawyers to draft an order reflecting his ruling and Anderson immediately placed his objection into the record. "Your Honor, I'd like to note that the objection is also based on the fact that your honor has not granted review of my brief and without reviewing my brief and the case law authority I believe I am being unfairly dealt with."

Judge Gray's face reddened and he angrily scowled at Anderson, "I have already told them what to put on that judgment. Now, that's all it's going to say, whether you like it or not!"

However, that was not all Gray's subsequent judgment order would say. The next day the defense lawyers faxed Anderson a copy of their Proposed Order. Despite the Virginian's strong objection, that it was "dishonest, deceitful and grossly corrupted, subverted and misrepresented Judge Gray's ruling and should accurately reflect the ruling, verbatim, and nothing more or less," Gray quickly signed it and it became the law of the case:

1. Plaintiff has failed to comply with the mandatory requirements of Article 17, G.S. Section 1C-1701, et seq., particularly the provisions of N.C.G.S. Section 1C-1703. 2. Plaintiff has not met his burden under the provisions of N.C.G.S. Section 1C-1705, nor has he complied with the North Carolina Rules of Civil Procedure. 3. The Judgment Plaintiff seeks to enforce is contrary to the public policies of the State of North Carolina, particularly the provisions of Chapter 1D of the North Carolina General Statutes. 4. Because the judgment Plaintiff seeks to enforce is violative of the North Carolina Public Policy, it is unenforceable pursuant to the provisions of N.C.G.S. Section 1C-1708. Based upon the foregoing findings of fact, the Court concludes as a matter of law that the above referenced findings, jointly and severally, mandate that Plaintiff's Motion to Enforce Foreign Judgment should be denied. IT IS THEREFORE ORDERED, ADJUDGED AND DECREED that Plaintiff's Motion to Enforce Foreign Judgment be and the same is, DENIED.

Anderson's objections and the deceitful, dishonest, subversive nature of the order mattered not to Gray.

Anderson immediately filed Notice of Appeal of Gray's Order. He was not about to allow the blatant dishonesty and deceit of the corrupt defense lawyers and the brash injustice of Judge Gray to go unchallenged.

Anderson then started down the slippery slope of the state's appeal process, making every effort to comply with the North Carolina Rules of Appellate Procedure.

He requested a copy of the video recording of the December 10, 2003, hearing from Judge Gray's Courtroom Clerk, Richard Lockhard. Upon receiving the video tape recording he sent it to Charlotte Court Reporter, Dianne Holt, to prepare a transcript. Upon receiving the transcript, Anderson prepared his Proposed Record on Appeal which contained all the materials from the record before the Mecklenburg County Superior Court that he felt necessary to give proper insight to the appeals court to help them decide the issues he would raise on appeal. The issues would be framed as errors of law made by Gray that Anderson contended warranted remedial action by the appeals courts.

On February 17, 2004, Anderson sent the defense lawyers, in timely fashion, copies of his Proposed Record on Appeal.

On March 9, Godley's lawyers responded with their Objections and Amendments and on March 12th, the Wades' lawyers responded with their Proposed Alternative Record on Appeal. This development set the stage, pursuant to the Rules of Appellate Procedure, for Anderson to request Judge Gray to set a hearing and settle the disputed parts of the proposed record on appeal, thereby deciding the final composition of the record on appeal that would go up to the appeals courts.

On March 12, Anderson sent Gray a timely, formal Request to Settle the Record on Appeal in compliance with Rule 11 of the Rules of Appellate Procedure:

...within 10 days after the appellee timely served amendments, objections or a proposed alternative record on appeal...appellant may in writing request the judge from whose order, judgment was taken to settle the record on appeal.

At that point, Rule 11(c) unequivocally mandated Gray's responsibilities to set a hearing to settle the record and then to timely settle the record on appeal:

...by written notice to counsel for all parties setting a place and time for a hearing to settle the record on appeal. The hearing shall be held not later than 15 days after service of the request for hearing upon the judge. The judge shall settle the record on appeal by order entered not more than 20 days after service of the request for hearing upon the judge.

The Rule 11(c) "shall" imperative afforded Gray no discretion to defy compliance. Notwithstanding, Gray chose to openly defy and violate the Rules and his clear obligations thereunder. He blatantly ignored both the request and his legal obligations to both set a hearing date and then to settle the record on appeal.

Dismayed, but not at all surprised, the diligent Anderson sent Gray a second such request, by both telefax and US Mail, on March 25, noting his previous request and again requesting the hearing be set to settle the record on appeal in compliance with Rule 11(c); the missive also inquired into Gray's health or other legitimate reasons for delay.

Once again Gray defied Rule 11(c). Instead of complying, he deviously arranged for his Courtroom Clerk, Richard Lockhard, to phone Anderson early the next morning and direct him to phone the Scheduling Clerk, Ms. Helen Stonestreet, to have a hearing date set to settle the record on appeal and to then send notices to the defendants of the action. Lockhard also informed Anderson that Judge Gray was not ill, that he was retired, and that he might not conduct the hearing.

The Virginian immediately complied with Judge Gray's directions, coming through Gray's courtroom clerk. Anderson phoned Ms. Stonestreet and informed her of Lockhard's call and instructions; she set a hearing date for May 5. It was to be heard in the same Courtroom 305 where Judge Gray had presided and where Lockhard served as courtroom clerk. Anderson then sent a proper Notice of Hearing to the defense lawyers along with a cover letter explaining the circumstances and details of the call from Lockhard.

The diligent Virginian then made a further effort to confirm Gray's capacity and health. Anderson phoned Gray's other clerk, Ms. Cathy Fletcher, and inquired about Gray's health, capacity and current activity on the bench. Ms. Fletcher was most helpful and informed Anderson that "although Judge Gray has been retired, he still sits and hears cases and was on the bench here last week with a case. He appears well."

At that point Anderson felt satisfied that he had acted diligently, in good faith, and that he was in full compliance with both the NC Rules of Appellate

Procedure and the instructions coming from Judge Gray through his Courtroom Clerk.

On May 5, 2004, Anderson attended the scheduled hearing to settle the record on appeal and was surprised to find another judge, Superior Court Judge Richard D. Boner, presiding. Judge Boner appeared to be a no-nonsense jurist. He indicated that he had taken the time to familiarize himself with the issues at hand and he had read all the materials in the record before him, including the plaintiff's Proposed Record on Appeal, and the defendants' Proposed Alternative Record on Appeal and their Objections and Amendments.

Anderson and the defendants' lawyers made their arguments concerning what they felt the settled record on appeal should contain. When Anderson objected to the exclusion from the record of his Memorandum, that Judge Gray refused to properly review prior to ruling, Judge Boner advised Anderson to later request the appeals court to include it in the record on appeal. Anderson thanked Judge Boner for his consideration and advice. At the conclusion of the hearing before Judge Boner, the defense lawyers did not repeat the same smugness and contemptuous smirks as they had at the conclusion of the hearing before their juice judge, Marvin K. Gray.

On May 24, 2004, Anderson timely filed the Settled Record on Appeal before the North Carolina Court of Appeals.

On May 28, the defendants' lawyers filed a Motion to Dismiss Appeal before the Court of Appeals. Their Motion contended that the record on appeal had not been filed with the court of appeals on April 16, in compliance with Rule 11(c) and, therefore, should be dismissed "for failure to timely docket the appeal."

The Virginian filed a Response brief, carefully documenting and laying out the sequence of events that resulted in the filing of the record on May 24, and showing that any delay was caused by the intentional violations of Rule 11 by Judge Gray on two distinct occasions coupled with his explicit instructions, through his courtroom clerk, to the plaintiff. Anderson laid out each step of the events showing how he had "diligently and in good faith complied with Rule 11(c) each step of the way while also fully complying with the instructions from Judge Gray coming through Mr. Lockhard."

Anderson's brief fully supported its irrefutable conclusion that "the defendants' Motion now makes it perfectly clear that Judge Gray's devious and intentional violations of the Rules, and then his subsequent ploy using his courtroom clerk, were intended to set the plaintiff up for the defendants' move to dismiss." Anderson strongly denounced Gray's "underhanded, reprehensible actions to rob plaintiff of an appeal and his constitutional rights to due process, equal justice and fundamental fairness." Anderson also contended that "the evidence supported plaintiff's contention that Judge Gray was acting in concert with the evil, corrupt defendants and their sleazy, dishonest, deceitful, corrupt lawyers."

Despite the Virginian's persuasive and well-documented arguments, on June 9, 2004, the NC Court of Appeals summarily issued its order granting the defendants' motion to dismiss the appeal. Although the ruling did not set well with Anderson, he understood the appeals court action as an expedient way to avoid hearing the case and having to expose, acknowledge and sanction the egregious misconduct of one of their state's superior court judges. The advice he had earlier received, concerning the injustice he should expect before the North Carolina state courts, was proving prophetic.

Although he expected no relief or justice, the Virginian took the final steps necessary to exhaust the North Carolina state courts.

On June 22, 2004, he filed a Notice of Appeal and a Petition for Discretionary Review before the North Carolina Supreme Court, followed by a Petition for a Writ of *Certiorari* to that Court on February 14, 2005. His petitions documented all of the dishonesty, deceit, misconduct and dirty tricks by the defense lawyers in concert with their home-town "juice judge." After carefully chronicling, in explicit detail, the entire sequence of brazen misconduct and grievous injustice, he laid out the shameful results:

> The ruthless, corrupt defendants stole the plaintiff's money and caused him severe damage ten years ago, and now their sleazy, dishonest, rogue, home-town lawyers through their home-town judge are robbing the plaintiff of his right of appeal and the enforcement of his valid foreign judgment. In doing so they are defying, violating and making a mockery of the US Constitutional Full Faith and Credit authority, the XIV Amendment, the rulings of the US Supreme Court and those of the Fourth and Sixth Circuit Courts of Appeal, and, ironically, the rulings of

this North Carolina Supreme Court and the North Carolina Court of Appeals. The actions of the evil, corrupt defendants, their dishonest, deceitful lawyers, and Judge Gray have tarnished the image of North Carolina jurisprudence.

Anderson's summary also chastised the North Carolina Court of Appeals' failure to do justice:

The NC Court of Appeals could have, and should have, been primarily concerned with justice and fundamental fairness and invoked its authority, pursuant to Rule 2, to preserve plaintiff's right to appeal and foiled Judge Gray's ploy to further defeat and defy justice, the US Constitution and controlling case law authority, and the enforcement of the valid foreign judgment. It is a manifest injustice that the Court of Appeals has chosen to penalize the honest and truthful, *pro se* plaintiff and dismiss his appeal for the reprehensible actions of Judge Gray while effectively condoning the unconstitutional misconduct of the trial judge and his intentional violation of the Rules of Appellate Procedure.

On April 6, 2005, the North Carolina Supreme Court issued a one liner order summarily denying discretionary review of Anderson's petition. The final action by the state's highest court opened the way for Anderson to place the gross injustice by the North Carolina courts on record before the US Supreme Court and to seek relief and justice before the federal district court in Charlotte, despite his grave doubts that any court in that state would be just.

In September of 2007, the *Charlotte Observer* ran an article describing how Arrowood had taken the oath of office, in a courtroom packed with his friends, for the North Carolina Court of Appeals. The headline trumpeted the fact that "Gay appellate judge makes history" and went on to relate how "Arrowood had just become the first openly gay person in a statewide elective office in North Carolina. A decade after such an event would have startled the NC capital, no one has made an issue of his sexual orientation."

North Carolina Governor, Mike Easley, who had appointed Arrowood to the bench, praised the appointment. Dan Ellison, president-elect of the NC Gay Advocacy Legal Alliance also applauded the appointment and the fact that Arrowood was an open and proud gay and bragged that General Assembly Senator Julie Boseman was also an open and proud gay.

A week later, Anderson crossed paths with the lawyer that had warned him about the "Charlotte snake pit" years earlier when the Virginian first took his Judgment to North Carolina to seek enforcement.

Over lunch, Anderson vented his frustration. "I understand Diehl's actions and motivation in this litigation and I don't blame him for milking Godley of his seven hundred and fifty dollar an hour fee plus expenses for as long as possible. What irritates me is how these North Carolina courts brazenly make a mockery of the Judgment of the Sixth Circuit and openly defile any measure of justice by protecting the interests of their home-town crooks and preventing their victim from recovering the monies they stole from him."

"Couldn't agree with you more; however, all of that and the justice factor have no relevance in a snake pit where the vipers prevail. I still believe that your only slim chance for justice will be before the Fourth Circuit and I doubt you will fare any better before the Charlotte Federal District Court where, most likely, the same influence will prevail that Margaret Godley bragged about when she warned you that they controlled the judges in Charlotte. As you now well know, she was not just whistling Dixie. Just be careful how you continue to handle those vipers."

CHAPTER X

SNAKEHANDLING: SEEKING CERTIORARI

UNITED STATES SUPREME COURT,
Washington, D.C.
*Paull Anderson v. Margaret L. Godley, Julius J. Wade,
Jr., James H. Wade, Godley, Inc., Wade & Wade,
Attys. At Law*

The United States Supreme Court is different from all other courts. It resolves Constitutional and important legal issues and decides fundamental political and social questions for the purpose of stabilizing and expounding legal principles for the general, social good of the nation not in the mere interest of the litigants. The Court purposefully avoids Constitutional issues, no matter how strongly pressed, if there is any other possible way to resolve the case. The cases it considers and resolves are strictly limited to issues that will have immediate national importance far beyond the specific facts and litigants that are involved.

Litigants wishing to have their cases considered by the United States Supreme Court must file a Petition for a Writ of *Certiorari* with the Court. The petition is simply the technical device by which the petitioner asks the Court to hear his case. The United States Supreme Court has complete discretion to decide which cases it will hear from the many thousands of Petitions for Writ of *Certiorari* that are brought before that Court every year. When the Court grants a petition, it then issues a writ of *certiorari* to the lower court that decided the case and the issues the petitioner is asking the Supreme Court to examine. That writ indicates to the litigants and to the lower court that the Supreme Court has decided to hear the case and it instructs the lower court to send up the record of the litigation from the lower court to the Supreme Court.

In granting or denying a petition, the Court gives no reason for its action. That action has absolutely nothing to do with the merits of the legal claim presented in the petition and it does not indicate that the Supreme Court agrees or disagrees with the actions or ruling by the lower court.

The Supreme Court's review of cases is strictly limited and controlled by the constitutional authority from which it derives its authority and the court's rules. It can only hear and re-examine issues from the lower courts involving questions of federal law. It can only consider legal issues that have been properly raised and pursued before the lower courts. It can only review state-court decisions that are final judgments or decrees that have been rendered by the highest court in a state in which a decision could be had or final decisions from one of the US Courts of Appeal. It will only consider a case concerning constitutional issues in which the complaining party has "standing"—where the petitioner can show that he has been personally injured or affected by the lower court action.

For cases from the federal courts to qualify for review, the case must meet strict "jurisdictional" requirements and involve suits between citizens of different states, qualifying as diversity-of-citizenship lawsuits. That policy complies with Article III of the Constitution and was implemented to protect out-of-state litigants from bias in the local state court where a litigant resides and could file the lawsuit to gain that advantage. However, the federal courts in such diversity cases are bound to apply state statutes and state decisions, no matter how unjust and appalling they may be—and reflect that the lower court judge has properly applied the state law of that state and before whom the federal claim was raised at the earliest opportunity in the state court action.

Rule 10 of the Supreme Court Rules further limits and explicitly specifies the consideration restricting and governing review on *certiorari*:

> Review on a writ of *certiorari* is not a matter of right, but of judicial discretion. A petition for a writ of *certiorari* will be granted only for compelling reasons. The following, although neither controlling nor fully measuring the Court's discretion, indicate the character of the reasons the Court considers:
>
> (a) a United States court of appeals has entered a decision in conflict with another United States court of appeals on the same important matter; has decided an important federal question in a way that conflicts with a decision by a state court of last resort; or has so far departed from the accepted and usual course of judicial proceedings, or sanctioned such a departure by a

lower court, as to call for an exercise of this Court's supervisory power;

(b) a state court of last resort has decided an important federal question in a way that conflicts with the decision of another state court of last resort or of a United States court of appeals;

(c) a state court or a United States court of appeals has decided an important question of federal law that has not been, but should be, settled by this Court, or that has decided an important federal question in a way that conflicts with relevant decisions of this Court.

Paull Anderson was well aware of the highly restrictive Supreme Court rules and that his petition would almost certainly be summarily denied because, historically, petitions by *pro se* litigants had virtually no chance of being granted and the issues he presented did not rise to the level of crucial political and social matters that the Supreme Court reviews. The US Supreme Court does not grant *certiorari* simply because the petitioner has been the victim of an injustice—regardless how obvious or reprehensible that injustice may be. Indeed, there have been many cases brought before the US Supreme Court by innocent victims of cruel injustice seeking justice but whose petitions for *certiorari* were arbitrarily denied and in too many cases after those innocent victims had been put to death their innocence was proven.

In the past few years, Barry Scheck's *The Innocence Project* has used modern DNA testing to confirm the shamefully large number of innocent victims of cruel injustice, routinely convicted and sentenced to death or long prison terms across the nation, whose cases were summarily denied certiorari and review by the United States Supreme Court. Unfortunately, only the venerable "Warren Court" proved to be the rare exception to that established practice. The "Warren Court" was famous as an "activist" Court that was overly concerned and dedicated to doing justice above all else and preserving an American's US Constitutional protections and rights to fundamental fairness, due process, and justice—even when that meant overturning long established legal precedent, as it did in the landmark *Gideon* case and other cases.

In contrast, the current "Roberts Court" could be fairly characterized as antithetical to the "Warren Court" regarding such issues. That chilling fact was well documented by *Newsweek* commentator Dahlia Lithwick's article, "Innocent Until Executed." She noted that the bloodthirsty Justices, Roberts, Scalia, and Thomas, had no qualms about putting an innocent man to death—so long as it results from "a full and fair trial." Scalia and Thomas expressly stated that "[T]his court has never held that the Constitution forbids the execution of a convicted defendant who has had a full and fair trial but is later able to convince a habeas court that he is 'actually' innocent."

Lithwick spotlighted a recent example of the application of those Justices' warped and shocking legal rationale in the recent case of a Texan, Cameron T. Willingham, who was executed "for an accidental house fire."

A week prior to Lithwick's article, a remarkable piece by author David Grann had appeared in *New Yorker* proving that the prosecution of the Willingham case and intentional distortion of the evidence had been "a train wreck"—as the detailed research of acclaimed forensic scientist and fire investigator, Gerald Hurst, had proven.

In his final moments of life, Willingham had lamented that the court was about "to kill an innocent man and doesn't care they're making a mistake."

Regardless, the Virginian had decided to afford the current Supreme Court a fair opportunity to do what would have been far more likely to have been done by the "Warren Court"—exact justice above all else.

However, the Virginia farmer also had a very practical and strategic reason for filing his petition before the US Supreme Court. He intended to include in his petition all of the violations of federal and constitutional law committed in the lower state courts and then to take what he filed before the US Supreme Court and file the same documentation as an exhibit before the US Federal District Court in Charlotte. This strategy would insure that all of the issues and controlling case law authority placed before the US Supreme Court would be in a comprehensive and complete package that would have to be reviewed and adjudicated by the US Federal District Court in conjunction with determining whether his Kentucky judgment was enforceable in North Carolina. Thus, he would be "making the record" in the most comprehensive fashion and "at the earliest stage of the litigation" before the Federal District Court for its adjudication of the relevant issues. This would insure that if he did not prevail before the Federal District Court he could later take all of those same issues up on appeal before the US Court of Appeals for the Fourth Circuit. Thus, it was crucial that he properly "make the record" before the Federal District Court to "properly preserve the issues for appeal" before the Fourth Circuit Court of Appeals.

On June 23, 2005, Paull Anderson filed his carefully crafted *Petition for a Writ of Certiorari* with William K. Suter, Clerk of the US Supreme Court. His petition fully documented the gross injustice he suffered before the North Carolina courts, their flagrant violations of his Constitutional rights, and raised the question of whether those courts should be allowed to prevent a victim from recovering monies stolen from the thieves that stole it while providing safe harbor for their hometown, career-criminal thieves.

As expected, on October 3, 2005, Mr. Suter graciously informed the Virginian that his petition for a writ of *certiorari* had been summarily denied by the "Roberts Court."

The official notification ended Paull Anderson's litigation in the North Carolina state courts and freed him up to pursue collateral action to enforce his judgment before the US Federal District Court in Charlotte where he hoped for the measure of justice blatantly denied him by the state courts. It would depend upon whether the corrupt defendants' bragging, that "We control the courts in this City," also applied to their hometown federal district court.

CHAPTER XI

SNAKEHANDLING: FEDERAL COURT
FIASCO

US FEDERAL DISTRICT COURT,
Charlotte, North Carolina
Paull Anderson v. Margaret L. Godley,
Julius J. Wade, Jr., James H. Wade,
Godley, Inc., Wade & Wade,
Attys. at Law
Paull Anderson v. Frank H. Godley

The Virginian had early on correctly anticipated that the North Carolina state courts would not respect and comply with the controlling constitutional and case law authority compelling the enforcement of his valid Kentucky judgment. Indeed, all of the warnings he had received, concerning the reprehensible tactics to expect from the "good old boys" and their "juice judges," had proven accurate harbingers of the egregious injustice that he later suffered before the North Carolina state courts.

Consequently, in anticipation of those results, on August 9, 2004, Paull Anderson had initiated a collateral action to enforce his Kentucky judgment in the Federal District Court for the Western District of North Carolina at Charlotte and on January 21, 2005, he filed a Complaint before that Court requesting a declaratory judgment.

Anderson's Complaint specifically noted that he had brought the action before the Federal District Court, at

Charlotte, pursuant to the superior, federal, statutory authority of 28 USC. Section 1963 which provided that such an action was proper and "in addition to other procedures provided by law for the enforcement of judgments." That federal statute provided for its enforcement independent of the North Carolina General Statute's Enforcement of Foreign Judgments Act, under which he had previously and unsuccessfully sought the enforcement of his Kentucky judgment in the North Carolina state courts.

The Virginian's Complaint also contended that his federal filing was "consistent with, the North Carolina General Statute at Section 1C-1701, Enforcement of Foreign Judgments Act which, at paragraph 1707, specifically provided that 'This article may not be construed to impair a judgment creditor's right to bring a civil action in this State to enforce such creditor's judgment.'" He was, thusly, requesting the federal district court to do, under their superior, distinct, federal statutory authority, what the state courts had refused to do under their separate North Carolina statutory authority. He was also thusly noting to the federal district court that such action was expressly authorized under the provisions of the North Carolina Enforcement of Foreign Judgments Act.

Anderson's Complaint meticulously described how his "previous efforts in the North Carolina state courts had been thwarted by the egregiously unjust, highly prejudicial, and mean spirited actions of Judge Marvin Gray in brazen violation of the constitutional Full Faith and Credit Clause, the Fourteenth Amendment, and relevant controlling US Supreme Court authority compelling the enforcement of the judgment." Anderson fully documented "the flagrant misconduct by Gray both at the hearing and thereafter, the corruption of Gray's ruling by the defense lawyers, Gray's repeated violations of the NC Rules of Appellate Procedure, and Gray's manipulation of his courtroom clerk to rob Anderson of his appeal and justice."

On March 8, 2005, Paull Anderson submitted a Motion for Summary Judgment to the Federal District Court, thereby asking the Federal District Court to avoid the long and drawn-out process of discovery and a trial, and instead, to rule that the judgment was enforceable, based upon the overwhelming abundance of controlling case law authority in Anderson's favor. Such a Rule 56 Summary Judgment would be proper where no issues of material fact existed and the prevailing case law authority favored the moving party. Under the Rules of Civil Procedure and controlling case law authority, issues of material fact usually required either a jury or bench trial to be determined. However, when no issues of material fact are at issue, and only issues of law required adjudication, Rule 56 authorizes the presiding judge to resolve those issues with his ruling prior to any discovery and trial process.

Anderson carefully laid out the Rule 56 authority supporting his Motion:

> The only issues involve those of law, and whether the valid money judgment of the Kentucky Federal District Court, affirmed by the Sixth Circuit, is enforceable in the State of North Carolina under the Full Faith and Credit Clause

and the Supremacy Clause of the Constitution. No triable issues of material fact exist. Consequently, under Rule 56 of the Federal Rules of Civil Procedure this Court should rule on those issues of law that Plaintiff's judgment is valid and enforceable in North Carolina pursuant to 28 USC. Section 1963 and for such other relief as to the Court may seem just.

Plaintiff has a valid Kentucky money judgment issued by a Kentucky Federal District Court and fully affirmed by the US Court of Appeals for the Sixth Circuit. The judgment is enforceable in North Carolina pursuant to the direct, compelling, controlling, authority of the Full Faith and Credit Clause of the Constitution and the other relevant, related, superior authority which plaintiff has raised before the North Carolina state courts, and recently before this Court, in his efforts to have that authority complied with and to have the judgment enforced in North Carolina. The honest, truthful, honorable, *pro se* plaintiff has diligently attempted to have his judgment enforced in Mecklenburg County, NC Superior Court; however, that Superior Court has refused to comply with the aforesaid controlling authority and to enforce the judgment. In addition, that same Superior Court Judge, Marvin K. Gray, subsequently, intentionally, repeatedly, violated the NC Rules of Appellate Procedure and intentionally deceived and misled the plaintiff, through his courtroom clerk, which resulted in the dismissal of plaintiff's direct appeal and right of appeal to the NC appeals courts without the merits being considered or adjudicated.

The plaintiff (1) sought relief from both N.C. appeals courts, (2) invoked his right to have his judgment enforced pursuant to the aforesaid Full Faith and Credit and other relevant authority, placing all of that authority before both appeals courts, (3) contested the actions of the Superior Court in refusing to comply with the aforesaid authority and to enforce the judgment, (4) contested and fully documented the improper, highly prejudicial actions by Judge Gray which resulted in the loss of the direct appeal, and (5) sought relief from those appeals courts pursuant to the N.C. Rules of Appellate Procedure which allowed them to grant relief. Both appeals courts repeatedly denied plaintiff's repeated efforts for relief, refused to comply with the aforesaid authority compelling the enforcement of the judgment, and refused to consider or adjudicate the merits of the judgment or the actions, misconduct and rulings of Judge Gray, refused to reinstate the appeal, and refused plaintiff's petitions for discretionary review to grant relief and do justice pursuant to the aforesaid authority.

After having thusly exhausted available legal remedies under NC state law in the NC state courts, plaintiff turned to this federal court and filed his Complaint seeking relief. Plaintiff's constitutional rights have been egregiously abused and violated by the NC state courts and the only avenue open to remedy is before this District Court. If an American is deprived of his constitutional rights and protections, as has occurred in the instant case, by the unjust actions of a rogue state court judge, then that American must have recourse to the federal courts. Otherwise, the state courts, and judges like Judge Gray, are free to trample and run rampant over their victims' constitutional rights with impunity knowing their brash injustice and blatant disrespect for the constitution has no significant chance of ever being held accountable, let alone remedied.

Further delaying enforcement of Plaintiff's valid federal judgment would violate, suspend and/or deny plaintiff's right to speedy justice, due process, equal justice, and fundamental fairness, guaranteed plaintiff under the Fourteenth Amendment, while creating more needless delay in, and further violation of, the enforcement of plaintiff's judgment pursuant to the Full Faith and Credit Clause. This would also further the effect of the Defendants reprehensible misconduct which they practiced throughout the arduous and protracted Kentucky litigation which Magistrate Judge Patterson, Federal District Judge Hood, and the venerable three Judges of the US Circuit Court of Appeals for the Sixth Circuit soundly denounced as 'obstructionist and delay tactics, gamesmanship and contumacious misconduct' and for which they were punished by those Judges.

Justice delayed is justice denied. To date the evil defendants have delayed the justice mandated by the Kentucky Federal District Court and the US Court of Appeals for the Sixth Circuit years ago. Their reprehensible 'obstructionist and delay tactics, gamesmanship and contumacious misconduct' should not be tolerated by this Federal District Court Judge any more than it was tolerated by this Court's brethren Kentucky Federal District Court Judge and Sixth Circuit Court Judges.

Summary judgment is appropriate pursuant to Rule 56, Fed. Rules of Civil Procedure, and the enforcement of plaintiff's judgment in North Carolina is compelled as a matter of law pursuant to the overwhelming, controlling constitutional Full Faith and Credit authority, US Supreme Court authority, and other relevant, superior, case law authority presented in plaintiff's Memorandum in Support of Motion for Summary Judgment and his Complaint.

WHEREFORE, plaintiff prays that his Motion be sustained, that the Court issue an Order granting summary judgment against the defendants, holding that plaintiff's Kentucky judgment is valid and enforceable in North Carolina against the defendants, that the process by which the state court decisions resulted is unconstitutional, and for such other relief as to the Court may seem just and proper.

For the next two years, the Virginian's case was shuffled back and forth among four of the area Federal Judges, Voorhees, Keesler, Conrad, and Whitney, as the case remained relegated to legal limbo. After his letters to Judge Conrad complaining of the shabby treatment were returned to Anderson, after having been refused delivery by Judge Conrad, the Virginian had become thoroughly frustrated with the lack of any progress. On January 25, 2007 Anderson sent the Clerk of Court a letter of complaint:

In several ways this situation appears to suggest a continuation of the unreasonable, unfair, unjust, and shameful treatment I previously received in the Mecklenburg County Superior Court, etc. while pursuing efforts there to domesticate and enforce my valid Kentucky foreign judgment, all of which is fully documented in the record in the instant case. The consequence appears to be that regardless of what I do before this Court, in my ongoing reasonable, diligent, and good faith *pro se* efforts to comply with the Federal Rules of Civil Procedure, my case will continue to be held hostage in legal limbo, and I shall continue to be denied fundamental fairness, due process, and justice with the knowledge that delay in this case greatly benefits the interests of the corrupt defendants while damaging the interests of their victim, myself. Indeed, the justice already unfairly delayed by this Court has insured I have been denied justice. Consequently, I see no real

prospects for fundamental fairness, due process,
justice, and the protection of my U.S.
Constitutional rights by this Court.

In the Virginian's mind the harsh braggadocio of
Margaret Godley that "We control the judges in this
City" continued to reverberate.

On the following day, Anderson learned Margaret
Godley had died on January 16, and he immediately
submitted appropriate documents before the federal
district court in Charlotte to protect his interests. He filed
a Suggestion of Death Upon the Record Under Rule
25(a)(1), placing notice of her death before the court,
along with a Motion for Substitution of the Proper
Parties, to have the court determine the proper parties in
interest to succeed and be substituted for Godley in the
lawsuit.

Margaret Godley's lawyers filed a Response
claiming that "the executor of her estate, her son, Johnny
C. Godley, should be the only proper party to be
substituted in this action" and argued that Anderson's
Kentucky Judgment was unenforceable in North
Carolina.

Anderson filed a Reply repeating the facts and law he
had previously raised that supported the enforceability of
his Judgment, notwithstanding the actions by the N.C.
State Courts, and noted that the enforceability issue had
yet to be resolved by that federal district court.

On March 28, 2007, the Virginian filed a Motion for
Joinder of Claims and Remedies and of Persons Needed
for Just Adjudication to bring the designated heirs of
Margaret Godley, her three sons James, Johnny, and

Frank, into the civil action. The Motion documented "the illegal actions and predicate acts by the ruthless outlaw, Margaret Godley and her interstate network of career criminal cronies, to steal from and defraud the Plaintiff and other victims out of millions of dollars by repeatedly peddling her worthless, bogus DeGroot patents Kentucky land title."

The Motion described how the "Plaintiff has recently acquired information and belief suggesting that the incorrigible career crook, Margaret Godley, as transferor, has conveyed her major assets to her transferee sons, constituting conveyances to defraud the Plaintiff giving them complicity in the aforesaid compounding and furtherance of the illegal actions and predicate acts by Margaret Godley." The Motion was intended to prevent the probating of Margaret Godley's estate to "enable the sons to keep the monies stolen from the Plaintiff by their mother and to prevent the sons' efforts to hinder, delay or defraud the Plaintiff and the enforcement, collection and satisfaction of his Kentucky federal money judgment."

After the defendants filed a Response arguing against Anderson's Motion he submitted a Reply in which he detailed the long history of peddling Godley's bogus title and the related transfers of Charlotte area real estate representing conveyances to defraud the Virginian:

> The conspirators' bogus title scam proved highly effective and over the decades it ripped off millions of dollars in cash and other ill-gotten gains from their numerous victims. The plaintiff

was only one of the many victims fleeced by the ruthless conspirators in their many similar schemes ("schemes") that centered around their bogus title scam in a pattern of related predicate acts. This pattern included, but was not limited to, at least the following separate but similar and related schemes:

a. $2,000,000.00 in cash defrauded from Ronald Manning of Lexington, Kentucky and his two business associates in the late 1980's.

b. $15,000.00 in cash defrauded from the plaintiff in 1993.

c. $65,000.00 in cash defrauded from John Walcott in 1993.

d. $3,000,000.00 in bogus tax deductions gleaned from the 1993 sale of the bogus title to the scam Indian Foundation with the assistance of Johnson, Mezvinsky, Campbell, and Brady. Margaret L. Godley subsequently used that bogus tax deduction over a period of several years to scam and defraud the IRS.

e. $3,088,315.05 in cash defrauded from the Christ is Our Savior ("C.I.O.S.") organization funneled through the scam Indian Foundation in 1993-1994.

f. The scheme to peddle the bogus title to the Wolford brothers of Louisa, Kentucky, for $28 million was perpetrated in 1995.

g. The scheme to peddle the bogus Godley title to Dr. William M. Knight, of Houston, Texas, for $28 million was perpetrated in 1999-2002.

These bogus title schemes involving millions in cash do not include other valuable assets, real estate, etc. acquired by Margaret L. Godley and her co-conspirators throughout her long career as a ruthless and incorrigible crook and ringleader of her notorious network of interstate, multi-convicted, career criminals.

The related transfers of some of the real estate, in the Charlotte area alone, representing conveyances to defraud the Plaintiff include the following:

1. Conveyance of property at 4720 Rozzells Ferry Road, Charlotte, N.C., on 5 December 1995, by Margaret L.Godley to Godley Auction Company;

2. Conveyance of property at Salem Church Road-Rozzells Ferry Road, Charlotte, N.C., on 31 December 1997, by Margaret L. Godley, Johnny C. Godley, Dianne W. Godley, James B. Godley, Frank H. Godley to MLG OF CHARLOTTE LTD. PARTNERSHIP;

3. Conveyance of 16.17 acres at Rozzells Ferry Road, Charlotte, N.C., on 2 January 2002, by James Godley to John C. Godley and Frank H. Godley;

4. Conveyances of various real estate in Charlotte N.C., by Margaret L. Godley, including but not limited to the following tracts:

- 31.27 Acres at 821 Oakdale Road
- 300 Carothers Street,
- 1.5 acres at Rozzells Ferry Road
- 16.17 acres at Rozzells Ferry Road,

- 1.13 acres at Rozzells Ferry Road,
- 4.03 acres at Rozzells Ferry Road,
- 3.53 acres at Godley Lane,
- and other tracts on Brookshire Blvd. and Duke Road.

On April 18, 2007, Jared E. Gardner, a junior lawyer in the same law firm as Arrowood and Diehl, filed a Notice of Substitution of Counsel announcing that he was "replacing John S. Arrowood as Lead Counsel and Attorney to be Noticed for Defendant Margaret L. Godley and in the representation of Mrs. Godley's estate and James, Johnny, and Frank Godley."

In checking out Gardner's credentials, Paull Anderson was amused to learn that Gardner was also a graduate of Boalt Hall law school at the University of California; it was the same law school that produced Margaret Godley's notorious, career criminal crony who was still serving time in a federal prison in Alabama–the disbarred Philadelphia lawyer and former US congressman, Edward M. Mezvinsky. The Virginian could only wonder about the coincidence and decided to leave it as such.

On May 30, 2007, Anderson received a Notice of Estate Administration from a Charlotte attorney, H. Morris Caddel, Jr., on behalf of the Executor and the Estate of Margaret Godley. Included in the Notice was a copy of a completed and filed Application for Probate and Letters Testamentary and copies of the Letters Testamentary verifying her sons as her heirs and son, Johnny, as Executor of her Estate.

Paull Anderson decided that he had to take further action to protect his interests in the Estate of Margaret Godley, to hold her sons accountable for their involvement in the conveyances to defraud him, and to enhance his efforts to enforce his valid Kentucky Judgment. Such action required that he file a distinct lawsuit in federal district court against one or more of the Godley sons alleging all of their illegal misconduct, in concert with their mother and her corrupt cronies.

Since Frank Godley had come to Bristol, Virginia, in one of the illegal acts alleged by Anderson he decided to file the Complaint only against Frank Godley in the nearby US Federal District Court in Abingdon, Virginia. Anderson hoped that jurisdiction would lie before that Court, in the diversity of interest case, because Frank Godley was a citizen of North Carolina, Paull Anderson was a citizen of Virginia, and Godley had committed one of the alleged illegal acts in the State of Virginia at that meeting. The Complaint included all of the allegations and supporting documentation previously raised in his Reply along with a detailed litany of the long history of illegal acts constituting civil RICO racketeering, civil conspiracy, common law fraud, fraudulent and wrongful concealment, and fraudulent conveyances in which Frank Godley was, directly and/or indirectly, involved.

However, soon after the Complaint was filed, the presiding judge, James P. Jones, decided it would be more appropriate if the newly-filed case was heard before the Charlotte Federal District Court where the companion civil action against Margaret Godley and her sons was ongoing and on August 7 [th], 2007, he transferred the case to the Charlotte Federal District Court.

Although the Virginian realized that pursuing his case against Frank Godley before Godley's home-town federal district court would most likely prove fruitless he was resolved to nonetheless attempt to seek justice in the Charlotte court.

Paull Anderson initiated discovery by submitting his interrogatories and requests for production of documents in compliance with the Federal Rules of Civil Procedure. He wondered about the tactics Frank Godley would use to foil discovery and if he would openly defy the rules as his mother and her cronies had done in the Kentucky and Virginia cases. Those defendants had claimed that compliance would force them to disclose information that "would tend to incriminate." To avoid such disclosure, criminal convictions, and imprisonment, they chose to defy and accept the far less serious consequences of Rule 37 default judgments in Anderson's civil cases.

In short order the Virginian learned that Frank Godley would employ a far different strategy to avoid disclosing incriminating discovery information without violating the rules and in the process force the dismissal of Anderson's case against him through a devious ploy that relied upon the crucial help of the local presiding federal judge. Such a ploy never could have succeeded in the federal courts of either Virginia or Kentucky before senior judges Glen Williams or Joseph Hood. However, in the Charlotte federal district court, before home-town Judge Martin Reidinger, the slick maneuver would be executed as easily as a snake slithers through a slimy swamp.

On August 31, 2007, Frank Godley's lawyer, Jared Gardner, sent Anderson a letter which included a copy of a Rule 11 Motion for Sanctions which Gardner threatened to file "unless you do not, within twenty-four (24) days from the date of this letter, withdraw your Complaint." The Virginian recognized the devious Motion as a slick, intimidation effort to improperly and illegally contaminate and sabotage his case and to force the Virginian to pay Godley's legal expenses and attorney fees. Anderson refused to be intimidated, and when Gardner later filed the Motion, the Virginian submitted a strong response denouncing the underhanded ploy:

The Defendant's Rule 11 Motion Constitutes a Reprehensible Ploy to Threaten, Intimidate, and Coerce the Plaintiff

On 4 September 2007, the plaintiff received a letter, dated 31 August 2007, from one of the defendant's lawyers, Jared E. Gardner, which the plaintiff found appalling and greatly disturbing. Notwithstanding the thin façade of a Rule 11 Motion for Sanctions that it came veiled behind, this action by the defendant's lawyers was primarily intended to threaten, intimidate, and coerce the plaintiff to abandon his litigation and just cause in this case. It constitutes a continuation, and the most recent predicate act, in the pattern of similar such efforts and tactics to force the plaintiff to abandon his litigation and just causes in the companion cases, in Kentucky, Virginia, and Tennessee, against this defendant's co-conspirators – one of whom was his mother, Margaret L. Godley.

Those prior, related, predicate acts in the ongoing pattern of threats, intimidation, and coercion began with anonymous phone calls late at night to the plaintiff's home threatening to "burn you out" if the plaintiff persisted in his litigation. They escalated to anonymous, threatening letters mailed to the plaintiff, to his family to his then lawyer, Christen Burkholder, to Federal District Court Senior Judge, Glen M. Williams, and they were placed before Federal District Court judge, Joseph Hood and Tennessee Judge G. Richard Johnson and the jurors in the Mezvinsky trial.

The efforts further escalated, in the Tennessee case in the trial of co-conspirator Edward M. Mezvinsky, into jury tampering by the defendant's brash, co-conspirators, Howard N. Johnson and Mary B. Brady. Although the jury tampering ended up landing Brady in jail and left Johnson serving a jail sentence, it succeeded in its intended purpose of getting Mezvinsky the mistrial he wanted and the opportunity to modify his testimony and other aspects of the first trial that subsequently allowed him to walk away from the charges at the retrial and continue on with his criminal career and the victimizing of many more victims out of millions of dollars in the years to come - until he was finally stopped through criminal prosecution in 2003 that finally put him in the federal prison where he currently resides.

In those prior, reprehensible actions to threaten, intimidate, and coerce the plaintiff the defendant's co-conspirators used the same tactics raised in this defendant's Rule 11 Motion. The same repugnant tactics were solidly denounced and struck from the records in the companion cases and should not be tolerated by this Court and should not be permitted to be deviously exploited by a shameless lawyer as a vehicle to once again emulate and repeat the previous, despicable efforts by this defendant's corrupt co-conspirators to threaten, intimidate, and coerce the plaintiff into abandoning his litigation and just cause in this case and to deny plaintiff his US Constitution rights to fundamental fairness, due process and justice.

It is a logical and reasonable certainty that the defendant's lawyers were not only fully aware of the previous, similar ploy by the defendant's co-conspirators which was successful in instilling fear and trepidation in the plaintiff and his family for their safety, but that these unscrupulous lawyers decided to repeat the same ploy to revisit in the minds and memories of the plaintiff and his family the same fear for their safety and lives they had earlier experienced by the previous, related, deplorable predicate acts of threats, intimidation, and coercion perpetrated by this defendant's ruthless co-conspirators. This despicable ploy by this defendant's shameless lawyers has certainly been successful since all of the past threats, intimidation and coercion, and their predicate acts that included explicit threats to "burn you out," their anonymous threatening letters, and brash jury tampering, are now back fully in the minds and fears of the plaintiff and his family – as a result of this defendant's recent, similar, predicate act in that ongoing pattern of despicable predicate acts to threaten, intimidate, and coerce the plaintiff and his family.

Any sleazy excuse the defendant and his lawyers should attempt to raise to mislead the Court concerning their intentional, willful, reprehensible, Rule 11 ploy should not be tolerated, just as the similar, earlier attempts to threaten, intimidate, and coerce the plaintiff to withdraw his complaints in the companion Kentucky, Virginia, and Tennessee cases, and to tamper with and contaminate the jury in the Tennessee case, were not tolerated by those judges. And just as the FBI and authorities were called in to investigate and deal with those similar instances, this Court should also seek their help in this most recent occurrence and predicate act in the same pattern of egregious, reprehensible actions by the body of co-conspirators to threaten, intimidate, and coerce the plaintiff to withdraw his complaints. This Court must not simply tolerate and condone such reprehensible behavior in its Court by members of the North Carolina Bar and in so doing simply turn a deaf ear and blind eye that tolerates and allows a *pro se* litigant and his family to suffer such threats, intimidation and coercion.

The previous brazen acts to threaten, intimidate and coerce the plaintiff, in the Kentucky, Virginia and Tennessee cases, were perpetrated by this defendant's corrupt co-conspirators through their anonymous threatening letters sent, across state lines through the US Mail followed by their jury tampering; this latest brazen, predicate act in that ongoing pattern was perpetrated by the defendant's Charlotte lawyers through a letter sent on their law firm's letterhead, across state lines through the US Mail from their law offices in Charlotte, NC to the plaintiff's home in Bristol, VA. The aggregate of these ongoing predicate acts and the threats, intimidation and coercion of the plaintiff likely constitute felonious acts, obstruction of justice, and other criminal conduct that this Court must not simply tolerate and sweep under the rug.

Plaintiff respectfully requests and moves the Court to have this matter referred to the proper authorities beyond the influence and reach of these Charlotte lawyers and their wealthy, powerful client's influences to insure justice and the protection of the *pro se* farmer, plaintiff and his family. The *pro se* plaintiff is bound to make the protection and safety of his family, and himself, paramount and if this Court will not do so the plaintiff will be forced to immediately bring the matter before the Fourth Circuit, via a Petition for Mandamus, Interlocutory Appeal, and/or any other available vehicle for relief. This heavy cloud of fear, oppression, threats, intimidation, and coercion must be removed from the plaintiff and his family and the plaintiff's constitutional rights to fundamental fairness, due process, and justice must be restored.

Apparently, the Virginian's response and assurance that he was ready to take the volatile circumstances to the higher US Court of Appeals for the Fourth Circuit for the protection of his family and himself and to find justice and due process finally prodded the Federal District Court in Charlotte into action. Just days after Anderson's Response was filed he received an Order from the Court indicating that the case had suddenly been "reassigned" to US District Judge Martin Reidinger, that all of the pending cases and motions had been "consolidated," and that "the parties are hereby prohibited from any further filing until the resolution of the pending matters." Finally, it appeared that the Federal District Court in Charlotte could no longer keep his case locked up in legal limbo.

On March 27, 2008, Judge Reidinger finally handed down a ruling which included language the Virginian found disturbing:

The Plaintiff has a valid Judgment, rendered by the United States District Court

for the eastern District of Kentucky against Defendants Julius Wade, James Wade and Wade and Wade, attorneys at law, and Margaret L. Godley and the validity of Plaintiff's Judgment has not been altered by any subsequent proceedings. Plaintiff's Judgment has been duly recorded with the United States District Court for the Western District of North Carolina, and is enforceable through such means as may be enforceable to the Plaintiff for the enforcement of a Federal Judgment, except that it may not be enforced through the state courts of the State of North Carolina...Some of Plaintiff's points may be well taken, and determination by the state courts may be utterly wrong. That, however, is of no consequence. Even if this Court were to perceive a miscarriage of justice in the state court's application of the law, it is this Court's obligation to treat the state court's final determination as exactly that: final...

Reidinger's refusal to do justice troubled Anderson. Under his doctrine the federal judge would as quickly have refused the Virginian relief even if Gray had unjustly sentenced him to death, it would be "of no consequence. Even if this Court were to perceive a miscarriage of justice in the state court's application of the law"—so long as the N.C. appeals courts had rubber-stamped Gray's appalling actions with "finality." And it would not matter that the North Carolina appeals courts had refused to even look at, let alone exercise their discretion and authority to remedy, Gray's brazenly unjust and reprehensible actions.

Paull Anderson found the cold, harsh, reality of Reidinger's legal doctrine, brazenly denouncing any concern for doing justice, deeply disappointing. The Virginian had grown accustomed to expect brash injustice from the North Carolina state courts but he had never experienced injustice before the federal courts. However, he recalled the earlier warning to expect as much in the North Carolina courts, and the haunting braggadocio of Margaret Godley, that "We control the judges in this city," was still fresh in his memory.

Reidinger's ruling did nothing to provide for the enforcement of the valid Kentucky judgment or any other relief that Anderson had sought. Instead, the ruling only made the Virginian's legal battle for justice far more difficult. The ruling established "the law of the case" and the laws governing appeals automatically attach a strong legal presumption that the lower court has acted correctly. This left Paull Anderson with the heavy burden of trying to legally overcome that presumption before the United States Fourth Circuit Court of Appeals in Richmond, Virginia.

Anderson was equally disappointed with another aspect of Reidinger's ruling that related to the lawsuit against Frank H. Godley and that directed Anderson:

> **...within ten days to amend his pleadings in that case to conform to the Rules of Civil Procedure or otherwise to conform to proper practice or otherwise to voluntarily dismiss his case.**

The directive included an explicit threat by Reidinger to exercise his discretionary right to impose severe sanctions upon the Virginian if he failed to properly respond. Reidinger's heavy-handed and coercive ploy forced Anderson to file a Motion to Dismiss, under protest, on April 4, 2008:

> The Court's Memorandum effectively forces the Plaintiff to "voluntarily dismiss his case."
>
> The Memorandum specifically directs the Plaintiff, within "ten days," to "amend his pleadings to conform to the Rules of Civil Procedure or otherwise to conform to proper practice or otherwise move to voluntarily dismiss his case."
>
> However, this effectively forces the Plaintiff to move "to voluntarily dismiss his case" because when the case was filed it was filed *pro se* and in the good faith belief that it did conform to the Rules of Civil Procedure and proper practice and a recent, careful review of that filing leaves the Plaintiff with the same opinion. Consequently, since the Court has not directed what must be changed, in its view, to make the Plaintiff's pleading conform to The Rules of Civil Procedure and/or proper practice, this *pro se* Plaintiff has absolutely no idea of how or what to change or amend. Thus, he is left—forced—to comply with the Court's directive in the only viable alternative and way that complies with the directive, which is to dismiss. Thus, he is now

doing so—to respectfully comply with this Court's directive and to avoid the intimidating threat of sanctions the Court has hung over his head and which has had a huge chilling affect upon the Plaintiff's *pro se* efforts to diligently and in good faith pursue litigation before this Court; however, the Plaintiff is respectfully doing so under protest that he is unjustly being denied due process and justice and in violation of his Constitutional Rights.

Consequently, the aggregate actions of this Court, as above documented, leave the Plaintiff convinced of the Court's deeply prejudicial mindset against the Plaintiff leaving him without any hope for fairness, justice, and the protection of his Constitutional Rights.

WHEREFORE, with a heavy heart, dismayed, distraught, and greatly disappointed and disillusioned the Plaintiff moves to voluntarily dismiss his case.

The Virginian was disappointed, but not surprised, that the North Carolina federal court, like the North Carolina state courts, had simply and conveniently manipulated the rules and laws to do injustice—and even brazenly declare that "injustice was of no consequence." In doing so, those courts had made a mockery of the mandate and warning by US Supreme Court Justice Benjamin Cardozo that "Justice is a concept by far more subtle and indefinite than is yielded by mere obedience to a rule" and the admonition of

Fourth Circuit Chief Judge Clement F. Haynsworth, Jr. "to do justice above all else."

On April 5, 2008, Anderson submitted a "Request for Permission to File a Motion to Transfer this Case to another Federal District Court where Plaintiff can be dealt with fairly and receive due process and justice," in an attempt to move his case to avoid further prejudicial actions by the Federal District Court in Charlotte. Reidinger simply ignored the request.

On April 23, 2008, Reidinger issued a brief order dismissing Anderson's case against Frank Godley.

Anderson quickly filed his Notice of Appeal of Reidinger's rulings and actions. Undaunted by the federal court fiasco, the Virginia farmer resolved to persevere in his tenacious battle for justice against the forces of evil—ever hopeful that the Fourth Circuit would "do justice above all else" and not be as ready as the North Carolina courts to prevent his recovery of the monies stolen from him and his damages. He would press on, *pro se* and to the best of his ability, to appeal Reidinger's ruling and actions before the US Court of Appeals for the Fourth Circuit in Richmond, Virginia.

CHAPTER XII

SNAKEHANDLING: FOURTH CIRCUIT FINESSE

US COURT OF APPEALS FOR THE FOURTH CIRCUIT,
Richmond, Virginia
Paull Anderson v. Margaret L. Godley, Julius J. Wade, Jr., James H. Wade, Godley, Inc., Wade & Wade, Attys. At Law, and Frank H. Godley.

In May of 2008, the Virginian submitted his Issues for Review with Supporting Facts and Argument before the US Court of Appeals for the Fourth Circuit:

Issues for Review with Supporting Facts and Argument
Issue 1. Whether the actions of the Federal District Court erroneously resulted in findings or conclusions that were unsupported by the evidence or were contrary to the evidence and whereas such actions more specifically include, but are not limited to, the following instances?

A. The District Court's Memorandum ("Memorandum") asserted that "In short, Plaintiff asks this Court to overturn the state court determination because the state courts were wrong on the merits. Plaintiff seeks a ruling of this Court overturning the state court's action as though this Court were the North Carolina Court of Appeals."

However, this assertion is contrary to the evidence. Plaintiff's Complaint seeks to enforce his valid Kentucky federal money judgment through the distinct authority of the federal courts – notwithstanding his prior unsuccessful attempts to enforce the judgment through the state courts. It clearly states that the Plaintiff has not asked the District Court to overrule the ruling and order of that inferior Mecklenburg County Court. Plaintiff challenges Judge Gray's state court ruling and order alleging violations of the Full Faith and Credit Clause of the Constitution and is thereby, by definition, not seeking appellate review and what he seeks is plainly within the federal-question jurisdiction of this Court. His Complaint challenges the constitutionality of the process by which the state court decisions resulted and the necessity of turning to the Federal District Court to remedy the violation of his constitutional rights by the state courts and to protect the Plaintiff's constitutional rights to fundamental fairness, due process and justice where the state proceeding deprived the party of a full and fair opportunity to litigate their claim so as to deny due process thereby removing preclusion from raising it in federal courts.

B. The Memorandum also erroneously asserts that "Plaintiff's Judgment is enforceable through such means as may be available to the

Plaintiff, if any, for the enforcement of a Federal Judgment, except that it may not be enforced through the state courts of the State of North Carolina. The Court makes no determination (and has not been asked to make any determination) as to whether there are any such alternate means of enforcement available to Plaintiff. Even if such had been sought, this Court would not have the subject matter jurisdiction to provide an answer. The exercise of judicial power under Article III of the Constitution depends on the existence of a case or controversy, and a federal court (lacks) the power to render advisory opinions."

However, this assertion is also contrary to the evidence. The primary, explicit and implicit, purpose of the Plaintiff's Complaint was to have his Judgment enforced through the Federal District Court via a ruling facilitating that enforceability. The Federal District Court touches upon the issue by stating the judgment "is enforceable through such means as may be available to the Plaintiff, if any, for the enforcement of a Federal Judgment," but then neither resolves the issue nor grants the subsequent relief requested by the Plaintiff, if his judgment is thusly enforceable, with an order enforcing the judgment in North Carolina.

In addition, the existence of the actual controversy is clearly specified and nowhere has the Plaintiff ever asked the Federal District Court to render any advisory opinion.

C. The Memorandum also asserts that the Plaintiff is to blame for the failure of the North Carolina State Courts to do justice and enforce his valid Kentucky federal money judgment, and that "the Plaintiff has come to ask this Court to fix the problem he created."

However, this erroneous assertion is also contrary to the evidence. The diligent, *pro se* Plaintiff proceeded before the North Carolina State Courts in good faith trying to enforce his valid Kentucky judgment; however, the actions by Judge Gray, the defendants' lawyers and the courtroom clerk at the hearing before Judge Gray, and thereafter, are what denied Plaintiff justice and effectively sabotaged his appeal and right of appeal. Any assertion attaching "blame" to the *pro se* Plaintiff is disingenuous and contrary to the irrefutable, documented facts.

Issue 2. <u>Whether the Federal District Court in Charlotte erroneously failed to enforce Plaintiff's Kentucky federal money judgment in North Carolina?</u>

The Federal District Court erroneously failed to provide the relief the Plaintiff sought, requested, and was entitled to. The Mcmorandum asserts that "Anderson does not seek relief in the form of enforcement of the Judgment through this Court."

However, that statement is also erroneous and seeks to avoid resolving the only reason for the Plaintiff's having brought his action before the Federal District Court. The Plaintiff has made it perfectly clear that after unsuccessfully attempting to enforce his valid Judgment through the N.C. State Courts he then brought it before the Federal District Court for enforcement. Plaintiff did not request an advisory opinion or anything less than whatever it took to have his judgment enforced by the Federal District Court. The Federal District Court's error of asserting that the Plaintiff "does not seek relief in the form of enforcement of the Judgment through this Court" was then compounded by its ruling that "the judgment is enforceable through such means as may be available to the Plaintiff, if any, for the enforcement of a Federal Judgment. The Court makes no determination (and has not been asked to make any determination) as to whether there are any such alternate means of enforcement available to Plaintiff." These statements allowed the Federal District Court to avoid ruling to enforce the judgment – thereby denying the relief sought by the Plaintiff and defeating the sole reason and purpose he had brought his case and cause before that Court: to recover the monies stolen from him and his serious damages inflicted by the corrupt defendants who are career crooks.

Issue 3. <u>Whether the Federal District Court improperly forced the Plaintiff to move to withdraw his Complaint, and then further improperly dismissed Plaintiff's Complaint, in the companion civil case, *Paull Anderson v. Frank H. Godley*</u>?

The District Court's Memorandum specifically directed the Plaintiff, "within ten days, to amend his pleadings to conform to the Rules of Civil Procedure or otherwise to conform to proper practice or otherwise move to voluntarily dismiss his case."

However, this effectively forced the Plaintiff to move to voluntarily dismiss his case because when the case was filed it was filed *pro se* and in the good faith belief that it did conform to the Rules of Civil Procedure and proper practice and a further, careful review of that filing left the Plaintiff with the same opinion. Consequently, since the Court did not direct what must be changed, in its view, to make the Plaintiff's pleading conform to The Rules of Civil Procedure and/or proper practice, the *pro se* Plaintiff had absolutely no idea of how or what to change or amend. Thus, he was left – forced – to comply with the Court's directive in the only viable alternative and way that complied with the directive, which was to move to dismiss, and to avoid the intimidating and draconian threat of sanctions the Court had hung over his head and which has had a huge chilling affect upon the Plaintiff's *pro se* efforts to diligently and in good faith pursue litigation before that Federal District Court; however, in doing so the Plaintiff noted his objection and express declaration that he was doing so under protest and that he was unjustly being denied due process and justice in violation of his Constitutional Rights

On 5 April 2008, Plaintiff submitted his Request for Permission to File a Motion to Transfer this Case to another Federal District Court where Plaintiff can be dealt with fairly and receive due process and justice. This was an attempt by the Plaintiff to move his case to avoid further prejudicial actions and further denial of fundamental fairness, due process and justice by the Federal District Court in Charlotte.

On 23 April 2008 Judge Reidinger issued an Order dismissing Plaintiff's case against Frank Godley and stated as follows: "The Court was reluctant to grant Plaintiff's Motion to Dismiss, because it appeared that the Plaintiff's action stemmed from a misreading of the Court's March, 2008, Memorandum of Decision and Order, which Plaintiff even misquoted in his Motion. In his Report to the Court, Plaintiff asserts that his handicap and poor health situation largely restrict travel for him, reflecting the burden that this case has become for Plaintiff. Based thereon and based on the record in this matter the Court finds that the best interests of the Plaintiff, the best interests of the Defendant, the best interests of the Court and the best interests of justice would be served by granting the Plaintiff's Motion and allowing the Plaintiff to voluntarily dismiss this case."

However, the facts are more revealing and make the Federal District Court's actions even more disturbing. Plaintiff's Motion mentioned nothing whatsoever about any handicap and poor health situation largely restricting travel. The Motion included no request that the Federal District Court in any way consider the Motion based upon the Plaintiff's "handicap and poor health situation largely restrict travel." And the assertion that this case has become some kind of a restrictive "burden" upon the Plaintiff is also a similarly, fabricated assertion that has no bases in fact. These facts are quite evident by simply reviewing the Plaintiff's Motion, which is in the record.

Plaintiff has never asked any court, including Judge Reidinger's, for any special consideration, favor, or indulgence based upon the Plaintiff's health situation and/or travel abilities. All of the briefs and filings before the Federal District Court make it quite clear that the Plaintiff is, and has always been, quite capable of proceeding *pro se*. If Judge Reidinger had any questions concerning those matters he could have, and should have, resolved them by inquiring about them, rather than simply leaping to a conclusion and unfounded assertion which, once again, was extremely prejudicial and destructive to the Plaintiff's case, and deprived him of fundamental fairness, due process and justice.

Also, if Judge Reidinger felt that the Plaintiff had submitted his Motion based upon "a misreading of the Court's March, 2008, Memorandum of Decision and Order, which Plaintiff even misquoted in his Motion," he could have, and should have, clarified such an important issue that involved a *pro se* Plaintiff, rather than, once again, leaping to a conclusion and unfounded assertion which, once again, was prejudicial to the Plaintiff, destructive to his case, and deprived him of fundamental fairness, due process and justice.

Finally, Judge Reidinger's assertion that what he did, in dismissing the Plaintiff's Complaint, was in "the best interests of the Plaintiff" is totally disingenuous and could not be further from the truth. The affect of his actions served only to further impede, frustrate and delay Plaintiff's ongoing, difficult, fourteen year struggle and "burden" to find justice and to recover the monies stolen from him and his damages.

Issue 4. Whether the cumulative actions of the Federal District Court have had a prejudicial and detrimental affect upon the Plaintiff and his case thereby denying Plaintiff due process, fundamental fairness and justice?

Paragraphs 1-3, supra, relate and constitute instances of specific actions by the Federal District Court that have prejudicially and detrimentally impacted upon the Plaintiff and his case. However, additional related prejudicial and detrimental actions have also occurred which include, but are not necessarily limited to, the following:

(A) Plaintiff's case has been needlessly shuffled back and forth between several different federal judges for years facilitating needless delay that benefited the Defendants and harmed the Plaintiff - it took more than three years to adjudicate the Plaintiff's Rule 56 Motion; (B) Plaintiff's diligent efforts to move his case out of "legal limbo" have been frustrated and defeated; (C) The Federal District Court has turned back and refused to accept US Mail from Plaintiff that was important to his case all the while knowing it was from a *pro se* litigant and important to his case; (D) The Federal District Court granted a motion by the defendant without first giving the Plaintiff any opportunity to file a response and contest the motion – pursuant to the FRCP. The Federal District Court unjustly hung the threat of severe sanctions over the Plaintiff's head while refusing to protect the Plaintiff and his family from threats and intimidation made by Defendant Frank Godley, his cronies, and his lawyers.

The aggregate actions of the Federal District Court, as above noted, have left the Plaintiff greatly troubled, dismayed, disappointed, and convinced of that Court's deeply prejudicial mindset against the Plaintiff leaving him without any hope for fairness, justice, and the protection of his Constitutional Rights before that Court.

Indeed, Plaintiff's disappointing experiences before the courts in Charlotte have left him haunted by the braggadocio and prophetic warning he received by Defendant Margaret Godley who insisted that Plaintiff's litigation to enforce his Judgment in North Carolina was doomed because "We control the judges in this

City." Those troubling experiences are in sharp contrast to the Plaintiff's past experiences before the federal courts in Kentucky and Virginia, and before the Sixth and Fourth Circuit Courts, in the previous companion cases – where he received a full measure of fundamental fairness, due process and justice.

Issue 5. <u>Whether the Plaintiff's Kentucky federal money judgment is enforceable in North Carolina by the Federal District Court in Charlotte?</u>

In the Plaintiff's filings he raised controlling authority compelling the enforcement of his judgment by the Federal District Court.

Issue 6. <u>Whether the actions of the Federal District Court improperly prevented the Plaintiff from recovering the monies stolen from him and his damages while protecting the interests of the corrupt Defendants that stole the Plaintiff's money?</u>

It is a fundamental doctrine of American jurisprudence that the laws and courts support a victim's rights and efforts to recover monies and goods stolen from him.

The Charlotte Federal District Court held that the Plaintiff's Judgment remains "valid" and "may be enforceable" against the defendants. However, if it cannot be enforced against them in North Carolina, where they reside and have located the millions in loot from their illegal actions and other huge assets, then the judgment is effectively worthless and makes a mockery of the rulings, actions and intent of the Federal District Court in Kentucky and the Sixth Circuit Court of Appeals that intended the judgment to be honored and enforced to do justice, to permit the Plaintiff's recovery of the monies stolen from him and his damages, to punish the "evil" Defendants, and to serve as a deterrent to these corrupt defendants and other crooks like them – as the language of those rulings explicitly states.

The bottom line is that the North Carolina State Courts, and now the North Carolina Federal District Court, have manipulated and applied the Rules and law to prevent the Plaintiff from recovering the monies stolen from him while protecting the interests of the home-town crooks that stole the money. Such actions and results are repugnant and contrary to the basic legal, moral and ethical doctrines of American law and justice - that it is wrong and illegal to steal and a victim is justly entitled to recover what is stolen from him. Actions of any court that violate and make a mockery of those doctrines, regardless of their smokescreen of "legalese" rationale or guise, only serve to enable, reward and encourage the evil motives and illegal actions of the thieves who stole the money while further punishing their victim.

To date, neither the Plaintiff nor any of the other victims have recovered any of the monies stolen from them or their damages from the ruthless, evil Defendants and their interstate network of notorious, convicted criminals – who

include former US Congressman Edward M.
Mezvinsky, former Kentucky State Senator
Howard N. Johnson, former FBI Special Agent
William B. Campbell, former bank executive
Mary B. Brady, real estate mogul Robert Krilich,
etc. It is high time that the corrupt, predator
Defendants be held accountable and forced to
return at least some of what they stole over the
decades. This Honorable Court has the authority
to insure that accountability and a small measure
of justice will finally be done.

Issue 7. <u>Whether the District Court erred in
denying Defendant Frank Godley's Rule 11
Motion seeking sanctions against the Plaintiff?</u>

The Defendant's Rule 11 Motion merits only
contempt and constitutes a reprehensible ploy to
threaten, intimidate, and coerce the Plaintiff. It
represents a continuation, and the most recent
predicate act, in the pattern of similar such
efforts and tactics to force the plaintiff to
abandon his litigation and just causes in the
companion cases, in Kentucky, Virginia, and
Tennessee, against this defendant's co-
conspirators – one of whom was his mother,
Margaret L. Godley.

If the Defendant's Rule 11 Motion was
legitimately motivated he could have, and should
have, raised it in timely fashion right after the
Plaintiff filed his Complaint before the District
Court in Virginia. However, he dared not do so
because he was well aware of what happened
when the Defendant's co-conspirators and

cronies, convicted career criminals Howard N. Johnson and Edward M. Mezvinsky, earlier attempted their similar, reprehensible ploys to threaten, intimidate, and coerce the Plaintiff, his family, and his then-lawyer, into forcing the Plaintiff to withdraw his complaint in that companion Virginia litigation, *Anderson v. Foundation, et al.* Senior Judge Glen Williams and Magistrate Judge Cynthia Kinser soundly denounced and severely punished those co-conspirators for their deplorable, shameful, reprehensible ploy.

And when the Defendant's corrupt and ruthless co-conspirators tried the same reprehensible ploy in the companion Kentucky case, *Anderson v. Wade, et al.*, and the Tennessee case, *Anderson v. Mezvinsky*, those co-conspirators were severely denounced, admonished, and punished by the presiding judges: federal judges Joseph Hood and Peggy Patterson and Tennessee Law Court Judge George Johnson. These irrefutable facts are well documented in the court records.

However, a few weeks after the case against the Defendant was transferred to his home-town Federal District Court his lawyer quickly perpetrated his reprehensible ploy to threaten, intimidate, and coerce the Plaintiff into withdrawing his complaint. In this latest predicate act, the Defendant's devious lawyers attempted to veil their ploy behind a brazen cover letter and deceitful Rule 11 Motion;

however, the ploy is quite obvious, and especially so in light of the past history of the similar actions, predicate acts, and intentions of the Defendant's brazen, career criminal, co-conspirators.

What is deeply troubling is that the Defendant and his lawyers dared not attempt the ploy in the Federal District Court in Abingdon, Virginia, but they had no qualms whatsoever about perpetrating the ploy in their home-town Federal District Court in Charlotte. And further troubling is the fact that their Federal District Court took no action to immediately react to and thwart such a reprehensible ploy and protect the Plaintiff and his family – even after the Plaintiff explicitly documented the nature of the reprehensible ploy and its relationship to the previous such ploys by this Defendant's corrupt, co-conspirator cronies and the strong actions taken by the courts against those cronies, and explicitly sought the protection of the District Court for his family and himself.

Instead, the District Court totally ignored the serious situation and took no action whatsoever - which was the opposite reaction of all of the other judges to the previous similar situations where the Defendant's co-conspirator cronies had perpetrated their similar, reprehensible ploys to threaten, intimidate, and coerce the Plaintiff into withdrawing his complaints against those cronies. The Charlotte District Court's act of omission in this serious matter served to deny the

Plaintiff fundamental fairness, due process, justice and the protections he was entitled to and received from all of the other courts, while enabling and encouraging the Defendant and his lawyers to continue with their deplorable ploy – and which his lawyer, Jared E. Gardner, further compounded with his letter of 24 April 2008 that explicitly and/or implicitly further threatened, intimidated, and coerced the Plaintiff from pursuing his appeal actions before this Honorable Court.

Unfortunately, these facts reinforce the troubling and disappointing reality of the District Court's deep prejudice against the Plaintiff, as the Plaintiff previously documented in his Issues for Review with Supporting Facts and Argument, Issue No. 4, which he submitted to this Honorable Court on 9 May 2008 re the companion case *Anderson v. Wade, et al.*, No 08-1468, as Plaintiff's Informal Brief.

And when these very troubling developments and circumstances are considered in the context of the brazen braggadocio of the Defendant's "evil" (as characterized by Judge Hood and the Sixth Circuit), ruthless, career crook, co-conspirator mother, Margaret Godley, that "We control the judges in this City" the matter becomes even more acutely troubling.

WHEREFORE, Plaintiff respectfully prays that this Honorable Court grant him the relief requested and any further relief he may be entitled to.

Relief Requested

Consequently, the Plaintiff respectfully requests the following relief:

1. A ruling that Plaintiff's judgment is enforceable in North Carolina by the Federal District Courts and that the Federal District Court in Charlotte enforce the judgment.

2. Reinstatement of Plaintiff's civil action, *Paull Anderson v. Frank H. Godley*, back in the Federal District Court at Abingdon, Virginia where it was originally filed and where the parties are certain to receive fundamental fairness, due process and justice.

3. A ruling affirming the denial of Defendant Frank Godley's Rule 11 Motion.

The Defendants subsequently submitted brief, weak, responsive arguments which Paull Anderson readily refuted in a further submission to the Sixth Circuit Court of Appeals:

The Defendants Response claims that the Plaintiff's allegations of the gross injustice he suffered in the NC State Courts was not documented with supporting evidence, "with no proof, affidavit or otherwise." The record clearly contradicts that specious claim. Attached to the Plaintiff's Complaint was an Exhibit which fully, clearly, and accurately documented the entire sequence of actions that comprised that gross injustice. It was sworn and attested to and properly notarized as any such Affidavit, attesting to its evidentiary value, and it made extensive references and quotes from the record and transcript of hearing to further support its accuracy. The defendants have never disputed the accuracy of the facts which have thusly been documented by the Plaintiff.

The Defendants' ongoing displeasure with the Plaintiff's accurate documentation of the truth and facts, and their claim that they are "not civil" continue to reflect their distaste for the facts and truth because they are indeed so vile and ugly and the Defendants cannot stand looking in that mirror. However, they are vile and ugly only because the Defendants made them so. It would be well for these incorrigible and inveterate career crooks, admitted/convicted criminals, disbarred lawyers, and totally corrupt Defendants to consider the words of the venerable, former US Supreme Court Chief Justice, Earl Warren, that "Truth in the pursuit of justice is always civil and to be respected, sought after, and appreciated."

The Defendants' claim, that "In reality, Mr. Anderson voluntarily chose to pursue dismissal" is absurd and totally contradicted by the Plaintiff's move to dismiss in which he explicitly articulated that he was being <u>forced</u> to file the motion, under protest and objection. Prior to that point, the Plaintiff had been vigorously pursuing, in good faith, his just lawsuit against Frank Godley and would have continued to do so had it not been sabotaged by the unjust, highly prejudicial actions of the Federal District Court in Charlotte.

The Defendants' Responses avoid a crucial issue – re the actions by the NC Courts, both State and Federal, to prevent the Plaintiff's recovery of the monies stolen from him and his damages from the defendants that stole it and damaged him.

The actions of the North Carolina Courts have subverted justice and contradict the overwhelming body of compelling and controlling legal authority that have always supported the right of a victim of theft to recover what was stolen and his damages from the thieves. In the instant case, the actions of the North Carolina Courts, both State and now Federal, have acted to protect the interests of their hometown, career crook, thieves while preventing their victim from recovering the monies they stole from him and his damages. In addition, the actions of those Courts have violated the US Constitutional Full Faith and Credit protections and relevant, compelling legal authority supporting the right of the Plaintiff to enforce his valid Kentucky federal money judgment in North Carolina.

NC Mecklenburg County judge, Marvin Gray initiated the brazen injustice through his actions at the hearing before him on Plaintiff's Motion to enforce his valid Kentucky Judgment and thereafter by sabotaging Plaintiff's appeal and right of appeal. In turn, the North Carolina appeals courts then repeatedly refused to remedy Judge Gray's injustice or even consider the merits. Finally, the Charlotte Federal District Court compounded the injustice by similarly acting to prevent the Plaintiff from recovering the monies stolen from him and his damages while protecting the interests of the home town, career crooks that stole from the Plaintiff.

Consequently, the aggregate actions of the North Carolina courts have: (1) made a mockery of the Judgment and intentions of the Federal District Court in Kentucky and the Sixth Circuit Court of Appeals, (2) made a mockery of the US Constitutional Full Faith and Credit protections and relevant, compelling legal authority supporting the right of the Plaintiff to enforce his valid Kentucky federal money judgment in North Carolina, (3) prevented the plaintiff from recovering the monies stolen from him and his damages, (4) protected the interests of the crooks that stole the plaintiff's monies and enabled them to keep what they stole and make a mockery of the judgment and justice of the Kentucky Federal District Court and the Sixth Circuit Court of Appeals, and (5) contradicted the overwhelming body of compelling and controlling legal authority that has always supported the right of a victim of theft to recover what was stolen and his damages from the thieves.

The actions of the North Carolina courts violate a fundamental, foundational, doctrine of both American Jurisprudence and International

Law – that the laws and courts protect the rights of a victim to recover what was stolen from him from those who stole it. Indeed, even an innocent third party must return stolen property to its rightful owner. American, British, and worldwide museums and collectors have been forced to return Egyptian, Greek, Roman, etc. antiquities stolen hundreds of years ago as well as art works and other valuables to their rightful owners, or the heirs of those rightful owners, stolen by the Nazis 60 years ago.

Many years ago, a very wise and dear friend, who also happened to be a distinguished jurist, Judge Sherman J. Bellwood, once solemnly assured the Plaintiff that "the measure of justice one receives depends not upon the laws and rules and courts, but upon the presiding judges and how they decide to apply the laws and rules to be just or otherwise." The past fourteen years of litigation have borne out that advice. The most excellent, presiding federal judges in the companion Kentucky and Virginia litigation have insured that the litigants received a full and fair measure of justice while the jurists in the North Carolina litigation have acted otherwise.

And many years ago, the Plaintiff also received some more legal insight from another of his dear friends who was very wise, cultivated magnificent tea roses, appreciated the fine arts, and also happened to be an accomplished jurist. Clement F. Haynsworth, Jr. was also a fellow Palmetto Gentleman of the utmost integrity who knew well and loved the law. He admired the Warren Court because he felt it exemplified his personal ideal, "to do justice above all else," and he deeply respected that Court's dedication to that ideal even when it was highly unpopular and meant changing well established and convenient laws, rules and practices. It was a tragedy and great loss for this nation when his confirmation to the US Supreme Court was unjustly sabotaged by a few misguided politicians and, as a consequence, our nation was deprived of the brilliance of a dedicated Fourth Circuit Judge who would have made a splendid Justice in the same tradition as the Warren Court. Notwithstanding, his commendable legal insight and ideal continue to guide and inspire most of our contemporary jurists "to do justice above all else." The Plaintiff was blessed to have such excellent judges presiding in the previous companion cases before the Federal District Courts in Kentucky, *Anderson v. Wade, et al.*, and Virginia, *Anderson v. Foundation, et al.*, and before the US Court of Appeals for the Sixth Circuit. However, it has been very disappointing to experience North Carolina judges that are not guided by that noble ideal and dedicated mindset "to do justice above all else."

The Federal District Court in Charlotte made it quite clear that doing justice above all else is hardly its primary focus and mindset, and especially when it can contrive and rationalize a more convenient and far less difficult path to resolving a legal issue. That Court emphatically noted that distinction in its ruling, in the instant case, that "some of Plaintiff's points may be well taken, and determination by the state courts may be utterly wrong. That however, is of no consequence. Even if this Court were to perceive a miscarriage of justice in the state court's application of the law, it is this Court's obligation to treat the state court's final determination as exactly that: final." Under that dogma, the Federal District Court in Charlotte would have as quickly refused the Plaintiff justice even if the Mecklenburg County judge had unjustly sentenced the Plaintiff to death – so long as the N.C. appeals courts had rubber stamped the sentence with their "finality," and even though those appeals courts had compounded the County Judge's injustice with further injustice and not even bothered to consider the merits of the *pro se* Plaintiff's case. Doing justice as the penultimate ideal and guiding principle "is of no consequence" to the Federal District Court in Charlotte, even when it perceives "a miscarriage of justice in the state court's application of the law." It was fortunate for the Plaintiff that the Federal District Court in Pikeville, Kentucky and the Sixth Circuit Court of Appeals in Ohio followed the ideal and mindset of the Warren Court and Judge Haynsworth rather than that of the Federal District Court in Charlotte.

The Federal District Court in Kentucky and the Sixth Circuit did all in their powers "to do justice above all else," and thereby assist the plaintiff to recover what had been stolen from him and his damages from the career crooks that stole from him and damaged him. In contrast, the North Carolina Courts, both State and Federal, have done the opposite by manipulating and subverting the laws and rules to enable their home-town thieves to keep what they stole from the Plaintiff and to prevent the plaintiff from recovering what was stolen from him and his damages. The result was a gross injustice, regardless of the legalese, rationale, and excuses that those North Carolina Courts have used to legitimize their actions. The North Carolina courts have effectively and constructively provided a safe haven for the corrupt defendants – a haven where they can steal with impunity as their courts prevent their victim from recovering what was stolen from him and his damages. Such a repugnant and patently unjust situation pleads for strong remedial action by this Honorable Court to bring those courts in line with the other courts within the Fourth Circuit that practice doing justice.

These career criminals should have been brought to justice long ago by the authorities; however, despite the plaintiff's best efforts to prod those authorities to do so the North Carolina scoundrels used their influence to escape the criminal justice system. Their cronies,

Mezvinsky, Johnson, Krilich and Campbell were prosecuted, convicted and imprisoned but Margaret Godley and the Wades neither spent a day in jail nor returned any of the millions they stole – thanks to their home-town North Carolina courts.

The Plaintiff now respectfully prays that this Honorable Court "will do justice above all else" and not allow the career crooks to keep the monies they stole from him, and prevent their victim from recovering his monies and damages, while making a mockery of the Full Faith and Credit Act, the Judgment and intentions of the Federal District Court in Kentucky and the Sixth Circuit Court of Appeals, and the fundamental doctrine of American and International Jurisprudence that protects the rights of a victim to recover what was stolen from him and his damages from the crooks that stole it and damaged him.

On December 5, 2008, the Fourth Circuit handed down a terse ruling that:

Anderson had a valid judgment that was unenforceable against the Defendants in the North Carolina State Courts because the enforceability of Anderson's judgment has already been determined by the North Carolina state courts.

The Virginian was disappointed that in its expedient disposition of the case the Fourth Circuit had finessed from doing justice above all else—by deciding against reviewing any of the issues he had raised, especially the flagrant violations of his US Constitutional rights to fundamental fairness, due process and justice by the North Carolina state courts. He felt that had the case been heard by the previous Fourth Circuit Court, where Clement F. Haynsworth, Jr. presided as Chief Judge, their practice and doctrine "to do justice above all else" would likely have produced far different results. Despite his disappointment, he accepted the reality that the ruling simply did not come from the "Haynsworth Court" and he recollected the wise advice he had received from Judge Bellwood, that "the measure of justice one receives depends not upon the laws and rules and courts, but upon the presiding judges and how they decide to apply the laws and rules to be just or otherwise."

He also realized that attempting to appeal the Fourth Circuit ruling by filing another petition for *certiorari* before the US Supreme "Roberts Court" would be a useless effort in futility.

After fifteen difficult years of litigation, the Virginian found himself with a "valid Kentucky federal money judgment" that could not be enforced against the ruthless, career criminals in their safe haven, home state of North Carolina where they and their family members were freely enjoying with impunity the millions stolen from the Virginian and other victims. The North Carolina courts had effectively prevented his recovery of what had been stolen from him and made a mockery of the rulings and specific intentions of the Kentucky Federal District Court and the Sixth Circuit Court of Appeals that the valid Kentucky judgment be enforced to do justice above all else.

A week after the Fourth Circuit ruled, Paull Anderson received a phone call from a prominent, investigative reporter who commended the Virginian "for your courageous battle against impossible odds. If there were more brave and dedicated citizens like you we might have a chance of reforming our largely corrupt legal system and maybe even clearing out the entrenched snake pits of Washington, DC, and Wall Street where the biggest and slimyest vipers thrive."

EPILOGUE

HINDSIGHT

Seventeen years ago Paull Anderson was "snakebitten" and embarked upon a fifteen year crusade of arduous legal battles against impossible odds in his relentless quest for justice. His quixotic legal adventures have left him acutely aware of serious problems, stark contrasts, and important issues that exist in civil American Jurisprudence on several levels.

Chief among them is the disparity between the quality and measure of "equal justice under law" provided from court to court and state to state in both the state and federal courts. He is troubled that some state legal systems are callously insensitive and grossly derelict in providing indigent and *pro se* litigants the necessary safeguards and protections mandated by law to insure them the equal justice guaranteed all Americans by the U.S. Constitution. He is critical of the disparity between the high quality and diligence of some judges versus the reckless incompetence and mean-spirited arrogance of too many others. He appreciates the honorable lawyers he has encountered and has no use for the scoundrels. His sharp criticism of the North Carolina courts reflects the grossly unjust treatment he suffered before them.

The Virginia farmer reflected back upon those difficult years and expressed his intriguing views and strong opinions concerning his experiences and those issues:

My experiences have left me convinced that American Jurisprudence is certainly not among the worst of the world's legal institutions; however, it has serious shortcomings. Among them is our "equal justice under law" myth. In fact, the ugly reality is that we have a dual system of justice—one for the powerful and wealthy haves, and another for the have-nots.

Too many American citizens do not enjoy equal justice under law. For them the words are pure hypocrisy and hollow—a cruel hoax. Unfortunately, the measure of equal justice one can expect under our legal system is directly proportional to one's wealth, power and influence. The wealthy and powerful top tier, and minority, of Americans are entitled to a full measure of equal justice under law while the majority of have-not, bottom tier Americans have to settle for a much smaller measure, if any at all. This fact has been well known and long accepted as the norm in American jurisprudence—as the way our legal system functions.

A wealthy citizen can afford the best stable of lawyers with huge resources of expertise, experience, and practical influence in their "good old boy" legal network that insures an overwhelming advantage over the adversary without comparable assets. The wealthy client's legal team can retain vast collateral assistance, such as investigators, research and trial expertise, and a wide spectrum of professional help that is far beyond the reach of the litigant with little or no financial means. Consequently, the wealthy litigant can expect to receive a large measure of equal justice under law while the indigent receives little or none.

In the matter of criminal litigation, the US Supreme Court, under Chief Justice Earl Warren's leadership, tried to affect some long overdue measure of balance and constitutionally guaranteed protections for a fair trial and justice when a citizen's life or liberty is at stake by mandating that all criminally charged litigants must be represented by a lawyer. That Court established the precedent in its landmark *Gideon v. Wainwright* case, *372 US 335(1963),* and Anthony Lewis later wrote a fine novel, *Gideon's Trumpet (1964)*, documenting the historical facts of that courageous ruling. That case and its progeny have clearly established and repeatedly confirmed that the question of whether one needs counsel when caught up in our judicial system is a *non sequitur*. The absolute need applies to both criminal and civil matters. Unfortunately, the US Supreme Court rationale mandating the need for a lawyer to represent an indigent in a criminal case has not been applied to the needs of an indigent party in a civil case.

In a civil matter, an indigent party is not entitled to counsel he cannot afford although the identical rational and legal reason applies in both criminal and civil matters concerning the conclusion that a party without counsel is equally handicapped in either a civil or criminal matter. This irrefutable conclusion was well developed during the *Gideon* case arguments by the distinguished Washington lawyer, Abe Fortas, who had been appointed by the US Supreme Court to represent Clarence Earl Gideon:

> The due process clause protects one's liberty and property as well as one's life. This case shows that no man, however intelligent, can conduct his own defense adequately...This case dramatically illustrates that you cannot have a fair trial without counsel...I think there is a tendency to forget what happens to these poor, miserable, indigent people in these strange and awesome circumstances. Sometimes in this Supreme Court there is a tendency to forget what happens downstairs... I was reminded the other night, as I was pondering this case, of Clarence Darrow when he was prosecuted for trying to fix a jury. The first thing he realized was that he needed a lawyer – he, one of the country's great criminal lawyers.

Fortas was referring to the fine documentary novel, *Attorney for the Damned (1957)*, by Arthur Weinburg, which provided further compelling argument and historic data to support the absolute need for counsel if the US

Constitutional safeguards for equal justice under law, due process, and fundamental fairness are to be affective.

Fortas' final argument quoted from the letter written to *The New York Times* by the distinguished legal scholars, Erwin Griswold and Benjamin Cohen, "The right of counsel, for the poor as well as the rich, is an indispensable safeguard of freedom and justice under Law."

On March 18, 1963, the US Supreme Court unanimously agreed with Abe Fortas' argument and held that all indigent defendants in criminal cases "had an absolute and constitutional protected right to counsel... [a]ny person haled into court, who is too poor to hire a lawyer, cannot be assured a fair trial unless counsel is provided for him. This seems to be an obvious truth." After Fortas was appointed a Justice on the Supreme Court he continued to champion the constitutional rights of indigent litigants in criminal cases.

Unfortunately, the same principles are not applied to indigent or *pro se* litigants in civil cases although the same basic need for competent counsel is obvious, to insure a fair trial and a real recourse to the same equal justice under law, as in a criminal case. The reasons for the distinction are twofold. The first is purely financial based upon the presumption that it would impose an impractical expense on the legal system, both federal and state. The second is that indigents and *pro se* litigants facing criminal charges have their life or liberty at stake whereas their counterpart litigants in civil cases have only their material assets at risk. However, both of these reasons have no substantial basis justifying the distinction, either by virtue of the equal justice under law guarantee to all citizens under the US Constitution or by virtue of practical considerations.

The philosophical argument has been made that in the criminal case there is liberty, and often life, at stake, whereas, in a civil matter it is usually merely a matter of money or some thing of material value. This relegates the issue of equal justice to the issue of competing priorities between incomparable values—life and liberty versus money and materiality—and it becomes a question of which is more worthy of the counsel necessary to insure a fair measure of equal justice. However, this avoids the greater constitutional issue of providing its protections in one instance but withholding them in another, although in both instances they are crucial and mandated under the Fourteenth Amendment. So why has American jurisprudence not honestly remedied this shameful disparity?

The bottom line answer lies in the same dollars and cents factor that controls so much of the practical reality of what actually drives and controls all American institutions— including American jurisprudence.

When the Warren Court forced American jurisprudence to remedy the problem facing indigent criminal defendants, the legal system was then burdened to pay the cost in dollars and cents. When ideals and righteousness end up costing real money, that is "crunch time." This is when the vested powers suddenly become very concerned about just how much righteousness they can afford. The *Gideon* case created a classic crunch as the state and federal judicial powers began to grapple with implementing, and more importantly, financing the mandate of the Warren Court.

An indigent citizen facing the loss of his liberty through a criminal conviction is entitled to counsel, regardless of the period of that loss of liberty. This applies in a situation where the accused faces a week or a hundred year period of incarceration. Certainly counsel is imperative in each and every instance of an accused facing loss of liberty; however, a further practical application merits consideration regarding the justification for counsel in one instance and denial in the other. Consider, on one hand, the litigant facing criminal charges that can land him in jail for a week or thirty days. He deserves and is provided counsel.

On the other hand, consider the instance where an individual has been defrauded or damaged in a devastating fashion where his only recourse for recovery lies through successful civil litigation. The unfortunate soul may have had his home, savings, and all that he accumulated through a lifetime of hard, honest work stolen from him as in the cases of the Enron, Adelphia, Trans-Global, Bernie Madoff, and other recent scandalous situations that have caught the public's attention. In such tragic circumstances, the victim's only recourse to recovery lies through civil litigation. However, the victim too often cannot afford counsel and is thus faced with the prospects of either proceeding *pro se* or abandoning any hope for recovery. Either way— he has no real recourse to recovery and equal justice under law.

When the situation of the individual facing the week in jail is placed on one side of the scale of Justice and the plight of the victim of the grave civil wrong is placed on the other side of the scale they hardly balance when subjected to the criteria of equal justice under law, fundamental fairness, or the level of damage, pain and suffering threatening each individual. Common sense and justice cry out that the victim of the civil wrong has far more to lose and deserves counsel equally as well as his counterpart facing a week in jail.

Consequently, the prospects for any measure of equal justice under law are slight for an indigent with a just cause requiring civil litigation. He has three basic choices. The first is to try to find a competent attorney who will take the case on a strictly contingent basis. Unless it is a "slam dunk, no brainer, no risk, no cost" case, such as an accident injury case, this prospect is nil, and if a contingency lawyer will take the case it will be for a huge contingency percentage, plus "expenses, etc.," from the recovery. The second choice is for the litigant to proceed *pro se*, representing himself, which has little or no prospects for success since most indigents have a very limited formal education, if any, let alone enough to begin to function in the complex legal arena. This leaves the third and last choice, which is to simply accept the fact that the cause must be abandoned for lack of money to afford counsel. These facts reveal the troubling reality facing a poor litigant with a *bona fide* civil cause of action under our current legal system, which is hostile and prejudicial to the little man's prospects for any measure of equal justice under the law.

In 2004, Tresa Baldas wrote an interesting article for the *National Law Review*, documenting the pressure upon the Ninth Circuit Court of Appeals concerning the serious problems of *pro se* litigants. In 2005, the Legal Services Corporation documented the justice gap in America that was short-changing low income Americans caught up in civil litigation.

I think that my cases demonstrate the vast difference in the way *pro se* civil cases are treated by the Kentucky and Virginia federal courts, versus the North Carolina state and federal courts. The federal courts in both the Kentucky and the Virginia cases diligently protected my constitutional rights to equal justice, due process, and fundamental fairness and strictly complied with the controlling case law authority insuring those protections. In contrast, the North Carolina courts refused to provide those same protections – in violation of the superior case law authority from the US Supreme Court and all of the US Circuit Courts of Appeal mandating those protections.

I was repeatedly reminded that the policy of the North Carolina state courts is to treat *pro se* litigants no differently than those represented by lawyers and to hold the *pro se* litigants to the same level of legal competence as a lawyer. Indeed, they made it very clear that the *pro se* litigant is expected to conduct his case within the same strict legal protocol and to know the law as expertly as the lawyers representing the other side. Judge Gray's explicit words and actions reflected this policy. His actions and legal rulings were subsequently fully condoned and rubber-stamped by both the North Carolina Court of Appeals and the North Carolina Supreme Court, emphasizing their concurrence with the policy and practice of holding *pro se* litigants to the same requirements and responsibilities as lawyers. When I specifically raised the controlling case law authority mandating the *pro se* protections, in *Hudspeth v. Figgins*, 584 F.2d 1345 (4th Circ. 1978) and in *Boswell v. Mayer*, 169 F.3d 384 (6th Circ. 1999), the North Carolina courts chose to ignore or defy that authority.

The November 11, 2004, *National Law Review* reported the findings by a federal task force that thoroughly investigated the national *pro se* problem. Its chairman, the distinguished Alaskan jurist, US District Judge James K. Singleton, noted that "One of the biggest problems that a self-represented litigant presents is the same problem that is presented by self-instructed plumbers and electricians and carpenters ... just as men and women would have a difficult time learning those trades, they also have a great deal of difficulty learning everything you need to know in order to effectively present a case." Judge Singleton could have taken his excellent analogy a step further and noted that the average citizen would find it much easier to act, with at least some minimal ability, as a tradesman whereas to expect that citizen to deal with the extremely complex requirements of presenting a case or otherwise fulfilling the professional requirements of a competent lawyer is absurd.

Circuit Court of Appeals Judge Paul Niemeyer noted that expecting a *pro se* litigant to be able to properly present his case, as it would be presented by a competent lawyer is a virtual impossibility. "It just doesn't and cannot work." He documented the severe handicaps facing a *pro se* litigant who is unable to afford an attorney and finds himself forced to either represent himself or forego his right to equal justice under law.

Obviously, the North Carolina courts adamantly disagree with this reality.

For decades prominent legal scholars, jurists and lawyers have recognized the flawed state of

American jurisprudence. Recently, distinguished defense attorney, F. Lee Bailey, lamented that "We all know that the (legal) system isn't working...what all the hypocrisy comes down to is the promise of a fair trial...we've got to put the emphasis on justice rather than game playing."

Attorney, legislator and highly successful author, John Grisham, also minced no words in describing the "broken criminal justice system—it is a mess. More than one hundred people have been sent to death row who were later exonerated because they weren't guilty or fairly tried...there is a lot that is wrong...and there are a lot of slimy lawyers to juice up the profession."

While I certainly agree with their criticism, I also believe that the goal of achieving equal justice under law can be served by remedying a major and fundamental flaw in our American legal system. This flaw is premised upon the well-established doctrine and practice that the American lawyers' first priority and legal obligation is to serve the best interests of their clients—rather than the emergence of truth and application of justice.

The practical reality of this is that our legal system is capitalistically-oriented and driven to winning cases. The most successful lawyers subsequently win the most cases and reap the greatest rewards: wealth, recognition and fame, which then allows them to charge greater fees and accumulate even greater wealth, recognition and fame as the progression continues exponentially—all based upon winning. Truth is not a factor, except when it can be exploited to win. Conversely, truth is to be readily subverted, defeated, and suppressed when it conflicts with winning. Indeed, the old law school adage is quite true that "The first victim in a trial is the truth." The successful lawyer knows how to manipulate facts and truth in order to serve his client's interests and his need to win, which in turn also serves the lawyer's best interests.

The only way this ugly flaw can be remedied would be to establish a different legal priority to the lawyer's obligations. This would require setting the emergence of truth as the top priority, doing justice as the second, complying with the standards of ethics as third, and serving the best interests of the client fourth. The effect of this would serve the interests of truth and justice because with all counsel striving, primarily, to bring forth the truth, it would then permit an honest and competent judge to justly apply the law to that truth and do justice. It would also mean that all of the operatives are on the same page—striving for the same goal of facilitating the emergence of truth to allow an even-handed application of the laws. There would be no counterproductive forces, as now exist, working to defeat the emergence of truth and justice—to serve the pecuniary interests of that client's lawyer and the selfish interests of a client whose winning would defeat justice. Such a system, focused primarily on truth and justice, would also level the playing field for all of the litigants and their advocates.

The wealthy litigant with the more competent and capable lawyers could not exploit that advantage to serve his best interest to defeat truth and justice. The client who could afford the more effective, expensive, powerful stable of lawyers would have no great advantage over the client with far less resources, and a less capable lawyer, since the primary efforts and goal of all of the lawyers would be to serve the same common interest. Consequently, the wealthy adversary's financial clout would be subordinated to the service of truth and justice. Such a system would also facilitate the role of the judge to more justly apply the laws and do justice. Unfortunately, such a truth-and justice-prioritized legal system would be at odds with the interests of our capitalistic society. Consequently, the interests of truth and justice in our legal system will always be effectively relegated to their places where they cannot and do not conflict with the capitalistic policies that continue to control our American legal, political and financial institutions.

My fledgling, two-hundred-year-old nation could learn much from your six-thousand-year-old civilization and its great wisdom, but our arrogant leaders look down their noses at China with the same disdain they have for the rest of the world—and especially for the Asian nations. American jurisprudence and our legal community would do well to be guided by the

Confucian concepts from the Daxue texts that examine the "Zhi ÖI" notion of justice and the noble goals to manifest exemplary character, to abide in the highest good, and to find truth to do justice. Unfortunately, my nation has evolved from the noble ideals and dreams of its founding fathers into an ugly and ruthless "capitalistocracy," as I characterize it, where a relatively few powerful and wealthy maintain a stranglehold on the masses through the laws and political body they control. That is the sad and practical reality of what my country has become. This is reflected in the general public's feeling of utter frustration and hopeless inability to drastically change our course and restore our identity—regardless of which party is in power.

I am writing a book which will document the past forty-four years of my legal battles against the forces of evil and it will have much to say about reforming our legal system from both within and without. Hopefully, one day this nation's legal system will actually provide equal justice for all. Meanwhile, I would encourage those who find themselves forced to fight for justice, even against powerful and wealthy adversaries and impossible odds, to be strong and persevere.

One can take heart from those brave souls, such as Clarence Earl Gideon, Robert Kearns, Mahatma Gandhi, Martin Luther King, and Nelson Mandela, who have done so. They all were exemplary champions of justice in my lifetime who bravely engaged in classic David versus Goliath battles against omnipotent adversaries and impossible odds.

Gideon was forced to fight, as a *pro-se* indigent, through the Florida courts and the US Supreme Court to affect fundamental changes in American jurisprudence of monumental significance which was well-documented in the inspirational novel, *Gideon's Trumpet*, and a subsequent movie with the same title, starring Henry Fonda.

Robert Kearns' epic battle against the Detroit powerhouses, Ford and Chrysler, was also well documented in the inspiring film, *Flash of Genius*. *Los Angeles Times* staff writer, Reed Johnson, noted that, "The lesson to be drawn from Kearns' remarkable struggle is that it takes a tremendous amount of guts, smarts and perhaps a touch of craziness to stand up to powerful interests in one's society. Those who do it must be prepared to sacrifice time, health, love, peace of mind or, in Kearns' case, all of the above."

The epic struggles of Mahatma Gandhi, Martin Luther King, and Nelson Mandela against injustice have inspired people of good conscience throughout the world.

Yes, indeed, the past fourteen years of litigation has been a learning experience. One of the primary lessons has been that the justice, or injustice, one receives has little to do with the laws and everything to do with the presiding judge. If you are fortunate enough to have a presiding judge who is competent and fair-minded, then you may have your case decided on the merits, rather than some red herring that gives the local boys an unfair advantage. If you are in the courtroom of an honest judge, chances for justice are great; if the judge is incompetent and/or a corrupt "juice judge," your chances for justice are slim to none—unless, of course, you control that judge—whereupon you have a lock on the outcome.

Most Americans are unaware that what happens on the lowest rung of the due process ladder can have the greatest impact upon whether they eventually are afforded the due process, equal justice under law, fundamental fairness, and all of the other protections guaranteed them under the US Constitution. They do not realize that the actions of their local, county judge in his little courtroom can have such huge ramifications.

Every legal action starts at the lowest rung of the due process ladder. In the federal court system that means you begin before a US district court judge with proper jurisdiction. In a state's legal system it is usually before the local county court. Both federal and state systems function quite independently of one another and under their own set of rules and statutes. While the same federal statutes and rules apply in every federal court in the nation, the statutes and rules of every state apply only in its state courts, and these state statutes and rules vary considerably from state-to-state. Unfortunately, the federal district courts are usually forced to apply the state statutes in which the federal district court is located.

Consequently, that first presiding judge handling the case at its onset has the authority to start it off along the path to justice, or to derail, cripple and prejudice it to the point that justice will never be served.

That first presiding judge will exercise his authority to establish crucial "findings of fact" and "conclusions of law" by his actions and rulings that establish the "law of the case." From that point forward, his actions can be appealed upward through the appeals courts; however, the policy of all appeals courts provides that the case comes before them with the strong presumption that the actions of the lower court judge and his findings of fact and conclusions of law are correct. This iron-bound doctrine leaves every appellant the "legal burden" of overcoming the difficult legal hurdles necessary to prevail and have the appeals court overturn the rulings in the lower court.

However, even if the appeals court finds that the lower court judge "abused his discretion" or committed significant errors and misconduct it can all be readily dismissed as acceptable "harmless error." It takes "overwhelming" proof of an obvious, very serious error of law by the lower court judge before the appeals court will remedy and overturn the action of the lower court. This doctrine is intentionally designed to attach great weight, credibility, and *gravitas* to the actions by the lower court judge. The practical and capitalistic application and result of this doctrine serves to greatly reduce the work load and expenses of the appeals courts.

Unfortunately, this current application of the "harmless error" doctrine actually works against the interests of justice and it should never have replaced the earlier rule regarding "harmless error." That previous rule should be reinstated – that "it is not harmless unless harmless beyond a reasonable doubt."

Under the current standard, too many unfair trial practices are upheld under the loose, catch-all standard of "harmless error" based upon the general and dubious assumption that the error probably did not make any difference. But what happens when it makes ALL the difference?

The Sixth Circuit Court of Appeals ruling in the *Maurino v. Johnson* case, No. 98-1332(6th Cir. April 2000), spotlighted the dire problem as it related to that case: "by the current harmless error standard that trial may as well not even have occurred because the defendant probably would be convicted anyway."

The actions by the lower court may reflect the mindset of a highly competent, fair-minded judge—dedicated to seeing that justice is served. If he is a sincere professional who complies with and respects the controlling case law authority, and insures the litigants' rights to equal justice, due process, and fundamental fairness are strictly protected—then any subsequent appeals process can function in the service of justice.

Unfortunately, many cases are crippled and fatally flawed and doomed to be denied justice in the appeals courts because of incompetent and/or corrupt lower court "juice judges." "Juice judges" or "just judges" make all the difference.

My cases vividly demonstrate the crucial importance of the presiding judges and contrast the high quality of those federal judges in my Virginia and Kentucky cases with the judges in the Tennessee and North Carolina cases.

The Kentucky case was favored, on its lowest level of litigation, with jurists of the highest quality, competence, and integrity: Federal Magistrate Judge Peggy Patterson and Senior Federal District Judge Joseph M. Hood. Similarly, the Virginia case was blessed with superlative jurists: Federal Magistrate Judge Cynthia Kinser, who has since been elevated to a seat on the Virginia Supreme Court, and Senior Federal District Judge Glen Williams. They all proved to be consummate professionals—extremely competent jurists who strictly respected and complied with both Constitutional and controlling case law authority while being sensitive that justice, not favoritism, was the ruling principle in their courtroom. Even their courteous manner from the bench reflected their attitude of deep concern to be fair to the parties and true to the law. Their actions and rulings started both cases on the straight and narrow path to justice and protected the rights of all the litigants. Both cases were subsequently appealed to the circuit courts where the actions of the federal district court judges and magistrate judges were reviewed and affirmed.

In stark contrast, my case before the North Carolina state courts to enforce my Kentucky judgment exemplified shameful and gross injustice. On the lowest level, the merits of the case were adjudicated by the presiding Mecklenburg County judge, Marvin K. Gray. The record clearly reflects his reprchensible bias and mean-spirited mishandling of the case and the serious impact of his highly prejudicial actions. One can draw his or her own conclusions as to the reasons behind those actions; however, the results reflect poorly upon Gray's competence, integrity, and obligation to be fair and just and to uphold his legal responsibility to do justice, to respect and abide by controlling case law authority, and to protect every litigant's right to equal justice, due process, and fundamental fairness.

During the hearing before Judge Gray, he appeared to take pleasure in berating me with the fact that he did not appreciate *pro se* litigants appearing before him and that he held them to the same standards as lawyers: "Since you're representing yourself you're presumed to know the law." He also made it clear that he neither agreed with nor complied with the doctrine mandated by the Fourth and Sixth Circuit Courts of Appeals rulings, in *Hudspeth v. Figgins*, 584 F.2d 1345 (4th Circ. 1978) and *Boswell v. Mayer*, 169 F.3d 384 (6th Circ. 1999), that "the filings and pleadings of *pro se* litigants are entitled to a liberal construction regardless how unartfully prepared."

Gray administered the same blistering, demeaning and harsh admonishment to another litigant who appeared *pro se* in a case that I happened to sit in on while waiting for my case to be heard. It mattered not to Gray that the doctrine protecting *pro se* litigants was well-established by mandates of the US Supreme Court and every US Circuit Court of Appeals. And Gray could not care less that his actions openly defied the explicit case law authority of the Fourth Circuit Court of Appeals whose rulings carry "compelling precedent authority" over every state in its Circuit, including North Carolina.

Tennessee Law Court Judge G. Richard Johnson's courtroom demeanor reflected the same strong bias and open hostility against *pro se* litigants and the rulings that mandated that they be treated fairly and with sensitivity in consideration for their lack of legal competence.

Judges with such strong prejudices towards *pro se* litigants and who refuse to afford those litigants the protections they are entitled to under the law simply should not be presiding in cases involving a *pro se* party. Better still, for the sake of American Jurisprudence, such judges should be persuaded to find another line of less harmful work, maybe pumping gas or parking cars. Besides tarnishing the image of American jurisprudence, they also create needless extra work, problems and expenses for the appeals courts.

Gray's mean-spirited actions also highly prejudiced and corrupted the appeals process, thereby compounding injustice upon injustice. In turn, both the North Carolina Court of Appeals and the North Carolina Supreme Court used their discretionary powers to simply refuse to review the merits of the case and Gray's actions which denied the remedial action and authority either appeals court could have exercised to do justice by confronting and correcting the serious problems and gross injustice created by one of their county court judges. This had a double negative effect: it left standing a gross injustice that could have and should have been remedied by either appeals court, and it effectively condoned and encouraged the continuance of such injustice by that rogue, lower court "juice judge." Cumulatively, the actions by Gray and the North Carolina appeals courts exposed some of the egregious and reprehensible flaws in North Carolina's judicial system.

Unfortunately, state court judges, such as Gray, in North Carolina, and Johnson, in Tennessee, exemplify maverick judges who know they can openly defy federal and constitutional mandates and controlling case law authority with impunity under the protective umbrella of their state appeals courts, state statutes, and fellow "club" members in their legal communities.

Johnson and Gray both refused to respect or comply with controlling authority, and especially federal case law authority. I would characterize their attitudes as an arrogant abuse of both their absolute authority in their courtrooms and their independence from any legal authority with which they did not concur. Reviewing the transcripts of hearings in their courtrooms emphasized these repugnant qualities even more than my previous memories and contemporaneous notes had recalled. I was shocked at their overt prejudice and arrogant disrespect for the law and any sense of fairness. The transcripts captured all of the highly prejudicial and mean-spirited reality. Their rulings also reflect their adamant refusals to respect and comply with the superior, controlling case law and constitutional authority they once took an oath to uphold. They validate and epitomize the "rogues in robes" and "juice judges" sobriquets by which such disreputable jurists are commonly characterized in the legal community.

My friend and mentor, Judge Sherman J. Bellwood, wisely noted that "the measure of justice one receives depends not upon the laws and rules and courts, but upon the presiding judges and how they decide to apply the laws and rules to be just or otherwise." He also concurred with Chief Judge Haynsworth's doctrine that every judge of good conscience should be bound "to do justice above all else," even if that required changing current laws and rules or *stare decisis* precedents. The bold actions of the courageous "Warren Court" reflected that doctrine in its most effective and practical application, and as the *Gideon* case personified.

Judge Bellwood's observation has certainly been repeatedly and dramatically proven to be accurate in each of my cases during the past fifteen years of litigation, whether the cases were in state or federal courts.

My civil case against Margaret Godley and the Wades was afforded due process, fundamental fairness and justice because of the even-handed and fair-minded Federal judges, Hood and Patterson, in the Kentucky case. Had that same case been filed before the Charlotte Federal District Court it is clear it never would have been similarly treated or received justice. Instead, it would have received the same heavy-handed, prejudicial, and unjust treatment that my later case against Frank Godley suffered. Both cases were before Federal District Courts but different judges made all the difference. Indeed, both cases were quite similar in factual and legal issues and even the language and allegations in the complaints were also very similar, except that my case against Frank Godley was much stronger because it incorporated the findings of fact and conclusions of law from the prior Kentucky case against his mother and the Wades.

Notwithstanding, the Charlotte Federal District Court quickly killed my case against Frank Godley in an obviously unjust, prejudicial, and heavy-handed fashion just as it would have done had I filed my case against Margaret Godley and the Wades before that Court instead of the Kentucky Court. In the Kentucky case that Federal District Court judge did everything to insure that the victim recovered what had been stolen from him and his damages whereas, the Charlotte Federal District Court judge acted otherwise and protected the interests of the home-town thieves and prevented their victim from recovering what had been stolen from him and his damages – in the same shamefully repugnant fashion that the North Carolina state courts had done.

The contrast in the actions by the Kentucky judges versus the North Carolina judges, even when the comparative analysis is limited to the actions between the federal judges in both states, is stark, dramatic, and revealing—and confirms Judge Bellwood's accurate observation.

When Judge Bellwood's observation is more directly applied to the actions by the North Carolina state courts versus the courts in the other states it becomes even more obvious that the presiding judge makes all the difference—for better or for worse. The actions by the Kentucky, Ohio and Virginia courts contrasted dramatically with those of the North Carolina courts. The Kentucky, Ohio and Virginia courts brought the incorrigible, career crooks to justice and acted to justly compensate their victim for his losses and force the thieves to return what they had stolen. In contrast, the North Carolina courts provided safe haven for their home-town thieves and acted to prevent me from recovering not only the monies stolen, but also the damages due.

The venerable courts in Kentucky, Ohio and Virginia chose to do justice above all else whereas the North Carolina courts deliberately chose to do otherwise; they violated my Constitutional rights to fundamental fairness, due process and justice.

The actions by the North Carolina Courts, and especially those reprehensibly unjust and mean-spirited actions by Mecklenburg County Judge Marvin Gray, certainly appeared to lend credence to Margaret Godley's naked boast that "We control the judges in this city."

North Carolina's entrenched system, with respect to its state judges, insures that their election and tenure on the bench is controlled by their "good old boy" cadre of fellow lawyers, jurists, politicians, and power brokers that put them on the bench and then control their re-election to the bench. Only reliable team players get on and remain on the state court benches. Lyndon Johnson aptly described the practice as

"The right man gets on the bench to go along so that everyone gets along."

The North Carolina legal community has embraced the Lyndon Johnson philosophy while choosing to ignore the explicit warning and admonishment by one of our nation's foremost modern legal authorities, United States Supreme Court Chief Justice Warren Burger, that "75 to 95 percent of American trial lawyers are incompetent, dishonest or both." Consequently, putting such misfits on the bench simply insures that they will bring the same deplorable incompetence and/or dishonesty to the bench. There is significant data supporting the wisdom of Chief Justice Burger's sound warning; ignoring it has resulted in instances of reprehensible misconduct and/or criminal behavior by the incompetent and/or dishonest "rogues in robes." Unfortunately, far too many bad judges avoid exposure and exploit their authority and influence to function with impunity and make a mockery of their sworn oaths as they continue to protect and perpetuate the selfish interests of themselves and their "good old boy" network that managed to put them on the bench and keep them there.

I was saddened to learn, firsthand, of the deeply entrenched corruption, intimidation, and coercion that plagues North Carolina's legal system. Any attempt to reform that disreputable legal system, whether from within or without, meets stiff resistance and eventually fails, noted

Ames Alexander, the *Charlotte Observer's* award-winning, investigative reporter, in a relevant expose.

In Alexander's May, 2005, documentary, *Judges Under the Influence*, he shone a light on the tip of the iceberg of North Carolina's rampantly corrupt judicial system where its powerful clique of "good old boys" lawyers intimidate and coerce, empower and tightly control their network of state court "juice judges" who subsequently do their bidding. It is the same "go along to get along" policy that Lyndon Johnson used to explain the creed of corruption that reflects the common practice among Washington lawmakers.

Alexander's interesting expose focused on two particular instances involving those all-too-rare state court judges who refused to kowtow to the clique. They would break ranks, refusing to remain in harness submissively going along to get along. He documented the circumstances involving Chief District Court Judge Lee Lumpkin who bravely declared that he refused to play their sordid game and that he "was not elected to cut deals with criminal lawyers" and "refused to take their money" and go along with their "blatant attempt to manipulate and control the court system."

After Judge Lumpkin refused to submit to their explicit threat to "play ball with us and you won't have any opposition for re-election," he lost his judgeship. Alexander's expose

documented how a senior member of one of the
state's largest law firms openly bragged that "We
went to work to kill (Lumpkin)."

The clique subsequently used the same dirty
tactics and threats to intimidate and coerce
another state judge who refused to play the state
legal system's dirty old game. They held up
Judge Lumpkin's fate as an example of what
happens to dissidents. North Carolina Superior
Court Judge Kenneth Crow had it thrown in his
face to "either play ball or face the same fate as
Judge Lumpkin." To Judge Crow's credit, like
Judge Lumpkin, he refused to submit to the
intimidation and coercion. He threw their threats
back in their faces and made it emphatically clear
that he had "no intention of being bullied or
intimidated" Both judges paid a heavy price for
refusing to conform to the role of "juice judge"
and "to go along to get along" in the corrupt
North Carolina state legal system.

Ames Alexander's expose also documented
the close ties and influence that the powerful
clique of North Carolina lawyers have with the
Governor's Office and, particularly, how they
funneled money into Governor Easley's office to
influence his judicial appointments. The
investigative reporter also focused on the related
"investigation by the NC Bureau of Investigation
concerning how judges return preferential
treatment to certain attorneys" and the powers
these attorneys wield to further "intimidate and
coerce" through their juice judges. Even

Morehead City Police Chief Wrenn Johnson was quick to acknowledge the rampant corruption and admit that "Judges are not abiding by the law"— notwithstanding the contrary position expressed by North Carolina Supreme Court Chief Justice I. Beverly Lake, Jr., who quickly stepped into the scandal and controversy to corral the wagons and defend his state's dubious integrity and reprehensible practices.

Alexander's expose and the unusual, public dissidence by state judges Lumpkin and Crow have caused the "good old boys" to close ranks and fiercely protect themselves from any further threats that could arise from either without or within their clique.

Alexander teamed up with fellow *Charlotte Observer* investigative reporter Gary Wright to further expose and document the corrupt practices in the state's legal system that supposedly provides lawyers for the poor.

After North Carolina was forced, by the federal courts, to provide legal representation for its poor defendants facing criminal charges, it set up a sham system that was actually a cash cow that allowed its network of "good old boy" lawyers to milk millions from the program. The program was purposely created without proper oversight and accountability which would allow its lawyers to submit bills for services and expenses they never performed. They do not even have to submit timesheets to the judges who authorize the payments and scamming of the system with a wink and a nod. Alexander and Wright exposed the scandal-ridden system in their March 12, 2006, documentary for the *Charlotte Observer*. North Carolina's chief district judge of Mecklenburg County, Fritz Mercer, finally admitted that the corrupt practice is "ripping off the state" and with a chuckle characterized the shameful abuse as merely "a bad joke."

The reporters documented how one prominent Charlotte lawyer, Lucky Osho, had milked "more than $700,000 from 2002 through 2004 with double billing and multiple billing" and Judge Mercer had to admit that the "lucrative" money Osho had been making milking the system is "unbelievable."

Mecklenburg County District Judge Nate Proctor also had to admit that "the money Osho's billing practices has reaped is staggering...no way to justify that much money...inexcusable."

Former Superior Court judge and president of the Mecklenburg County Bar, Shirley Fulton, also admitted that "The system, as it currently operates, is broken."

North Carolina's Indigent Defense Services director, Tye Hunter, who manages the state wide system, admitted that the practices are "probably not unique to Mecklenburg County."

Attorney Osho's lawyer contended that "any errors by his client were unintentional," although the state's Indigent Defense Services began an investigation of Osho and removed him from its listing of lawyers authorized to defend the poor. Osho counter-charged that the real problem is that most judges put the "bottom line" interests above those of adequate representation for the poor and "should be ashamed" for their deplorable conduct.

Osho adamantly stated, "I do not apologize." He admitted, however, that he just "didn't follow all the rules," although the investigative report documented scores of specific instances of multiple billing.

The *Charlotte Observer* investigative reporters also spotlighted other Charlotte lawyers, Chiege Okwara and Christofer Sanders, for similarly milking the system of $540,000 and $370,000, respectively, from 2002 through 2004. Okwara quickly denied engaging in "any fraudulent or illegal billing practices" and Sanders raised his "solid reputation for dependability, reliability and competence" in response to the allegations. Notwithstanding, the practices of both lawyers have been solidly criticized by the Indigent Defense Services.

The long and sordid history of North Carolina's legal system is rife with brazen injustice and rampant corruption. Recently, the press exposed how Ronald Cotton was victimized and sent off with a life sentence for a rape he never committed. His tragic tale was documented in *Picking Cotton Our Memoir of Injustice and Redemption* (2009). In 2007, the nation was appalled by the bizarre developments in the Duke

University rape case where the ruthless Durham County, North Carolina, prosecutor, Michael Nifong, attempted to prosecute and imprison three innocent Duke students to enhance his re-election prospects. That case was well documented in *Until Proven Innocent* (2007).

Unfortunately, these disclosures represent only the tip of the sordid iceberg that is North Carolina's corrupt legal system. My numerous efforts to remedy the instances that related to my cases there proved futile and demonstrated how the system reacts to protect its "good old boy" operatives against any threat of reform. I repeatedly brought the instances of blatant injustice, corruption and misconduct before the North Carolina authorities: the North Carolina Court of Appeals, the North Carolina Supreme Court, the Federal District Court in Charlotte, and the North Carolina Bar Association, and I fully documented my allegations with irrefutable, compelling evidence and controlling case law authority—all to no avail. My experiences proved to me that the North Carolina appeals courts do little more than rubber-stamp the actions of the lower courts. Lower court injustice, even on a flagrant level, gets the "good old boy" wink and nod.

When I learned of John Arrowood's appointment to the North Carolina Court of Appeals by Governor Mike Easley I denounced it in my subsequent briefs to the courts: "Indeed, Arrowood's appointment to that Court emphasizes the shamefully deplorable condition of the North Carolina state courts, even on the appeal court level. Appointing a person to that Court who has proven to be brazenly dishonest, deceitful, devious, and without integrity is reprehensible..."

Arrowood's appointment to the high court further angered the public and critics of Governor Easley. In a *Charlotte News & Observer* article Staff Writer Jay Price reported the numerous scandelous actions reflecting wrongdoing during Easley's governorship that were under investigation by a grand jury. They included how, in 2005, Easley's staff and NC State Chancellor James L. Oblinger had secured a $170,000 University sinecure for Easley's wife, Mary, with an 88 percent pay increase that brazenly violated UNC-system policy. After the facts were publicly exposed Oblinger was forced to resign and Mary Easley was fired. Arrowood's appointment had simply added to the sordid list of sleazy actions reflecting business as usual within the North Carolina cadre of "good old boys – and girls."

Obviously the North Carolina "good old boys," their Court of Appeals, their Supreme Court, and even their governor all found Arrowood's dishonesty, lack of integrity, and lifestyle perfectly acceptable, worthy of acclaim, and excellent qualifications for a seat on North Carolina's second highest court.

No, I do not consider it appalling, or even unusual, that career crooks steal whenever and from whomever they can. What I find appalling are judges who rationalize and justify their brazen injustice with their warped legal doctrine that "miscarriage of justice is of no consequence."

What those North Carolina career crooks did to me was certainly criminal and repugnant; however, it was consistent with their incorrigible, criminal mindsets. On the other hand, what the courts in North Carolina did to me was far more appalling, grievous and worthy of scorn than the actions of their home-town crooks. The corrupt Margaret Godley and the Wades were able, on their own, to steal thousands from me and millions from their other victims. However, they would not have been able to prevent me from recovering the $15,000 they stole from me and cheat me out of the $611,000 legally won with my valid Kentucky judgment without the crucial, legal help from their home-town courts. So those corrupt and/or unjust courts bear direct culpability for making it possible for their home-town crooks to keep what they stole from me and then to cheat me out of what was legally due me. Those courts had numerous opportunities and the necessary authority to do justice but, in each instance, they deliberately chose to do otherwise and they had no qualms about doing so. In fact, Judge Reidinger made no bones about it in his ruling, with his bold statement that "miscarriage of justice is of no consequence."

I find this openly proclaimed and liberally applied legal policy appalling; however, it does reveal their rationale that justified the injustice they did to me as inconsequential, of no concern or significance, in their minds. But far more grievous and shamefully appalling is the fact that those courts robbed me of my basic, US Constitutional protections and rights to fundamental fairness, due process and justice— the sacred rights and protections I served to protect while overseas in the military.

The appalling actions by those courts proved that they are corrupt and/or shamefully unjust and merit nothing but scorn and disdain by every American who reveres their US Constitutional protections and rights. Unless the present corrupt and/or unjust aspects and operatives of the North Carolina legal system are reformed and purged, many more Americans will be victimized in the future, just as it ruthlessly victimized me, Ronald Cotton, the Duke University students, and many others in the past. So long as the current creed, that "miscarriage of justice is of no consequence," continues in the Tar Heel State injustice will prevail. This fundamental defect will persist as long as the North Carolina "good old boys" continue to stack the State's deck of jurists with the likes of Marvin Gray and John Arrowood. For these individuals, the miscarriage of justice is of no consequence; the injustice and same dirty old game will continue. And so long as they continue the practice of elevating the likes of Arrowood, whose actions proved he was brazenly dishonest, deceitful, devious, and without integrity, to the State's highest courts the icon of North Carolina justice will yet be blind, deaf and dumb. Mostly dumb.

The citizens of North Carolina who are honorable, have integrity, and who reject the aspects of their State's legal system that are shamefully unjust and corrupt, should feel deeply offended by the deplorable condition of that sordid legal system and force major reforms in those factions of its courts, judges and lawyers who perpetuate its corrupt and/or unjust practices.

History has recorded many examples of nations, states and governments with an abundance of laws and rules but no justice. Nazi Germany and Idi Amin's brutal dictatorship are but two of the more appalling examples. And, tragically, from time to time here in the United States our citizens have found themselves victimized by laws and rules that were applied to defeat justice, as in the enforcement of slavery and the disenfranchisement of equal rights for women. Today, my case reflects that the shameful practice is still alive and well in the North Carolina courts. Those courts used their laws, rules and authority to prevent me from recovering the $15,000 stolen from me by their home-town career criminals and to beat me out of the damages I was due and awarded by the federal court in Kentucky and the Sixth Circuit Court of Appeals in Ohio; they subverted, defeated and made a mockery of even the most basic concept of justice – let alone equal justice under law.

I have also learned that another important factor affecting the quality of justice among state legal systems, in a state-to-state comparison, are the bar associations in each state and the policies they practice concerning the behavior and standards of their members. This largely determines and controls the quality of their lawyers. However, these differ considerably from state-to-state, practically and philosophically. North Carolina perpetuates a legal system that best serves the selfish, vested interests of their most influential bar association members and jurists.

I have had occasion to witness and deal with lawyers on both ends of the spectrum during this litigation. I must place Chip Burkholder among the very best. He has absolute integrity and the strongest sense of honor. He is top notch when it comes to competency and cares with all his heart to both do his very best for his client and to strictly adhere to the highest principles of what a lawyer should be. He has a keen sense of balance and solid common sense. I am sure he would make a terrific judge; however, he is not a political animal. He is content to be a small town lawyer caring for his neighbors. He is much like a brilliant physician that could be making a big name and big bucks in a high profile, elitist setting, but instead chooses to return to his small town roots to make a difference to his people. The highest legal standards and dedication to serve the interests of justice beat in the heart and soul of this small town, Virginia lawyer.

During the Kentucky litigation I was pleased to have fought honorable and competent lawyers that represented the Wades and Godley: John Burrus, Frank Heaberlin, and David Stratton. It is to the great credit of John Burrus and his reputable law firm that when his clients tested the issues of his integrity, honesty, and loyalty to his oath as a lawyer that he chose to uphold his integrity and that of the federal court system over the big bucks the Wades and Godley were waving in front of him. The record and Judge Hood's express recognition and ruling attesting to John Burrus's commendable actions to protect the integrity of the court confirm what a fine man and lawyer he truly is. Likewise, I can only say good things about both Frank Heaberlin and David Stratton. All of these Kentucky lawyers, as the record reflects, fought me hard but fairly, honorably, and in strict compliance with both the letter and spirit of the rules and their obligations as lawyers.

During the Virginia and Tennessee litigation I encountered the same type of excellence and competence in the lawyers representing my adversaries: Fred Rowlett and Barry Proctor from Abingdon, Virginia, and Frank Johnstone from Kingsport, Tennessee. Again, they also fought me long and hard every step of the way, but always as honorable lawyers in every sense of the word.

When the North Carolina litigation commenced I had already been forewarned to expect an entirely different type of "good old boy" Charlotte lawyer to make an appearance. I think the warning went something to the effect that I would be stepping into the vipers' home-town snake pit. In any event, the warnings proved prophetic and I found myself confronting lawyers who were the opposite of those I had faced in Kentucky, Virginia and Tennessee.

Once I discovered the ugly reality of those big-town, high-priced, big shot, Charlotte lawyers, I decided to repeatedly remind them of who and what they are, under their glitzy, "Queen City" facades. On all of the correspondence I sent them, from that point forward, I included the quote of Chief Justice Warren Burger that *"75 to 95 percent of American Trial Lawyers are incompetent, dishonest or both."* Needless to say, the practice did not endear me to the defendants' home-town lawyers. The gesture was intended to force them to look in the mirror and, hopefully, to relent and repent of their ways. I also suggested that they try to learn from and emulate their clients' fine

Kentucky lawyers and they read Judge Catherine Crier's powerful book, *The Case Against Lawyers(2002)*; that only served to further vex them. Everyone should read her excellent book.

Perhaps I should note, in all fairness, that I have been exposed to a few very fine North Carolina judges and lawyers, notwithstanding the bad apples I have previously mentioned. I have often expressed my admiration for, and appreciation of, the fine qualities, competence, and effort to be fair that I received when the Mecklenburg County, North Carolina, judge, Richard D. Boner, briefly presided in my case to enforce my judgment. He certainly provided an excellent contrast to his fellow jurist, Marvin Gray, and yet they are peer judges in the same Charlotte courtroom. I came to know and admire another top notch North Carolina Circuit Court judge in the person of the Honorable Lee Lumpkin, whose brother, Parker, is a North Carolina attorney of impeccable character, competency and integrity. Thus, I am certain that there is a small group of honorable, competent judges and lawyers in the Tar Heel State. However, until the many rotten apples are purged from the barrel, the problems and further contamination will only continue and North Carolina will remain far behind its neighbor state of Virginia in providing equal justice under law.

In response to that question, I must say that, no, I have never had any inclination to become a lawyer and I have litigated in these cases only because I have been forced to do so. The only real satisfaction I get in the courtroom involves my *guardian ad litem* work in the juvenile courts as a court-appointed special advocate battling for the best interests of "my kids"—the abused and neglected children that I fight for. I have found it interesting, that for the past few years I have received many personal invitations to join The Association of Trial Lawyers of America from some of this nation's most prestigious law firms and most distinguished lawyers, including an invitation from the legendary Jerry "Racehorse" Spence—whom I have always admired and respected for his integrity and stellar legal skills.

Looking back with hindsight over these past fifteen years leaves me impressed with how, early on in the litigation, US Attorney Guy Blackwell recognized and characterized the network of incorrigible, career criminals that I was battling as "an endless den of snakes." In turn, Senior Federal District Court Judge Joseph Hood specifically characterized and denounced the defendants as "evil." Both characterizations have clearly proven to be accurate.

Yes, I do have regrets: that I have had to spend so much of my time and energy fighting these civil cases for the past fifteen years. It would have been far more productively spent in the juvenile courtrooms doing my advocacy work for "my kids." And I would have preferred to have spent that time and energy raising money for the fine charitable causes that need all the help I am able to channel to them. Ironically, one of those causes is the Baptist Children's Homes of North Carolina, which is down there in the Wades' and the Godleys' backyard.

I regret that despite my best efforts in the end I was unable to enforce and collect the judgments in either the Kentucky or Virginia cases. Those proceeds were pledged to reimburse my fellow victims for their losses and the balance was designated to be sent to the wonderful charitable causes I support that help children.

I also regret that it took me so long to close down the notorious, interstate, criminal network of Godley, the Wades and their cronies; had I been able to do so sooner it would have spared losses by some of their other victims. And it is most regretful that despite my best efforts to bring them all to justice Margaret Godley's and the Wades' backyard courts provided them with safe haven, thwarted justice, and allowed them to avoid criminal prosecution. They deserved imprisonment right alongside their cronies who did not escape criminal prosecution and justice.

There are many criminals serving long sentences in prisons across the United States for stealing much less than the fifteen thousand dollars stolen from me. Had those felons been able to avail themselves of the North Carolina safe haven they also likely could have avoided prosecution and justice.

My final regret is that I have had to take priceless time away from my wonderful family who remained a replenishing source of light and strength through the darkest and most difficult hours. Throughout this ordeal I was also blessed with the steadfast support of my loyal friends and brethren veterans.

Regardless, I would do it all over again if I knew then the heavy price I would have to pay—simply because that is who and what I am which goes back to the way I was reared back on my grandfather's farm. He was a splendid role model of absolute integrity and uncompromising principles who championed the belief that any man worth his salt was obligated to stand fast against the forces of evil and injustice. One of those principles, which he often repeated and attributed to Edmund Burke, was that "The only thing necessary for evil to triumph is for good men to do nothing." Another, from Plato, was that "Of all the things of a man's soul which he has within him, justice is the greatest good and injustice the greatest evil."

He also taught me to be proud of my heritage and ancestors—the "sons of liberty" who came from our farm community and faced their British oppressors and the gallant men in our family who have fought and bled for the cause of freedom and justice throughout this nation's history.

As an old sea dog now in my seventieth year, I am too old to change my principles. I have remained dedicated to recovering the monies stolen from me and my fellow victims, and I wanted both those victims and the fine charities that I support to benefit from that recovery. However, that recovery has always been the secondary issue. The main issue and my primary motivation have always been and will remain—to fight for justice against the forces of evil.

The fifteen year record of Paull Anderson's arduous struggle seeking justice is a remarkable testament to his willingness to confront daunting adversaries and problems while enduring considerable hardship and expense, in support of his principles.

The Virginian refused to submit to the injustice perpetrated upon him or to allow the perpetrators, regardless how wealthy and powerful, to victimize him and his fellow victims with impunity—although most victims in his situation would hardly have dared to even consider confronting and battling such odds and adversaries. In the same inspirational and exemplary fashion as Clarence Earl Gideon, Robert Kearns, Mahatma Gandhi, Martin Luther King, and Nelson Mandela, the Virginian has proven to be a tenacious and dedicated champion of justice and a fearless adversary against the forces of evil.

Jai Bez
Beijing, Yi Chou 4707

NOTES

Considerable information came from the archives and legal filings of Paull Anderson.

Page **Chapter I**
24 US Federal District Court (Pikeville, Kentucky), *Bessie Berry, et al. v. Cyprus Coal Co., et al*, unpublished opinion No. 53 (E.D. Ky. March 20, 1992), aff'd, unpublished opinion 1993 WL 78780 (6th Cir. March 19, 1993).

41 US Federal District Court (Abingdon, Virginia), Case No.94-CV-57 *Anderson v. Foundation, et al.*, "Complaint." April 7, 1994.

41 US Federal District Court (Pikeville, Kentucky), Case No. 94-111 *Anderson v. Wade, et al.*, "Complaint." April 27, 1994.

Chapter II
45 US Federal District Court (Pikeville, Kentucky), Case No.94-111 *Anderson v. Wade, et al.*, "Complaint." April 1994; unpublished opinion No. 94-911 (E.D.Ky. June 14, 2000.

48 US Federal District Court (Pikeville, Kentucky), *Bessie Berry, et al. v. Cyprus Coal Co., et al*, unpublished opinion No. 53 (E.D. Ky. March 20, 1992), aff'd, unpublished opinion 1993 WL 78780 (6th Cir. March 19, 1993).

58 US Court of Appeals for the Sixth Circuit, *Anderson v. Wade, et al.*, aff'd, unpublished opinion No. 00-6249 (March 29, 2002).

Chapter III

59   US Federal District Court (Abingdon, Virginia), Case No. 94-111 *Anderson v.* Foundation*, et al.,* "Complaint." April 1994; unpublished opinion No. 94-CV-57(W.D.Va. May 22, 1996).

71   US Court of Appeals for the Fourth Circuit, *Anderson v. Foundation, et al.*, aff'd unpublished opinion, No. 96-2221(4th Cir. September 1998), aff'd, unpublished opinion No. 99-1508(August 1999).

Chapter IV

72   Washington County Law Court (Johnson City, Tennessee), CA No. 17452, *Anderson v. Mezvinsky*, "Complaint." January 1995.

73   Oklahoma Office of the Secretary of State. "Certificate of Incorporation, Foundation for the Advancement, Education and Employment of American Indians, an eleemosynary corporation, Articles of Incorporation and By-Laws." December 9, 1976.

74   Moore, Robert. "History of Organization's President Packed with Color." *Citizen Tribune* (Morristown, Tennessee), August 2, 1995.

75   Bell, Betty and Steve Rogers."Sumner-based foundation faces Fed prosecutors." *The News Examiner* (Gallatin, Tennessee), August 14, 1995.

75   Carter, Rochelle. "Group's loan to employee questioned." The *Tennessean* (Nashville, Tennessee), August 1995.

75   US   Federal   District   Court   (Greenville,
      Tennessee),   "Transcript   of   Proceeding,
      Sentencing   Hearing   of   Mary   B.   Brady."
      September 25, 1995.

Chapter V

89   "Fraud   Case   Sentencing   Scheduled,"   *The
      Courier*, Florida, 1973.

90   "Johnson Gets 3 Year Sentence," *The Courier*,
      Florida, October 8, 1973.

90   Oklahoma Office of the Secretary of State.
      "Certificate of Incorporation, Foundation for the
      Advancement, Education and Employment of
      American Indians, an eleemosynary corporation,
      Articles   of   Incorporation   and   By-Laws."
      December 9, 1976.

91   Wells, Garvin. "Sworn Statement of Garvin
      Wells." Law Office of Atty. Christen W.
      Burkholder, Bristol, Virginia, June 10, 1994.

92   Schroeder, Joan V and Lewis Burwell. "Last of
      the Old-Time Con Men." *Blue Ridge Country*,
      September/October 1994 Issue.

92   Rakes, Hugh N. Rakes' journal and personal
      papers; letters between Rakes and Godleys
      (Margaret L. and Marvin R.). 1970 – 1994.

92   Middleton, D.M. "Interview with Hugh R.
      Rakes." Floyd, Virginia 1993-1994.

96   US   Federal   District   Court   (Chattanooga,
      Tennessee),   CA   No.   1:94-cv-227   *John   and
      Donna Mousourakis v. Foundation, et al.*
      "Complaint." 1994.

99   US Court of Appeals for the 7th Circuit, *USA v. Robert R. Krilich*, "Opinion," May 11,1999.

100   Moore, Robert. "Brady Sentencing Delayed – Restitution Loan Questioned." *Citizen Tribune* Morristown, Tennessee, June 27, 1995.

100   Moore, Robert. "History of Organization's President Packed with Color."*Citizen Tribune* (Morristown, Tennessee), August 2, 1995.

100   Bell, Betty and Steve Rogers. "Sumner-based foundation faces Fed prosecutors." *The News Examiner* (Gallatin, Tennessee), August 14, 1995.

102   Carter, Rochelle. "Group's loan to employee questioned." *The Tennessean* (Nashville, Tennessee), August 1995.

102   US Federal District Court (Greenville, Tennessee), "Transcript of Proceeding," Sentencing Hearing of Mary B. Brady, September 1995.

104   Rogers, Steve. "Foundation must pay $4.8 million." *The News Examiner*, (Gallatin, Tennessee), October 7, 1996.

104   Associated Press. "Former congressman on trial for cheating Bristol businessman." *Bristol Herald Courier* (Bristol, Virginia), June 27,1997.

105   Moore, Robert. "Brady Jailed For Contempt." *Citizen Tribune* (Morristown, Tennessee), June 27, 1997.

105   Moore, Robert. "Anderson: Mezvinsky Knew of Donations." *Citizen Tribune* (Morristown, Tennessee), June 29, 1997.

105   Moore, Robert. "Attorney Files Motion to Convert Grigsby Bankruptcy."*Citizen Tribune* (Morristown, Tennessee), August 31, 2000.

105   US Bankruptcy Court (Knoxville, Tennessee), Case No. 00-31509, *RE:Debtor/Defendant Samuel F. Grigsby, Sr.* "Motion to Dismiss Debtor's Petition for Fraud and Deception Upon the Court and Creditors and for such Appropriate Action to Protect the Integrity of the Court and the Interests of the Creditors," June 4, 2001.

111   Paine, Ann. "Foundation Director Sentenced." *The Tennessean* (Nashville, Tennessee), February 15, 2000.

113   US Bankruptcy Court (Nashville). Debtor-*Foundation for the Advancement, Education and Employment of American Indians.* "Petition for Bankruptcy," May 20, 2002.

113   Staff Reports. "Greer makes $1 million judgment against company with Morristown ties." *Citizen Tribune*(Morristown,Tennessee), April 12, 2009.

Chapter VI

123   Green, Michelle and Andrea Fine. "Woman on the Run." *People Magazine*, August 10, 1992.

124   Clinton, Hillary. *Living History—Hillary Rodham Clinton*, Scribner 2003, p.179.

124   Clinton, Bill. "Hero of the budget battle in the House lost her wealthy suburban Pennsylvania district in the next election." *My Life—Bill Clinton*, Vintage Books 2004, pp. 535, 630.

126   US Federal District Court (Abingdon, Virginia), Case No. 94-111 *Anderson v. Foundation, et al.*,

"Complaint." April 1994; unpublished opinion No. 94-CV- (W.D.Va. May 22,1996), aff'd unpublished opinion, No. 96-2221(4th Cir. September 1998), aff'd unpublished opinion No. 99-1508 (4th Cir. August 1999).

126 Washington County Law Court (Johnson City, Tennessee), CA No. 174 *Anderson v. Mezvinsky.* "Complaint." January 1995.

126 Associated Press. "Former congressman on trial for cheating Bristol businessman." *Bristol Herald Courier* (Bristol, Virginia), June 27, 1997.

126 Moore, Robert. "Anderson: Mezvinsky Knew of Donations." *Citizen Tribune* (Morristown Tennessee), June 29, 1997.

126 Kruger, John. "Mezvinsky acknowledges role in scam foundation." *The Hill* (Washington, DC) January 12, 2000.

126 Rubin-Erdely, Sabrina."The Crash." *Philadelphia Magazine*, May 2000.

126 Rees, Matthew. "The Long Slide – the mess that Mezvinsky built." *Regardie's POWER* (Washington, DC). November/December 2000.

128 Levy, Michael L "News Release, US v. Edward M. Mezvinsky." US Attorney's Office, Philadelphia, PA, March 22, 2001.

128 Schogol, Marc and Ralph Vigoda "Edward Mezvinsky indicted on fraud charges." *Philadelphia Inquirer*, March 22, 2001.

128 US Bankruptcy Court (Philadelphia, PA), *Re Debtors, Edward Mezvinsky and Marjorie-Margolies Mezvinsky.* "Bankruptcy Petition." January 2000.

128 Vigoda, Ralph. "Mezvinsky charged with fraud." *Philadelphia Inquirer*, March 23, 2001.

128 Philadelphia County Court of Common Pleas Civil Action. No. 002971 *Edward M. Mezvinsky and Margorie Margolies-Mezvinsky v. Roche Holding.* "Complaint." March 23, 2001.

128 Smith, Jim. "Squirmin." *Philadelphia Daily News*, March 23, 2001.

128 Vigoda, Ralph ."Indicted in fraud, he cites medicine." *Philadelphia Inquirer,* March 24, 2001.

128 Smith, Jim. "A Hard Pill to Swallow ." *Philadelphia Daily News*, March 28, 2001.

128 Vigoda, Ralph. "Ed Mezvinsky pleads not guilty." *Philadelphia Inquirer,* March 29, 2001.

129 Vigoda, Ralph. "D.A. says malaria-drug defense is malarkey." *Philadelphia Inquirer* March 30, 2001.

129 Porter, Jill. "Oh, the shame of it all." *Philadelphia Daily News*, March 30, 2001.

129 Todt, Ron. "Mezvinsky to plead insanity on fraud charges." *Philadelphia Inquirer*, July 5, 2001.

130 Duffy, Shannon P. "Margolies-Mezvinsky's Ignorance Plea Fails to Sway Bankruptcy Judge." by *The Legal Intelligencer*, August 21, 2001.

132 Vigoda, Ralph. "US Judge tightens bail for ex-Rep. Mezvinsky in fraud case." *Philadelphia Inquirer*, September 7, 2001.

132 Vigoda, Ralph. "The incredible tale of Ed Mezvinsky." *Philadelphia Inquirer,* November 4, 2001.

132 Vigoda, Ralph. "Mezvinsky faces more allegations." *Philadelphia Inquirer,* January 15, 2002.

132 King, Larry. "Electronic monitoring ordered for Mezvinsky." *Philadelphia Inquirer*, January 24, 2002.

132 Vigoda, Ralph. "Medical experts dispute Mczvinsky defense." *Philadelphia Inquirer*, March 16, 2002.

133 Rubin-Erdely, Sabrina. "Crazy Eddie." *Philadelphia Magazine*, April 2002.

133 Vigoda, Ralph. "Attorney for Mezvinsky asks to be removed from case."*Philadelphia Inquirer*, March 9, 2002.

133 Vigoda, Ralph. "Judge says Mezvinsky must hire an attorney by tomorrow." *Philadelphia Inquirer*, April 16, 2002.

133 Vigoda, Ralph. "Judge says Mezvinsky may not use mental health defense." *Philadelphia Inquirer*, June 3, 2002.

133 Vigoda, Ralph. "Mezvinsky can't use disorder as defense." *Philadelphia Inquirer*, June 4, 2002.

134 Vigoda, Ralph. "Mezvinsky guilty plea ends saga." *Philadelphia Inquirer,* September 28, 2002.

137 Zauzmer, Robert A. "US Attorney's Office News Release, Update to Interested Parties, US v. Edward M. Mezvinsky." US Attorney Office (Philadelphia, PA), October 3, 2002.

137 Zauzmer, Robert A. "Government Sentencing Memorandum, *US v. Edward M. Mezvinsky,*

Criminal No. 19106-1756" US Federal District Court, Philadelphia, PA, December 17, 2002.

137   Zauzmer, Robert A. "US Attorney's Office News Release Update to InterestedParties, US v. Edward M. Mezvinsky." US Attorney Office (Philadelphia, PA), December 30, 2002.

160   Vigoda, Ralph. "Mezvinsky to serve 6 years for scams." *Philadelphia Inquirer*, January 10, 2003.

160   Vigoda, Ralph. "Mezvinsky gets six years for fraud." *Philadelphia Inquirer*, January 10, 2003.

160   Zauzmer, Robert A. "US Attorney's Office News Release,Update to Interested Parties, US v. Edward M. Mezvinsky." US Attorney Office (Philadelphia, PA), January 10, 2003.

160   Kilen, Mike. "Whirlpool of lies swallows Mezvinsky." *Des Moines* Register, August 3, 2003.

162   Kessler, E.J. "Chelsea's Jewish Beau – Chelsea Clinton Goes Public with New Beau."*Forward*, November 22, 2005.

163   Author unknown. "Chelsea's Secret Honeymoon in India – Hillary and Bill's Outrage." *Globe*, February 6, 2006.

164   Rhee, J., Sandholm, D. "Will Father of the Groom be Welcome Figure at Chelsea Clinton's Wedding?" *ABC News*, December 1, 2009.

Chapter VII

Information re Hugh Ramon Rakes, Margaret L. Godley, and Marvin R. Godley from interviews with Hugh Rakes, Eleanor H. Dunn, and letters, journal, and personal papers of Hugh Rakes.

166 Schroeder, Joan V. and Lewis Burwell. "Last of the Old-Time Con Men." *Blue Ridge Country*, September/October 1994 Issue.

178 US Federal District Court (Pikeville, Kentucky), *Bessie Berry, et al. v. Cyprus Coal Co., et al*, unpublished opinion No. 84-53 (E.D. Ky. March 20,1992) *affd* unpublished opinion 1993 WL 78780 (6th Cir. March 19, 1993).

180 US Federal District Court (Pikeville, Kentucky), Case No.94-111 *Anderson v. Wade, et al.,* unpublished opinion No. 94-911 (E.D.Ky. June 14, 2000), affd. unpublished opinion No. 00-6249 (6th Cir. March 29, 2002).

Chapter VIII

189 Keane, Chris. "Jake Wade has been around the league for 45 years, coaching kids 10 to 12 and 'they learn from me, he says.' " *Charlotte News & Observer*, April 7, 2002.

192 Chandler, Liz. "Prominent lawyer pays for 'terrible mistake.' " *Charlotte News & Observer*, January 9, 1994.

192 North Carolina State Bar, Case No. 93 DHC 34, RE: Julius Jennings Wade, Jr. "Order of Disbarment," March 16, 1994.

192 DeAngelis, Mary Elizabeth. "Lawyer receives probation in embezzling case." *Charlotte News & Observer*, June 28, 1994.

192 Mecklenburg County General Court of Justice (Charlotte, North Carolina), Case No. 94 CRS 040951-(01)(02)(03). *RE: Julius Jennings Wade, Jr.,* "Plea agreement, judgment, and sentence for

multiple criminal charges," June 27, 1994. North Carolina State Bar, Case No. 00G 1307. *RE: James Hunter Wade ,* "Order of Disbarment." January 19, 2001.

Chapter IX

Chapter X

228 Sheck, Barry. *The Innocence Project* at Cardozo School of Law

229 Lithwick, Dahlia. "Innocent Until Executed," *Newsweek*, September 2009.

229 Grann, David. "Cameron Todd Willingham, and the death penalty," *New Yorker*, September 2009.

Chapter XI

232 US Federal District Court (Charlotte, North Carolina), Case No.3:03CV33, *Anderson v. Wade et al.*: "Plaintiff's Complaint," January 21, 2005; "Plaintiff's Motion for Summary Judgment," March 8, 2005.

240 "Plaintiff's Notice of Suggestion of Death of Defendant Margaret L. Godley," February 9, 2007; "Plaintiff's Motion for Substitution of the Proper Parties," February 9, 2007."Defendant's Response to Plaintiff's Motion for Substitution," February 26, 2007. "Plaintiff's Reply to Defendant's Response," March 9, 2007; "Plaintiff's Motion for Joinder of Claims and Remedies," March 28, 2007; "Defendant's Response to Plaintiff's Motion for Joinder," April 16, 2007; "Plaintiff's Reply to Defendant's Response," April 25, 2007.

245 "Plaintiff's Complaint against Frank L. Godley," June 4, 2007.

247 "Defendant Frank Godley's Rule 11 Motion for Sanctions," September 25, 2007.

247 "Plaintiff's Response to Defendant's Rule 11 Motion," October 11, 2008.

Chapter XII

Epilogue

293   Baldas, Tresa. "9th Circuit Court Feels *Pro Se* Pressure" *The National Law Review* November 18, 2004.

293   Legal Services Corporation. "Documenting the Justice Gap in America: The Current Unmet Civil Legal Needs of Low-Income Americans," 2005.

294   Federal task force findings. *The National Law Review,* November 11, 2004.

296   Bailey, F. Lee and Aronson, Harvey. *The Defense Never Rests*, Signet Books,   1971, pp. 308,313.

296   "John Grisham will now take your questions." *Time Magazine*, February 4, 2008, p. 6.

300   Johnson, Reed. "Robert Kearns' flawed 'Genius'" *Los Angeles Times*, October 3, 2008.

313   Alexander, Ames. "Judges Under the Influence" *Charlotte News & Observer,* May 15, 2005.

315   Alexander, Ames and Gary L. Wright. "Defenders of the poor use an honor system that's vulnerable to abuse and errors" *Charlotte News & Observer*, March 12, 2006.

317   Thompson-Cannino, Jennifer. *Picking Cotton Our Memoir of Injustice and Redemption*, St. Martin's Press, 2009.

318   Johnson, K.C. and Taylor, Jr., Stuart. *Until Proven Innocent*, St. Martin's Press, 2007.

319   Ingram, David. "Gay appellate judge quietly makes history" *Charlotte News & Observer*, September 8, 2007.

319   Price, Jay. "Mary Easley is fired; Oblinger resigns" *Charlotte News & Observer*, June 9, 2009.

326 Crier, Catherine. *The Case Against Lawyers*, Broadway Books, 2002.

328 Moyer, Liz. "It Coulda Been Worse, Bernie" *Forbes Magazine*, July 13, 2009.

ACKNOWLEDGMENTS

This book was possible because of the gracious cooperation and support of several individuals and data sources. Among them, and especially helpful, have been the following: Tommy Zhou, Lu Wang, Mike Middleton, Hugh Rakes, Jai Dismas, Paull Anderson, and Infometrics.

In appreciation, the author has pledged proceeds from the sale of this book in the United States and Canada to the following fine causes to benefit children: St. Jude Children's Hospital, Shriners Children's Hospital, Doctors Without Borders, CASA, the Oprah Winfrey Foundation, and the Baptist Children's Homes of North Carolina.

INDEX